Working with
Human
Service
Organisations

To Drew, with thanks for the company on the journey.

Working with
Human
Service
Organisations

CREATING CONNECTIONS FOR PRACTICE

Fiona Gardner

OXFORD
UNIVERSITY PRESS

OXFORD
UNIVERSITY PRESS

253 Normanby Road, South Melbourne, Victoria 3205, Australia

Oxford University Press is a department of the University of Oxford.
It furthers the University's objective of excellence in research,
scholarship, and education by publishing worldwide in

Oxford New York

Auckland Cape Town Dar es Salaam Hong Kong Karachi
Kuala Lumpur Madrid Melbourne Mexico City Nairobi
New Delhi Shanghai Taipei Toronto

With offices in

Argentina Austria Brazil Chile Czech Republic France Greece
Guatemala Hungary Italy Japan Poland Portugal Singapore
South Korea Switzerland Thailand Turkey Ukraine Vietnam

OXFORD is a trade mark of Oxford University Press
in the UK and in certain other countries

National Library of Australia
Cataloguing-in-Publication data:

Gardner, Fiona.
Working with human service organisations:
creating connections for practice.

Bibliography.
Includes index.
ISBN 0 19 555303 9.

ISBN 9 78019555 3031.

1. Human services — Textbooks. 2. Social work administration —
Textbooks. 3. Organisational effectiveness. I. Title.

361.006

Typeset by Mason Design
Printed in China by Golden Cup Printing Co. Ltd.

Contents

Figures

Acknowledgments

This is a book about ideas: ideas about how we as workers can be active and dynamic in our relationships with the human service organisations we work in and engage with. These ideas have developed for me from working and participating in organisations over many years. The aim or hope is that using these can encourage workers to wrestle with the inevitable dilemmas of organisational life in a way that is congruent with their values as human service professionals. The book then suggests ways of thinking about organisations; and tools for engaging with organisational life.

The development of such ideas never happens in a vacuum but rather from experience, past theory, and discussions and explorations with other people. There are vast numbers of people who have contributed both in shared experiences and discussions of many kinds. I would like to thank them all, but there are too many to name all of them individually, so I have decided not to name any. Their many contributions are seen in the examples used in the book. Some of these examples are clearly identified as coming from existing organisations and I particularly want to thank them for sharing their experiences. The others have germinated from experiences I have either had myself or heard about from a wide range of discussions with clients and colleagues, managers, workers in other organisations, students, family, and friends over a very long time. They have all been changed to safeguard confidentiality; while still reflecting the experience of life in or with human service organisations. Thank you all for your example, encouragement, and challenge in writing this book.

This is the first book I have written and I do want to thank Debra James; as the publisher for this book, she demonstrates all that a new author could want in terms of her support and clarity.

Introduction: Starting Points

Human service organisations come in many shapes and sizes with different structures, management styles, and visions about how to provide effective services for clients. From my experience, it seems that often the greatest challenge for workers in human service organisations is in dealing with their employing organisation rather than their direct work with clients. For clients too, the organisation is often a somewhat mystifying source of authority with its own peculiar rules and expectations. Front-line workers have to negotiate between the hopes and sometimes fears of their clients and the expectations and requirements of the organisation. This book aims to enable potential and current workers to grapple with the dilemmas and opportunities of working in organisations.

Why is it so challenging for professionals to deal with organisations? I suspect we tend to assume that the organisation we work for is simply there to support us. Of course, in part it is, but organisations also have their own agendas. Professional training tends to focus on the skills and knowledge needed for working with clients towards change; how to negotiate such change in the context of the organisation is not always so clear. Training also encourages us as professionals to develop and articulate a set of values and beliefs about how things should be done. Professional workers are not value free: they generally come to organisations committed to beliefs about the worth of individuals and the desirability of a just and fair society (Fook et al. 2000). Added to that is an expectation of thinking independently, a confidence in our knowledge and skill, and often an enthusiasm to make a positive difference in the world with a focus on client and community issues.

The organisation, on the other hand—influenced by the current political, social, and economic context—has its own values, agendas, and ways of operating. Ideally, and reasonably often in practice, there is overlap between the values of professional workers and their organisations. However, there are also clearly times when there are different agendas and expectations. Human service organisations tend to be large, with complex systems of rules and processes to ensure consistency in work practices and a focus on managing resources and funding. The current focus on funding programs according to narrowly defined categories, for example, limits organisational and thus professional flexibility and responsiveness. The example of Ruth in the case scenario below highlights some of the current issues for clients and workers.

Case scenario

Ruth is a 25-year-old woman who was referred to me at a family counselling agency for 10 sessions on anger management. Her son, Tom, now about 3 years old, had been taken into care when Ruth was convicted of drug-related offences. He was now living with Ruth, one of the conditions of which was that Ruth learn specific strategies to deal with anger.

I was the worker allocated to see Ruth. As I explored further what was happening with her, I was somewhat intrigued to learn that I was one of a series of workers. She had an alcohol and drug worker to check that she wasn't using drugs, a parenting worker to teach her how to look after Tom, a family support worker to offer general support and encouragement in developing supportive relationships, and a family services worker who was helping with financial and housing issues. There was also a case manager to help coordinate all these workers, although Ruth was clearly doing some of this herself. I was interested to know what Ruth thought about all this; how did she feel about the range of people she was now involved with? Ruth was initially cautious, saying simply that this was what needed to be done to keep her son with her, so she was doing it. She did add that, because she had no car and had to use public transport, keeping up with visiting workers and looking after Tom meant she was very busy and she had no time to develop supportive relationships.

Over time, it became clear that Ruth's anger was related to a very complicated family background and a series of traumatic experiences including sexual abuse. Who then was to deal with the scars of this? Ruth had already had sessions with a sexual abuse counsellor. What seemed to be missing was someone who could work with her on the background issues that in many ways were impacting on her life.

Ruth's experience demonstrates several issues for clients and workers. While clearly not all services or agencies operate like this, her story illustrates the dangers of services that have a relatively narrow focus. Good practice emphasises the capacity to see the person in the context of their community. Not only was Ruth's connection to community lost here, but the capacity of workers to see and work with her as a whole person was limited. I suspect information about the needs of people like Ruth at a more fundamental level may also have been lost. Each service provider was gaining a sense of how many people need their particular service, which would perpetuate those services. It does not seem that anyone was asking what would be most helpful for Ruth if any kind of service was possible.

However, the picture is not all gloom. Organisations do vary and the potential to work creatively and effectively is always present. Even large and bureaucratic organisations can encourage innovative and client-responsive work. This depends partly on the assumptions and values of particular managers: some consider that workers are professionals who should be trusted to work well, others tend to see workers as dubious characters who need to be controlled. Some large, apparently bureaucratic organisations have teams or groups of workers who manage to operate in a more participatory way, sharing decision-making across the team. As Argyris and Schon (1996) suggest, organisations are dynamic, not static—they constantly change depending on who is in them (workers and managers).

Organisational structure is a key aspect of organisational life. Power and influence in organisations partly relate to a person's place in the structure. Over the years, I have seen many agencies experiment with organisational structure, some exploring what would work best from a client perspective. There is a growing interest in what I will call a more integrated way of working, that is using structures that allow workers to operate across a range of work domains depending on the issues and resources of the individuals and communities they work in. If the aim of practice is to achieve broad social change, an integrated approach is more likely to be effective than focusing solely on work with individuals and families, community work, or social policy (Garbarino and Eckenrode 1997; Pierson 2002). In the United Kingdom too, there are moves 'towards community-based practice and collaboration rather than a competitive market approach to health and social care and towards greater flexibility of budgets' (Smale et al. 2000:23).

What then are the aims of this book?

In their work with clients and/or communities, workers generally see themselves as active agents, with 'agency' meaning 'the capacity of people to act, now and in future' (Adams 2002:304). The primary aim of this book is that workers will also come to see themselves as active agents in dealing with their employer or other organisations. This might mean being active in advocating for change or in preventing the erosion of valued activities or perspectives. Rather than feeling over-whelmed by the complexity of organisational issues and dynamics, workers will consider these critically and creatively, using appropriate frameworks to consider organisational practices and potential for change. This will include looking at their own interactions with the organisation, reflecting on how they contribute to organisational life and culture.

Second, implicit in this for professional workers is being able to acknowledge the centrality of their values and how to express these in the workplace. We often talk about worker idealism and the reality of on-the-ground work as if they are opposites rather than seeing them as an important combination. Workers need ideals—clearly expressed values—about what they are doing, and why, to sustain them in their working life at the same time as having strategies to ground these values in practice. Affirming values can help workers maintain clarity about overall direction. Ideally, human service workers work in organi-sations that are congruent with their values or at least where there is creative and ongoing discussion about values. However, given that this is not always the case, workers need to find ways to maintain their sense of value about their work while working within the organisation for change.

A third aim is to provide useful knowledge and tools to enable workers to be critical participants in their organisation. To be active in organisations, workers need specific frameworks and tools for analysis and change.

Fourth, this book aims to explore a model of integrated practice for working in organisations. This model provides a framework for work-ers to consider how their work in organisations connects with broader values and principles. Integrated practice is about maintaining a broader vision of practice, moving towards more holistic work with clients and/ or communities, seeing the interactions between clients and their communities, and looking for ways to connect practice areas. In this approach, workers—and organisations—need to value clients' perspectives. Clients are likely to want to be seen as whole people, with workers who are adaptable but can find specialised resources when needed, in flexible organisations able to work to fit client issues, and who understand the client context.

Although my own background is in social work, and this is reflected to some degree in the examples I use, I have chosen to talk about workers in human service organisations rather than focusing on a particular discipline. This is for two reasons: first, my experience in working in many human service organisations is that workers from a wide variety of disciplines are employed to do essentially the same work. The emphasis for workers tends then to become how to work together effectively. This is clearly not the same across all human service organisations: teachers and nurses, for example, have some specific training for work in schools and hospitals that could not be done by any other worker. However, within nursing and teaching, as within social or welfare work, workers are trained to be able to work in many different ways— as community or school focused workers, workers with different age groups, home-based workers, and/or supervisors and managers.

The second reason for talking about workers in general is that I want here to focus on what is common, given that professional training will already focus on what is different. While it is important to recognise the contributions different disciplines make to organisational life, it is also useful to acknowledge the shared experiences of working in human service organisations: there are similar tensions and prospects for all workers in human service organisations.

This connects to the reason for the title of this book. It is about making connections at many levels:

- connections across disciplines or professional groups
- connections between ideas about how to work with clients and how to work with organisations
- connections between kinds of work; seeing, for example, how community work and work with individuals and families are linked
- connections in skills and knowledge
- connections between the personal and professional
- connections between issues for individuals and families and the social structures in which they operate.

Outline of chapters

In order to facilitate lively debate in tutorials and workshops and to encourage students and human service workers to think critically about the issues, people, and structures within organisations, I have included a large number of examples and case scenarios, drawn from my experiences of working in the field. The case scenarios may be used by students and lecturers to help visualise the various constraints and resolutions that clients may face in their dealings with organisations. Reflective practice sections in each chapter are intended to help students and workers engage with the issues raised, critically reflecting on implications for effective and active practice in organisations.

Part One: Current issues and approaches

Part One focuses on current experience and thinking about working in human service organisations. The aim here is to provide information useful for workers contemplating how to be active in influencing their organisation.

Chapter 1 explores what it is like to be a professional worker in a human service organisation, looking at the major dilemmas and tensions for workers in human service organisations. These include, for example, fragmented service delivery, an emphasis on outcomes rather than process, and fear of risk. To balance this I will also acknowledge some more positive prospects—the development of interest in community, the exploration of social exclusion as an issue, and increased understanding of the importance of social capital. This chapter also looks at two areas that are both tensions and positives: the changing view of what it means to be a professional and new approaches to research and evaluation.

Chapter 2 will identify current thinking about human service organisations that will help workers look critically at organisational practices. I will consider relevant theory about the structure of organisations, particularly understanding the nature of the bureaucratic organisation.

In Chapter 3, I will consider how theories generally used for direct service work can be used for thinking both about organisations and how they operate, and how we might act as workers. This will include understanding the general impact of postmodernism and critical theory, as well as how more specific approaches such as narrative, systems, and psychodynamic thinking can be used to reflect on organisational life.

Chapter 4 explores the culture of human service organisations, how culture is developed and maintained, including the dangers of a 'fear of risk' culture. The culture of a 'learning organisation' and how this relates to a culture of supervision is considered. The chapter finishes by looking at the influence of personality differences in organisations.

Chapter 5 takes the idea of workers being 'active agents' in the organisation, looking at what this might mean in terms of promoting and resisting change. This connects with power, authority, and leadership in organisations—who has what kind of power, who can exert leadership capacities, and how this influences change. This chapter also includes the role of clients in the organisation, particularly in relation to change.

Part Two: Integrating practice

The second part of the book will propose and explore a more integrated approach to working in organisations—that is, what might an organisation look like that enabled workers to work in active, creative, and flexible ways—focusing on the whole person as much as possible and making links to their communities. We will consider what it would mean for workers to develop their own sense of integrated practice in the context of their own organisation and community.

To do this we will start in Chapter 6 with key elements and principles of integrated practice. This will include such principles as breadth of vision; capacity to work across domains and working towards wholeness; awareness of context; active articulation of the importance of values; acknowledging common beliefs and skills; and reciprocity and shared knowledge.

Chapter 7 will then explore how these principles might translate into practice. Rather than having a prescriptive model of integrated practice, the aim would be for workers to develop their own model. Three dimensions of integrated practice are identified that workers can use to match their own skills and interests with the context they are working in—community, practice, and agency dimensions. To ground these ideas, a wide range of case scenarios of integrated practice are outlined in detail. These include examples for individual workers, workers in teams, geographically integrated practice, practice integrated across work areas, and practice integrated across practice domains.

Chapter 8 identifies a list of possible skills and knowledge for working effectively in organisations. These include considering how workers can be effective in negotiating between their personal values and beliefs and their organisational roles. Partly this relates to workers being able to articulate clearly their personal and professional values and to think through what this means about their practice.

Chapter 9 focuses on the tools workers can use to maintain their sense of their own capacity while negotiating organisational issues for themselves and their clients, particularly from an integrated practice perspective. The tools also enable workers to think creatively about their work practice and about how they might be supported in the process. Three main areas are identified:

- *tools to encourage reflecting critically on practice* in human service organisations, including use of supervision, critical incidents, reflective writing, and a set of questions for thinking about integrated practice
- *networking* for effective and integrated practice, using small groups for peer or group supervision, mutual support groups, and critical friendships
- *evaluation and research* for effective and integrated practice, with several examples of research and evaluation tools.

Finally, some strategies for integrating practice in an organisation are suggested.

Chapter 10 concludes by drawing together issues for workers in organisations and the creative use of integrated practice. We return to the initial aim of the book—finding ways for workers to be active agents in their interactions with human service organisations.

Finally, a note about language, often a vexed issue in human service organisations. I have chosen here to use the word 'client' for people using a human service organisation. Client is still the word most commonly used in organisations, though some feel it has negative connotations. Consumer or customer has become more popular, but for me reflects a more market-oriented approach, implying a relationship where the person is in control of buying a service. 'Client' implies a more complex relationship between clients and human service organisations: issues of choice are less clear, services are often provided rather than directly paid for, and there are expectations of quality and professionalism for all clients. For these reasons, I will talk about 'clients' as people in a professional relationship with an organisation and its workers.

1

Current Issues and Approaches

Working with and generally in human service organisations is an inevitable part of professional life. Organisations in turn are inevitably affected by the context in which they operate: the general social and political environment interacts with the organisation, influencing its aims and operations. Ideally organisations are also able to influence their broader environment, generating changes in policies and processes that reflect their knowledge of their communities of interest.

In order to be active and effective, workers need to be conscious of this context, how it impacts on them and their organisation, and opportunities for influencing change. Having an understanding of the broader environment enables workers to see particular organisational approaches in context. The issue of fragmented service delivery, for example, can be seen as a function of general government policies rather than as a specific reaction by one organisation.

Because of this, Part One begins in Chapter 1 by exploring the broader context for human service organisations, first raising current issues, the dilemmas and tensions of working in organisations, as well as more positive developments. Some issues of course express both—this is seen most clearly in changes in what it means to be a professional and the rise of interest in evidence-based research. Each issue generates dilemmas for workers, but also the potential for constructive change.

Chapters 2 and 3 provide a broader context in a different sense—each chapter provides useful background theory for thinking about human service organisations and how they operate. Chapter 2 focuses on theory about organisations. Chapter 3 starts with some broad theories surrounding post-modernism and critical social theory, which are influential in the general social and political environment as well as in organisational life. This is followed by exploring how direct service theories can be helpful in considering life in organisations.

Chapters 4 and 5 focus more specifically on life within human service organisations: Chapter 4 on the culture of organisations; Chapter 5 on how workers can be active in their organisation. Again, these will be influenced by the broader context—and hopefully will influence it as well.

1

Current Issues and Prospects

We are confronted in our work with the problem of implementing a holistic approach to client or community problems. Human services workers usually believe in a holistic approach. They usually do not see people as an aggregation of little boxes of need; people are seen as integrated beings. Health, for example, affects psychological well being which affects relationships, and vice versa.... In other words, humans are seen in 'systems' terms. ...The development of our services however, ...(the) growth of specialisation and the resultant division of responsibilities between different professions, different departments, and indeed different organisations leads to major problems in integrating and coordinating the total effort. (Liddell 2003:23)

Introduction

The context for organisations is an important background to this chapter, which begins by exploring some of the current major tensions when working in human service organisations. I have chosen to talk about these tensions as workers often describe their experience from inside the organisation—the limits and frustrations of funding, working to rules and procedures, fear of risk, and increasing complexity of issues. This is balanced in the second half of the chapter by identifying some of the positive 'prospects'—signs of change and opportunity for workers in the field. These include a rising interest in what community means, the use of critical reflection and reflective practice, and the interest in working in partnerships. The chapter finishes with looking at the changing nature of what it means to be a professional and new approaches to research end evaluation—both potentially either a frustration or an opportunity.

Background

Organisations do not exist in a vacuum; each organisation is constantly interacting within a broader context. Currently, that context is increasingly complex, with pressure to think globally, act economically, and respond technologically, even in organisations delivering services to individuals and families. Barnett (1999) suggests we live in an environment of 'supercomplexity'—that is, a situation where there are many conflicting frameworks through which we are trying to see the world. For example, a doctor may feel that their role is becoming more that of a counsellor, a counsellor that their role is becoming a coordinator of services, and so on.

Part of the 'conflicting frameworks' relates to how human service organisations have been influenced over the last 15 to 20 years by a more business-oriented, or what is often called a managerialist approach, to their work. The focus here is on efficiency and the effective delivery of services, rather than on flexibility to suit client needs. Workers often remark how language has changed; that their human service organisation now talks about its core business, marketing their services, and having clear outcomes for its customers or consumers. For workers expecting to operate as professionals with their focus on what is best practice for clients, this can create tensions in itself. Organisations have often become larger, providing more services in response to funding bodies seeking economies of scale. At the same time, funding bodies have required agencies to apply for funding for increasingly specific programs. Rather than having workers operate across programs, agencies have generally continued to deliver services separately. This does, of course, make it easier to account for program activities to satisfy funders that money has been appropriately spent. In practice, it means that for clients, services come in relatively narrowly defined packages. Clients can end up feeling that they need to fit the packages, that services are not organised to suit them.

State and federal governments provide much of the funding for human service organisations. Currently, there is a belief at both levels that an economic rationalist approach is preferable to the previous, more flexible, form of service provision. This approach provides services on the basis of specific services leading to distinct outcomes at a defined cost. Pusey (1991:153) points out that this 'is by no means a "value-free" and innocent means of greater coherence, consistency and commensurability of reference'. In talking about changes to the Australian federal government departments with the introduction of economic rationalism, he says 'In the central agencies or coordinating departments this process of rationalism has been invested with a transcending and universalistic moral significance that accusingly defines those against whom it is applied as having more particular, "narrower"and more pointedly still "vested" interests...Those who drive the process of rationalism believe in it and deploy it very powerfully as an evaluation framework that throws a difficult onus of justification on anyone who seeks to oppose them with defenses based on social needs or on values such as equity, compassion, common sense wisdom, courage and integrity'(Pusey 1991:154).

Ife's (1997) book, *Rethinking Social Work*, explores these issues through comparing four competing discourses in human service organisations. Two that he sees as having a major and generally negative impact are the managerial and market discourses. The managerial discourse (based on an economic rationalist approach) emphasises 'measurable outcomes, effectiveness, the efficient use of resources, rational planning...rather than on meeting the felt or expressed needs of human beings' (Ife 1997:48). Here the welfare recipient is a consumer and the social worker is the 'case manager'. In the market discourse, the welfare recipient is seen as a customer and the social worker either as the broker who helps the customer to 'purchase the most appropriate service, at the lowest possible price from the range of both government and non-government programs on offer' or as the entrepreneur seeking 'to create a market and to provide a program people will pay for' (Ife 1997:52). Disability services and respite care often provide instances of this where, for example, clients can choose which respite services and/or which kind of respite they prefer to use. In practice, this is not always as good as it sounds: in rural areas, choice about type of service is limited and even in more populated areas with more services, the pressure of demand can limit choice.

The emphasis in both these discourses is on efficiency: completing tasks quickly and effectively, maximising outcomes and minimising costs. This reflects a business rather than a traditional human service orientation where the questions are more about: what is the need here? What are the issues? How can this person/family/community best be supported and enabled? While the focus is still on change, it is in the context of values—often professional values of respect and empowerment, and broader questions of how the person will be worked with. This reflects to some degree Ife's next discourse: the professional discourse, which he also has concerns about. While this discourse does emphasise service to clients, with the service recipient seen as the client and the social worker as a service professional, Ife considers that the worker generally retains much of the control in the relationship with issues of power and decision-making. Ideally, Ife suggests we move towards a fourth discourse—the community discourse that emphasises welfare as 'social activity, or participation in a community context...it is more of a process than an outcome. It is "people helping people", and is grounded in the relationships and transactions that occur between people within the context of human community' (Ife 1997:50). Here service recipients are citizens and the role of the worker is community worker or enabler. Ife's diagram illustrates this:

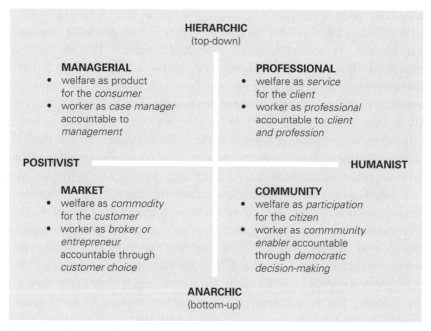

Figure 1.1 Competing discourses of human services

Source: Ife 1997:56

One way of describing what is happening for workers is that they feel caught between these discourses—or conflicting frameworks in Barnett's terms. Their human service organisation expects to operate in a businesslike fashion and to a greater or lesser degree will need to express a managerial and market-oriented capacity in order to receive funding. The worker will have been trained to act professionally with a focus on what is best practice for the client. I would argue that at least some professional training would also include an awareness of the fourth discourse proposed by Ife, that is, a desire to work jointly with clients in a community-oriented way. Managing to operate between and across these discourses is challenging for workers and the resulting tensions are not often articulated.

Current tensions for workers

Limits and frustrations of funding

One of the major issues for workers and clients is the way funding limits how services can be provided. Some talk about the fragmented nature of service delivery or delivering services in 'silos'. What this means is that services are funded according to particular categories or functions. At the broadest level this can be seen in the division of government departments into such areas as family and children's services, health, housing, and education when clearly all of these have major and direct impacts on families. More significantly, within each of these major divisions, specific programs are developed to respond to particular target groups.

In order to access services, people need to be assessed as 'having' a particular issue or problem, which might be anything from being an adult with an acquired brain injury, a family with inadequate housing, or a family conflict. Workers are expected to focus their work on these target areas and to refer issues that are not directly related to them elsewhere. As Smale et al. (2000:33) illustrate vividly, this categorisation of funding for different groups 'leads to the image of a row of lifesavers lined up on the river bank each with a different colour of hat. None of them can enter the water unless the drowning person wears a matching colour. If their lifeguard is busy, people have to change the colour of their hat to get saved. People without clothing that matches a coloured hat do not attract attention and are not rescued. Because they or their organisations, only get paid when they enter the water, none of the lifesavers go upstream'.

Many implications can be drawn from this analogy. First, it means that it can be difficult for clients to see a worker who will work with them across a range of issues. Very few services offer to work with the whole family or individual. Ruth's situation (see the case scenario in the Introduction) illustrates this very well. She was in regular contact with six different workers, each with a role to play. This required her telling her story to six different workers, endeavouring to build relationships with them all, visiting them regularly, and completing tasks to satisfy each one. It was hard for Ruth to keep track of appointments as well as what each worker expected. In a situation like this, it would seem reasonable to ask why the workers could not cover a wider range of roles. The family support worker or family services worker, for example, might have been able to talk about parenting and managing anger, while the alcohol and drug worker would have the skills to deal with financial and housing issues.

Second, it means that for many clients, no one is working with them as a whole person or as a whole family. This was certainly true for Ruth. She commented that each worker was only interested in the part of her that they were seen to be responsible for. The alcohol and drug worker was only concerned with drug use and to some extent leaving behind the drug subculture. The family services worker focused on finance and housing and, ironically, was not interested in how Ruth was managing with her child. No one asked Ruth how she was in a more basic sense; how she was feeling about her life and her sense of herself in it. Given that this question was at the heart of Ruth's drug use, her difficulties in parenting, and her lack of connections and net-works, it seemed a fundamental question, yet was missed.

The third implication is that to be a client you need to have a clearly identified issue that matches what is on offer. This creates difficulties both for potential clients who do not feel their issues match what is on offer or those who have a range of issues and want two 'lifesavers' at once. Clients with dual disabilities, for example, who want services from both mental health and physical disability services might well be in this situation. Some potential clients, of course, are not sure what they want or what will best serve their needs. Sometimes it becomes clear that what would best suit clients does not exist. Workers are then faced with a dilemma: do they compromise with what does exist or negotiate what is often a minefield of procedures to try to match client needs. There are clearly dangers in trying to fit clients into boxes. A report from the United Kingdom on research into child protection says 'Clients suffered whenever professionals became preoccupied with a specific event, ignored the wider context, chose the wrong "career avenue" for the child, or excluded the family from the enquiry' (cited in Winter and Munn-Giddings 2001). Unfortunately, the pressures of work and the inflexibility of the system mean that workers do look for what there is rather than what there might be.

Finally, the fourth implication is that there is no one to 'swim up-stream' and find out why so many people are 'in the river'. It may be that if we looked at the underlying causes for service demand, we might take a different approach. Sadly, so much funding goes into providing the services or lifesavers, that often little is left for looking at prevention. Martinez-Brawley (2000) points out that there are considerable costs in having such fragmented services. However, there are some signs that this may be changing with an increased interest in the importance of community (see the discussion later in this chapter).

It is important here to mention case management, which partly developed as a means of managing this fragmentation of services for clients. The idea was that a case manager would act as a coordinator of services for the client and act as a central point for information. Essentially, as Payne (1997:55) suggests, case management approaches are an 'administrative system' within which work can be provided. There are many views about case management and its success, Ife (1997:52), for example, is critically suggesting that such work is 'technical, controlling and dedicated to the achievement of measurable results using available resources in the most effective way. There seems little room...for a feeling of common humanity with another, for personal growth, for empowerment, for empathy, or for self fulfillment unless these are seen in strictly instrumental terms'. Other writers suggest that case management provides a much needed service, enabling clients to find the most appropriate services in a bewildering service system. Guransky et al. (2003) found that case management worked well in some situations and not so well in others. They suggest that the aims and underlying principles are generally positive; it is the delivery that is the issue, with limited funds, and pressure to focus on outcomes rather than responding flexibly to client issues.

Certainly, case management can and does provide coordination. However, it also perpetuates a system where clients work with many workers for small amounts of service. In Ruth's situation, for example, this meant that no one worked with what she saw as her most significant issues—how she felt about herself and her life—but many workers worked with her on specific issues. Guransky et al. (2003:199) suggest that 'what is often neglected in discourses about case management is acknowledgement that the approach does not supersede service provision'.

Clearly, one worker is not able to provide all of the knowledge and skills needed by every family or individual. The debate here is partly about what range of areas it is reasonable to expect a worker to cover. In practice, this varies considerably. In the United Kingdom, for example, social service workers in some areas can be expected to work across all age groups and deal with a wide range of issues from family crises to older people needing supported accommodation. Rather than having a prescriptive view about what can be done, a more helpful question to ask is what range is possible.

Increased complexity of issues

When I talk with experienced practitioners about how their practice has changed compared to 15 or 20 years ago, they often raise the increasingly complex nature of practice. Generally what they mean by this is that the individual and family situations they see present a greater range of complex issues. The challenges of working with these relate partly to changes in organisations and how services operate.

So what do practitioners mean by this? First, while increased complexity is not necessarily seen as negative, and in fact adds to the diversity and richness of life, this complexity needs to be recognised as needing more time and energy to engage with rather than less. Practitioners often feel that they are expected to deal with more issues in less time with fewer resources, or to focus on one issue in isolation when it is clearly affected by others.

One of the major changes relates to deinstitutionalisation; many people now being supported in the community would have been in institutions 20 years ago—people with intellectual and physical disabilities as well as those with psychiatric disabilities. While workers see this as a positive development with increased quality of life for many clients, it does mean for many families—and for workers—another layer of both richness and challenge with which to engage.

Second, family structures are more varied and this can also present challenges. The complications of 'blended' families with multiple layers of connections again means for families, as well as workers, that many different needs, issues, and values need to be taken into account.

Third, workers talk about having more contact with a greater diversity of cultures and backgrounds. For some, this is about contact with migrants and refugees and trying to understand life from other perspectives, including experiences of severe trauma and dislocation.

Fourth, other workers raise the issue of a greater sense of anger and tendency for violence to erupt; they point to the increase in safety mechanisms in offices—barriers between receptionists and clients, emergency alarms in waiting rooms. They see this as part of a greater sense of alienation; perhaps related to people not feeling heard in the wider social system and/or to the widening gap between the aspirations of a consumer society and what is possible for most people.

Fifth, workers also talk about the complexity of the systems they and clients need to deal with. The fragmentation of the service system means that it is often confusing to work out which services will fit best. Rules and procedures (explored further below) can be perplexing for workers as well as clients. Sometimes it seems as if the system has been set up to cause the most possible obstructions to finding help. Workers, like clients, struggle to find the service that seems appropriate, then struggle also with the paperwork to make a referral. Schon (1983) suggests that the rate of change, and the range of knowledge needed to keep up with it, also contributes to this sense of increasing complexity: 'Professionals are called upon to perform tasks for which they have not been educated' (Schon 1983:14).

Case scenario

Kate works for an aged care service. She saw a family recently who had been looking for nursing home care for George Jones' mother, Joan. The family had visited ten nursing homes and contacted twenty others looking for a place. Joan had been living with the family for 10 years and now has the beginnings of dementia. George remarried 12 years ago and his partner, Susie, had two young children, now 14 and 16 years old. George and Susie now also have two young children of their own. Having Joan live with them initially worked well, but they are now stressed with the combination of lack of space, the different needs of the children, Joan's health, and maintaining often difficult relationships with their ex-partners. When Kate explains the complexity of the aged care system and lack of available beds, George explodes and abuses her. Even though she can see why he is so frustrated, she is shaken and finds it hard not to take it personally.

Pressure to work to established routines and procedures

A third major tension for workers is the expectation of working to established routines and procedures at a time when client issues are increasingly complex. Exactly what this means varies depending on the organisation and its context. An obvious example would be the increased emphasis in child protection procedures. Some of these procedures are determined by law and the requirements of the court system; others by policies within a particular government agency. Workers can feel this limits their ability to work creatively and intuitively with the client, to acknowledge the process of the interaction with the client. Instead the focus becomes completing the necessary paperwork and ensuring deadlines are met. Jones (2001:553) in an article about social workers employed by the state in Britain says that often 'the contact (with clients) is more fleeting, more regulated and governed by the demands of the forms which now shape much of the intervention'.

Another aspect of this is the expectation that clients will be seen for a set number of sessions with the assumption that major issues can be dealt with often in a relatively short time. In some areas, agencies as diverse as centres against sexual assault and family counselling services limit clients to six to eight sessions, partly as a way of dealing with limited funding and resulting waiting lists. Given that the issues being raised by clients are often of long-standing, clients may feel they have only just begun the process when it has to be stopped. While some practitioners would argue that brief, solution-focused work can be as effective as longer processes (de Shazer 1991), this is not true for all clients. Setting such limits negates client diversity and the need for services to meet client needs.

In this context, measuring outcomes for clients is likely to be an agency focus. This is not easy to do—how do you measure client change? Often agencies resort to measuring events and activities rather than change. For example, workers are asked to identify how many sessions they have had with clients, for how long, topics discussed, and actions undertaken. As Orme (2002:239) suggests, 'the problem with such measurements is that they take no account of the quality of service which might be given and the purpose of the social worker being involved in the first place'. Similarly, in nursing, Street (1990:17) says, 'The nurse cannot treat a unique case as an instrumental problem to be solved by the application of known rules. Instead, the nurse needs to rely on knowledge, experience, improvisation, invention and new strategies relevant to the given situation'. Again workers are caught between the expectations of the agency and their own desire to work as professionals.

Fear of risk

The emphasis on established procedures may reflect an increasing concern about accountability; a sense for workers as well as clients of being at risk in some way. Parton and O'Byrne (2000:1), writing in the social work field, say 'we have become concerned that social work both in the way we think about it and practise it has become very defensive, overly proceduralised and narrowly concerned with assessing, managing and insuring against risk'. This certainly fits with my recent contact with workers in human service organisations where a common comment has been something like 'you need to make sure you have covered yourself, when things go wrong, you feel very much on your own'. Taylor and White (2000:3) suggest that in the health and welfare fields generally, the 'external pressures upon professionals to make good judgements and decisions have increased in recent years'. They suggest three reasons for this—public awareness and media coverage into, for example, child deaths; a more consumer-oriented approach; and the move to seeing welfare services as businesses rather than as professional domains.

While it is clearly reasonable that workers should be accountable, there are dangers in this approach. Workers can become so focused on 'covering their backs' that they lose sight of what is important and effective in their work with clients. Banks (2002) suggests that the balance between being accountable and responsive has become distorted. One of the social workers she interviews gives an example: 'One of my clients hung himself in the garage, yesterday afternoon. The first thing I was asked was: "Is the file up to date?" Because it's so important that the file is up to date and that nobody can be held to be responsible' (Banks 2002:34).

Experiences such as these are likely to make workers work to rule, rather than thinking creatively about effective client contact. This is damaging to both clients and workers, particularly since 'health and welfare work is a messy and complicated business in which there are often no right or wrong answers. Workers are confronted by situations in which risk and uncertainty prevail' (Taylor and White 2000:5). Unfortunately for workers, it seems that the organisational response to this is often to aim to standardise and control activities. Vince (2002:1202), for example, says 'Fear of failure and risk reinforced fear of conflict and conflicts were therefore covered over rather than dealt with....Managers' difficulties with conflict, both personal and organisational, undermined the extent of their authority to act corporately'. Instead organisations could seek ways of ensuring that work is of high quality to minimise mistakes and support staff when inevitably mistakes are made.

Prospects: possibilities for change

The situation with human service organisations, however, is not all negative—there are signs of positive change. Organisations interact with and are affected by their environment, including the communities they relate to. There is an increase in interest from governments, particularly about the need to consider community context, and this will ultimately have an impact on human service organisations and their workers.

There is also an increased interest in critical reflection; a theory and a process for enabling workers and their organisations to look more critically at practice. This again will have a positive impact on organisations. Third, there is more interest in working in partnerships that may allow for more creative ways of working with clients and communities.

This chapter concludes with two areas that can be seen as offering both tensions and possibilities. First, there is interest in what it means to be a professional; clarifying expectations about professional roles may mean that professionals are seen more realistically and able to work more collaboratively. Second, there is interest in more research and evaluation, often talked about in terms of 'evidence-based practice'. While this may reinforce a limited view of research, part of it is also a broader desire to use research and evaluation to explore and deepen the understanding of issues in human service organisations.

Rise of interest in community context

All individuals and families are part of a community at some level, whether it is a community of interest or a geographic community. How people interact with their community is often significant in terms of how they deal with change and crisis. However, the importance of this community relationship is not often recognised by organisations and so in turn not seen as a valid area of interest for workers. Opportunities are then lost for looking with families at their interactions with their community, what mutual support there might be, and how families' resources might complement each other.

There is a growth in research that connects family well-being with their community. Coughy, O'Campo, and Brodsky (1999), for example, reinforce the importance of neighbourhood and larger societal factors in the health and well-being of communities. Their research suggests that positive individual and community outcomes on a range of health measures are connected to:

- a lower level of crime and higher perception of neighbourhood safety
- community organisation and a positive sense of belonging to a community.

They give an example where the risk of low birth weight for highly educated women living in poorly organised neighbourhoods was almost two and a half times the risk for poorly educated women living in well-organised communities. Vinson's (2004) research also links internal and external issues as important to communities: in his study of disadvantage there were significant differences in rural areas in terms of community strengths compared to urban areas. He suggests that while this is an exploratory study, it does suggest that in some areas of disadvantage 'compensatory inner strengths may be a formidable ally to community renewal initiatives' (Vinson 2004).

Similarly, Garbarino and Eckenrode (1997) identify the need for an ecological approach that aims to strengthen communities as well as families. Garbarino and Barry (1997) identify four working assumptions from their research into neighbourhoods that are likely to be 'high-risk' in relation to child maltreatment. These include economic forces that are significant but not exclusive determinants of neighbourhood character; residential segregation based on socioeconomic factors that threatens family well-being because it produces concentrations of high-need, low-resource families that lack positive role models, opportunities for mutual nurture and feedback, and the capacity to share. Results such as these suggest the value for human service workers of making connections with communities to be effective in work with individuals and families.

The organisation itself is part of a community, again at varying levels. Some organisations see themselves as operating almost as if they are removed from the community; instead they are operating from policies and procedures handed down a central level. Some of course *are* quite separate such as the rapidly expanding call centres where the staff may be located hundreds or thousands of kilometres from their clients. However, organisations must be in some kind of relationship with at least their community of interest—that is, the client groups to whom they owe their existence. More positively, some organisations act as community members, paying attention to community issues and responding accordingly. Being interested in the community can provide benefits for organisations as well as for their clients.

Case scenario

Shared Action is a community development project in an area with few physical resources and community activities. One of the area's few resources, the primary school, had been sold by the government to an employment and training agency. This caused considerable resentment in the community. Volunteers and staff at Shared Action asked the agency to provide some funding to help with the newly developed under-13 football team in the local community. Vandalism at the agency dropped dramatically and the community began to see the agency as a potential resource. The agency was able to work with the community to develop training programs that provided short-term employment and long-term skills for community residents.

My sense is that there is some feeling of optimism that change may again be developing both in how our society wants to operate in terms of community and in service provision. Saleeby (1997) suggested in the 1990s, for example, that there was a beginning reawakening of interest in community work in reaction to the impact of economic rationalism, a desire to move away from seeing individuals in terms of outputs and more as whole people in relation to their communities. There has been an increasing interest in the idea of community in general. For some people there is a longing for a greater sense of being connected to others, reflected in talking about communities. This is reflected in popular writing by Scott Peck (1987), as well as writing in the professional field (McMillan and Chavis 1986; McKnight 1997). Much recent writing incorporates a strengths-based approach to communities, emphasising the importance of acknowledging a community's resources and capabilities as well as what needs to change (LeCroy 1999).

Writing about social capital has been particularly important in generating interest in community. Again this seems partly a reaction to the dominance of talking about economic capital. Putnam (2000:19) has been particularly influential, describing social capital as 'connections among individuals—social networks and the norms of reciprocity and trustworthiness that arise from them'. Eva Cox suggests that developing social capital requires 'opportunities for trust and cooperation....if most of our experiences enhance our sense of trust and mutuality, allowing us to feel valued and to value others, then social capital increases'(Cox 1995:17). Healy and Hampshire (2002:232) suggest that for workers the notion of social capital is helpful first in terms of reinforcing the links between the 'social' and 'economic', and the 'micro' and 'macro'. It also gives workers a language to 'evaluate the social capital effects of their activities'; to be conscious of 'directing resources to the kind of social capital development that we are trying to achieve'.

Vinson's (2004) study on community adversity and resilience supports the importance of social capital and social cohesion. He researched the distribution of social disadvantage across postcode areas of Victoria and New South Wales. The results showed significant differences between urban and rural communities in terms of community strengths. He suggests that while this is an exploratory study, it does indicate that in some areas of disadvantage 'compensatory inner strengths may be a formidable ally to community renewal initiatives' (Vinson 2004:80). However, he continues to emphasise the need to balance recognising the resilience and health of some communities with awareness of the impact of macro-economic policies and the importance of external resourcing.

The valuing of social capital and focus on community is not to suggest that the experience of community is always positive. Communities like families and individuals are enormously variable and people experience community very differently (Cox 1995; Brodsky, O'Campo and Aronson 1999). Communities can operate to exclude people who are perceived as different or disruptive of the prevailing norms—which is all too clear in the world community at present. There is a danger in seeing a community as a united entity when it is generally more realistic to think of communities as a complicated mixture of cooperation and conflict.

Some governments are again starting to pay attention to generating positive community building. In Victoria, the government is funding local communities to assess their own needs and resources and to develop local responses. The Federal Government is funding community initiatives under its community capacity building initiative. The two broadly desired outcomes clearly reflect the influence of thinking about social capital:

1 Improved community capacity as indicated by improvement in skills and access to resources, and increase and improvement in leaders, networks and partnerships.
2 Community capacity applied as indicated by an increase in opportunities or activity to address local problems (Family and Community Services Department 2000).

In Britain and the USA, there is also currently significant interest in funding major projects to generate what is often called 'community capacity building' or working towards 'social inclusion'. The 'New Deal for Communities' aims to tackle multiple social issues in what are seen as the most disadvantaged communities in England, as part of the National Strategy for Neighbourhood Renewal. In the USA, the Robert Wood Johnson Foundation has funded an Urban Health Initiative to address health and safety issues for children and youth in distressed urban areas. These projects all have in common a desire to work from a broader community focus to resolve issues affecting individuals and families. Depending on the program and the particular government emphasis, communities or neighbourhoods are encouraged to develop plans around key goal areas such as employment, education, or what the community perceives as community-building strategies.

However, it is important to note the limits to this approach. The expectation is that communities will identify expected outcomes in their application for funding, but a more community-oriented approach would allow outcomes to emerge as the process developed. A second concern can be that governments expect change quickly: three-year programs are not likely to be sufficient for communities that have experienced major disadvantage over many years. Vinson's (2004) notion of balancing the external and internal is important here too; there can be a danger in governments expecting communities to become more self-supporting, drawing on their own internal resources when they also need realistic amounts of external resourcing in order to build greater capacity and social capital.

Interest in critical reflection and reflective practice

Over recent years, interest in critical reflection and reflective practice has increased remarkably across a wide range of professional disciplines, including teaching (Brookfield 1995; Cowan 1998), adult education (Mezirow 1991), nursing (Johns and Freshwater 1998), and social work (Kondrat 1999; Parton and O'Byrne 2000; Fook 2002), as well as in research and evaluation (Everitt and Hardiker 1996) There are many definitions of reflective practice; often it seems that writers focus on writing within their own discipline, although this is starting to change. Cherry, for example, talks about 'action learning rather than reflective practice—that is, 'experience-based learning' where 'the individual is asked to access direct personal experience and practice in 'real life' situations: this contrasts with reading about other people's experience and ideas or simply thinking about ideas in a training situation' (Cherry, 1999:8).

Essentially, reflective practice encourages workers to stop and think about their practice—often using a particular incident from practice, taking into account both what they think and feel about it. The process usually includes analysing practice in the sense of exploring assumptions and values that influence how they work so that workers look at these consciously and consider the implications of this for practice. The 'critical' element adds an expectation of exploring practice in the context of the social system in which it operates, looking, for example, at the influence of dominant social expectations about gender, age, disability, culture, sexual orientation, and class. It also includes looking at assumptions developed from family and other life experiences where these impact on working relationships.

Kondrat (1999:464) makes a useful distinction between:

- *Reflective self-awareness*. This assumes a subject-self who reflects on an object-self's behaviours, emotions, thoughts, and actions. The aim is to be aware of the impact of the subject self, in terms of biases, for example, so that such biases can be reduced or eliminated.
- *Reflexive self-awareness*. This is the realisation that we cannot totally stand aside from ourselves because we are so influenced by our own history, culture, and language. Workers become aware of those processes by which the self interacts with others to create meaning and identities.
- *Critical reflectivity*. This is the synthesising perspective where self is seen as 'inextricably emersed in society's structures both as agent and as product'. Workers need to be aware of how at individual and social levels they maintain or change social structures.

While reflective practice may be any one or more of these for some writers, for others reflection is inextricably critical (Johns and Freshwater 1998; Kondrat 1999; Fook 2002). Kondrat (1999:465), for example, says: 'the self that emerges in this framework is a self who cannot escape his or her day-to-day involvement in the ongoing construction, maintenance or renewal of the structures of society....In one manner of speaking, then, self-reflection is always a reflection on society and vice versa.'

Using a critical reflection framework, then, reflects a particular way of looking at the world. It helps generate an awareness of the influence of context and structure and the subjective meanings that affect interactions. For reflection to be critical, it must also include the capacity to consider social structures and power relationships analytically and apply this analysis in practice. The critically reflective practitioner develops the capacity to deconstruct knowledge and assumptions, in order to 'develop (reconstruct) their own practice in inclusive, artistic and intuitive ways which are responsive to the changing (uncertain, unpredictable and fragmented) contexts in which they work; and in ways which can challenge existing power relations and structures' (Fook 2002:41).

Such a framework can encourage practitioners to articulate their own subjective meanings, to analyse these in terms of the social and institutional structures with which they are involved, and to seek change in the light of this understanding. Critical workers ask, for example, what assumptions they unwittingly make that perpetuate stereotypes and inequities and seek to change both their own and other people's assumptions and the structures they reflect. Part of the process is paying attention to feelings. Murphy and Atkins (1994:13) suggest that:

> Reflection is initiated by an awareness of uncomfortable feelings and thoughts which arise from a realization that the knowledge one was applying in a situation was not itself sufficient to explain what was happening in that unique situation. The focus of learning is upon critical analysis of these unique practice situations. It is important that this analysis involves an examination of both feelings and knowledge so that the knowledge required for professional practice is illuminated.

Implicit in critical reflection is an assumption that the personal and professional cannot be separated. As we will explore further (see Chapter 8), we inevitably express who we are in how we react and interact. The process of articulating assumptions can unearth assumptions from family or past personal history as well as from work-related experiences. Some assumptions connect across areas of life—for example, a worker might realise that their assumption that conflict should be avoided is part of their family and work life. This is easier for some workers to acknowledge and use than others. Duke and Copp (1994:103), for example, in working with nursing students say that:

> those students who have previously believed that to be professional in your approach to care means that you are detached personally have found using reflection fundamentally difficult since they are now being encouraged to look at themselves. Furthermore, reflection exposes

personal beliefs, motivations and vulnerabilities. Recording and expressing experiences and feelings in writing makes explicit an individual's reaction to these things and this can be both a painful and powerful experience.

So why this surge of interest in critical reflection across many disciplines? Again this may be a reaction to the pressure to act in more routine and inflexible ways, to focus on outcomes, and follow procedures. Critical reflection and reflective practice affirm that practice involves creative processes that are intuitive and subjective, reflecting the personal and cultural influences on workers. Reflecting critically encourages workers to explore their hidden assumptions and values so that they can be made explicit and lead to change. Feedback from workshops using critical reflection shows that workers value the intuitive and dynamic in their work; they want to be able to use their 'self', as well as their knowledge, skills, and values. Critical reflection also enables workers to look at their organisation more critically and to see issues of power and authority in a more complex way. The process of reflecting critically often enables workers to see how they can become more confident about seeking change in the organisation.

Working in partnerships

One of the implications of the more business-oriented approach to service delivery was to encourage a more competitive attitude between services. This was partly because the method of funding changed; rather than services being allocated to agencies on the basis of history, experience, and/or demonstrated needs, agencies had to tender for services, demonstrating why they would be able to provide them more effectively and efficiently. This was in response to the federal government's agenda for increased competitiveness. The Hilmer Report (1993), the *National Competition Policy Report by the Independent Committee of Inquiry*, reflected a market-oriented view in Ife's terms; a belief that 'competition is a positive force that assists economic growth and job creation. It has triggered initiative and discovery' (Hilmer 1993:xv). The report recommended a Competition Policy that would encourage competition to 'promote efficiency and economic growth'. It is important to note that Hilmer (1993:xvi) added 'while accommodating situations where competition does not achieve or conflicts with other social objectives'. However, government desire for a competitive approach was so strong that this approach eventually extended to the human service field in the form of competitive tendering.

You could argue that this is a reasonable approach: it means that new agencies have opportunities to prove their worth, rather than the same agencies always receiving services even if they are not working well. However, the compulsory competition for funding also lessened cooperative relationships between agencies, generating an atmosphere where agencies became protective of their information and resources so that they were better placed to compete (McDonald 2002). Agencies had to allocate considerable amounts of time and resources to tendering for services. Larger agencies were generally better placed to deal with the costs of this and so smaller agencies tended to miss out, leading to the development of fewer and larger agencies. Ironically, initially the tendering process encouraged 'collaboration', which in practice tended to mean smaller agencies working with larger agencies and were eventually incorporated into them.

There are some signs now that governments and other funding bodies are wanting to create more positive cooperative working relationships across agencies. Many tender documents now require agencies to demonstrate that they will be working cooperatively with other agencies in the delivery of services. Language such as 'partnerships', working 'collaboratively', and 'cooperative working relationships' has become desirable. Funders have recognised that to be able to provide services effectively in communities, agencies need to be able work together, while still being able to maintain independence.

Darling (2000), writing from the USA, talks about the 'resurgence' in the social systems approach where individuals and families are seen in the context of their communities and social structures. This links to a movement to a partnership approach in community- and family-centred practice. Darling sees this happening in reaction to fragmented, rule-oriented service delivery, similar to what we have been talking about here. What this means in practice has been, for example, the development of early intervention services often based in schools, with many services under one roof so that they are accessible and can be easily coordinated. The USA, like the United Kingdom, has also developed Family Centre programs that 'are intended to be preventive and supportive rather than corrective' (Darling 2000:28). Partnership here is about professionals and clients working together as well as agencies working effectively with each other. Taylor (2004) writes about change in the United Kingdom, with increased funding to major projects based on partnerships between organisations with service delivered jointly at a local level.

Tensions and possibilities

Changing views of what it means to be a professional

Being a professional worker can seem a mixed blessing in the current climate. Ife's (1997) discourses show how professionals in human service organisations can be operating from a number of contradictory discourses, taking on roles that fit particular ideologies. Historically, being a professional was valued: professionals were seen as having useful expertise. Professional workers were expected to have been trained to be able to operate confidently and independently, with a commitment to the public good. However, Schon (1983) identifies a change in views from the 'triumphant professions' of the early 1960s, to the scepticism and unease of the 1970s and early 1980s. Ivan Illich is well known for his criticisms of the disempowering nature of professionalism (Illich 1972). Ife (1997) too questions the relative power of the professional in relation to those they work with.

The traditional view of the professions developed with modernist thinking that will be explored more in Chapter 3. Essentially, in terms of professional practice, modernism encouraged a view that identified 'the major professions as those with unambiguous ends, a knowledge base that is firmly bounded, strictly scientific, standardised and located within a positivist epistemology' (Cowley 1999:6). Professional practice then was about clear and definite answers, professionals as experts with knowledge often seen as difficult for the layperson to understand. Notice that Cowley talks here about the *major* professions: this would originally have been professions such as medicine, law, and accounting that lend themselves more easily to a scientific orientation. Fook et al. (2000) point out that professions are also defined in status terms, with some—often those seen as more women's professions—being less scientific and having less status, the 'semi-professions' of social work, teaching, and nursing. Professional groups can also be seen as seeking to control particular areas of knowledge in order to exert power. In our current social system, the scientific professions are generally seen as more powerful, so the 'semi-professions' have often aimed to become more scientific. In social work, for example, there has been much debate about whether social work is a science or an art.

For the sake of this discussion, we will assume that workers in human service organisations are professional workers, who do have power by virtue of this status. Cowley (1999:4) suggests that what professionals in human service organisations have in common is that they use skills based on a specific, if not unique, theoretical knowledge base and have education and training in these skills, have to pass competency tests by a professional body, and have 'professionals status... associated with the performance of service for the public good'. Matheson (1998), in exploring whether senior public servants can be considered to be professional, considers professionalism as a continuum rather than an either/or: 'All that we can say is that when located on the continuum between a full profession and a non-profession, it falls roughly half way...its members possess specialist expertise, a degree of collegiality and some autonomy'. He goes on to compare this with 'a full profession...as there is no relatively definite and teachable skills, no course of training for entrants, no standard and indispensable qualifications, or admission and mutual control exercised by means of peer review and recommendation' (Matheson 1998:22).

The modernist definition of professionals led to common myths and assumptions that still cause tensions, particularly for those working in human service organisations. Traditionally, professionals were placed —and often wanted to be placed—on pedestals, and were seen as experts able to direct and instruct people in what should be done. Inevitably, it became clear that professionals did not always know best and did not always agree. However, some professionals continue to take on board these myths or assumptions, thus creating unhelpful relationships with clients.

Common myths about professionals

Professionals always know best and should therefore make decisions for their clients

Clearly professional workers have knowledge, skills, and experience that we value as clients—that is usually why we see them. Professionals operate with varying amounts of professional discretion—the ability to make decisions on their own based on training and experiential knowledge. However, when we are clients, we are aware that we also have our own knowledge, of our own situation at least, our likely reactions and preferences, and skills that we can use in general as well as in making decisions. We generally do not want to hand over decision-making to professionals, but rather to work with them to make our own decisions about what to do. Clients often say to us, 'we are the ones who will have to live with the situation, so we need to decide what will suit us'. This suggests the need to work collaboratively instead: Higgs and Titchen (2001:12), speaking for a group of professionals, propose, 'we recognise and value the uniqueness and individuality of people as both recipients and providers of professional services, or more desirably as partners in professional practice. To achieve this... requires professional artistry or creativity and expertise in doing, knowing, being and becoming'.

Clearly there are some situations where workers as professionals in human service organisations do have to make decisions. This is easier to see in some situations than others. In working with involuntary clients, for example, workers do, at times, have to make recommendations or decisions based on their knowledge and experience. A court wants a recommendation based on professional knowledge and judgment. However, even here the aim is to work with clients as much as possible. A plan for change is more likely to work if it is one conceived of or at least shared by those expected to carry it out.

Obviously the degree of influence of the professional will vary depending on the situation. A health care worker might recommend a particular rehabilitation program for an older woman based on her knowledge of the woman's health issues and the range of services available. The older woman might agree that this would be useful in theory but in practice decide that she just does not feel she has the energy to take it up.

Another aspect of professional discretion is how much should workers be able to make decisions themselves based on their professional judgment rather than having to be answerable to a more senior worker. This partly relates to myth four (see later in the chapter), that professionals are always operating for the public good. Professionals often value independence in decision-making, but no one is infallible. Lipsky (1980) points out some of the dangers of what he calls 'street level bureaucrats' having discretion—seeing some clients as more deserving than others, for example, or being swayed by particular experiences. Baldwin (2004:46) suggests that discretion is an inevitable part of work in human service organisations; the problem is that 'intuition can be based on prejudice, empathy can be experienced by others as patronizing and discriminatory, and values can be based on unchecked assumptions'. He suggests using critical reflection rigorously to counter this.

Finally, 'knowing best' implies that there is a best or a right answer for every situation. More realistically in professional domains, there are many possible answers to any situation, and a variety of alternatives can be equally realistic. 'Professionals work in indeterminate practice arenas' (Schon 1983) where there are many possibilities/ alternatives available and many choices to be made from among them. 'For instance, there are often no right or wrong decisions in teaching, only judgements that this knowledge or this learning strategy is more or less appropriate in this context with these learners' (Ewing and Smith 2001:19). Our own preferences can mean that we think clients will want a particular action, which may not be the case. The following case scenario demonstrates this.

Case scenario

Alice broke her hip and was in hospital for several weeks. After she was discharged, she requested home help and was visited by the local government's Home and Community Care coordinator for assessment. A week after the visit, Alice received a letter telling her that she was entitled to home help twice a week, meals on wheels daily, and a home handyman visit monthly, and that these services had been arranged to start from the day she received the letter. Alice was furious, as she had been quite specific about what she wanted. It took several phone calls over the next two hours to cancel services she had not requested. She was too late to cancel the first meals on wheels delivery and received a bill for a meal she did not need or want. She wrote to her local councillor pointing out that professionals needed to listen to their clients and not make decisions on their behalf without communication.

Professionals have the same training (that is, share a knowledge and skill base and so will always agree)

One of the aspects of professional life that surprises workers and clients alike is that professionals do not always agree. This can be perceived in different ways: clearly it is exasperating to have professionals generating a number of ways of looking at something when, as a client, you want consistent and unambiguous answers. People who are sick, for example, want to know what will make them better. The court system wants to know that the professionals have worked out the best alternative for a child or offender.

At the same time, as workers and clients, we often know that there are rarely clear answers. We cannot know for certain that one answer will necessarily work, and we do know that the same answer often does not work for everybody. Cowley (1999:6) suggests that the '"real world" of practice tends to be unstable, shifting, unpredictable, unique and contradictory; for this a different form of knowledge that Schon calls "professional artistry" is needed'. Her perspective is that life rarely has clear answers; instead it is a matter of working out what seems most reasonable to try in a given situation.

Professionals are objective and unaffected by their own experience
Traditionally, professionals were trained to be, or to appear to be, consistently calm and objective, able to operate without emotion, and able to separate the personal and professional. Higgs and Titchen (2001:10) say 'Terms like "clinical", "academic" and even "professional" have understandably acquired connotations of distance, reserve and dominance, through such factors as exclusive education, privileged knowledge bases and technical expertise, but these connotations are also attributable to professional socialisation programmes which result in adopted and learned models of professional conduct, and which commonly encourage maintaining professional distance'. Training of social workers in the 1960s, for example, discouraged social workers from accepting cups of tea offered by clients on the basis that this was not a sufficiently professional interaction. While we might laugh at this now, there are still debates in training for professionals about what is appropriate behaviour.

Workers still struggle with how to be 'professional'; to what degree can they express their personality at work. Clearly, professionals are affected by their own experience and their strength is in how to use this. Bolton (2001:45) says 'We do not practise with one part of ourselves, and live a personal life with another, all the elements of ourselves are each a part of the other'. This acknowledgment of the private and personal, is a positive aspect of changing attitudes to what it means to be a professional. More realistically, current writing acknowledges the complexity of the interaction between the professional and personal. Effective workers are aware of their own reactions, emotions, and thoughts and can use them as part of their tools of practice.

Professionals are only interested in the public good rather than their own
This is another aspect of the dispassionate and objective professional. While from my experience it is fair to say that most professionals working in human service organisations do have a high degree of desire to work for the public good, they generally also get satisfaction and/or other rewards from their work, or they do not usually stay in it. It is important to acknowledge this for several reasons. First, accepting

there is mutual benefit in the relationship can remove a disempowering element from the relationship between worker and client—a sense of the professional as all-giving and the client as all-receiving. Instead, the relationship can be seen as mutually beneficial. Second, it helps to remove a sense of otherness—that is, worker as distinct from client, to create more of an attitude of partnership.

The community's experience of professionals is mixed and for some professionals the public good is clearly much less significant than what they feel is good for themselves. This creates a degree of cynicism for some clients about some professionals in human service organisations, and means that each professional has to develop their own credibility with clients, rather than being able to rely on a common goodwill towards all professionals.

Current views about professionals

Professionals in human service organisations face both issues or tensions and a sense of new possibilities. Often it seems workers talk about the struggle to have their professional skills and knowledge recognised and valued. The checks on what individual workers can do means that their capacity to make decisions themselves are eroded at least in some organisations. The issues we identified in the first part of this chapter also relate to frustrations for professionals—for example, the increased expectations of working to routines and procedures, the reduced flexibility given funding guidelines, and the focus on risk rather than creative and proactive practice.

However, there is also an increasing desire for professional practice that fits the 'real world of practice' that is reflected in a range of current writing and research. Higgs and Titchen's book, *Professional Practice in Health, Education and the Creative Arts*, for example, comes from a 'cooperative inquiry'—a group of professionals from the creative arts, health, and education spending a week together exploring what it might mean to talk about professional practice (Higgs and Titchen 2001:viii). Together they generated the 'development of a conceptual framework which represents a vision of people-centered, accountable, context-relevant professional practice, suitable for the demanding world of human services which we are facing today and tomorrow'. As part of the discussion they considered the curricula of many professional courses and concluded that courses tend to focus on skills and knowledge, and were 'less about how knowledge is generated, understood and critiqued in their professional context'.

Fook et al. (2000) carried out an extensive research project looking at professional expertise. They decided to work with a definition of professionals that focused on what was common across all professional groups regardless of status or field. What they saw as common was 'the imperative to practice effectively, using a given body of knowledge, in a constantly changing and complex environment' (Fook et al. 2000:3). This is a helpful definition for this book given that here we too are looking at working across professional groups working in human service organisations. In using this definition, we can see that professionals:

- Focus on *practice*—they aim to be doing, to incorporate relevant theory into specific activities.
- Aim to practise *effectively*—they want to make sure that what they do is helpful and constructive, and leads to positive rather than negative change.
- Use a *specific body of knowledge*. The knowledge used by professionals will vary depending on their background and their field of practice. The common feature is that professionals are aware of the value of knowledge and how to use it.
- Manage *change and complexity*. Professionals are trained and have an expectation that their work will have many uncertainties and that they have the capacity to manage them creatively rather than expecting work to be routine.
- See the importance of the *environment*. The context in which workers operate both at an organisational and community level will inevitably affect what they are able to do.

Compared to the myths about professionals, these approaches would encourage us to think about professionals and clients as people who have skills, knowledge, and experience to offer. They would be working collaboratively with clients for possible options for change rather than seeking 'the answer'. Such professionals would be aware of context, consciously able to use their selves in their work and interested in a range of views about how things could be done.

New perspectives on research and evaluation

In recent times, there has an increased interest in research and evaluation from many perspectives. I have included this section here because some writers and practitioners have mixed feelings about these. Generally, the value of research and evaluation is not questioned as both are fundamentally about asking questions: often, for practitioners, about what works and why, what processes influence positive outcomes, and how to ensure that practice is effective.

Part of what has been positive has been interest in developing an organisational climate where practitioners are interested in and able to be continuously evaluating their own work. This is partly about creating in organisations what Winter calls a 'culture of inquiry' (Winter and Munn-Giddings 2001:13) so that rather than research and evaluation being separate from practice, they become an integral part of practice. There has been an upsurge in the literature about approaches that seek to work in a collaborative way involving clients and other interested parties such as: action research (Wadsworth 1997), collaborative inquiry (Heron 1996), utilisation-focused evaluation (Patton 1997), and empowerment evaluation (Fetterman 2000).

The differences between research and evaluation have become increasingly blurred. Research can tend to be more about exploring a question or issue—asking, for example, what is it like to be a client with a particular disability living in this community? Evaluation tends to be more about asking what that client's experience of a particular service has been in order to decide whether it is effective. However, a research project could compare, for example, the experience of clients using different practice methods. An evaluation project could work with program participants to identify what is happening in a program.

Owen and Rogers (1999:41–6) have a helpful division of evaluation into five categories:

1 *Proactive evaluation*—takes place before a program is designed to help look at what is needed—for example, needs assessment, research review, review of best practice.
2 *Clarificative evaluation*—the evaluator works with those designing or considering a relatively new program to identify the internal structure and functioning; sometimes called the program logic.
3 *Interactive evaluation*—here the evaluator and program workers, and possible users of services, work together to consider how a program or part of a program is being delivered or implemented. This form of evaluation supports programs that are constantly developing and changing. For example: action research, developmental evaluation, empowerment evaluation.
4 *Monitoring evaluation*—more often used for established programs to check whether goals are being achieved and targets being reached. Methods, for example, are devolved performance assessment, systems analysis.

5 *Impact evaluation*—used to assess the impact of an established program, including whether to continue funding. This is called summative evaluation if the aim is to decide on the value of the program in relation to future funding.

This increased interest in research and, particularly, evaluation is demonstrated in the current interest in what is called evidence-based practice. This partly relates to being accountable for public spending; it also reflects a desire to ensure that services are effective. Evidence-based practice basically means critically examining the relevant research and evaluation to justify the practice approach you are taking. Clearly this is a good idea. Checking for effectiveness means programs can be better developed and previous problems avoided.

However, it is also important to recognise the tensions related to evidence-based practice, particularly the issue of what kind of research and evaluation is seen as acceptable. Organisations, and researchers and evaluators, may feel differently about what evidence they consider valid or what research methods they prefer. Some writers (Hollister and Hill 1995; Webster and Osborne 2005) talk about the need for the 'gold standard' of evaluation, meaning randomised control trials, where one group of clients or communities receive resources and the other does not and outcomes are statistically compared for significance. These are often difficult to achieve in human service organisations: there are ethical issues about providing services to one group and not another. It can also be difficult, if not impossible, to make sure that the groups are sufficiently similar for comparison. Statistical data is also limited in value—often it generates more questions than it answers. Knowing that a community receiving resources now has less vandalism leads to questions about why, what processes were important, and what the influence of context was.

Winter and Munn-Giddings (2001), on the other hand, advocate action research as a form of responsive evaluation, which may illuminate practice rather than emphasising statistical outcomes. They suggest the need to ask 'what sort of judgments are to be made and what sort of evidence is therefore appropriate?', adding 'It is thus highly misleading when the advocates of so-called "evidence-based practice" attempt to hi-jack the term "evidence" to mean, exclusively, statistical evidence of the sort generated by randomised control trials' (Winter and Munn-Giddings 2001:47). The debates about evidence-based practice reflect the tensions about professional practice—for example, do the professions need a scientific knowledge base, and where does the creativity of practice and the knowledge of practice wisdom fit?

There is also concern about whose voice will be heard in an evidence-based practice approach: 'There is much emphasis now on evidence-based practice but social problems are not like physics and engineering and the knowledge on which we base our practice must include the experience and expertise of users and carers as well as research' (Smale et al. 2000:8). This may also relate to the politics and power issues involved in deciding what outcomes are seen as important—for example, will the views of clients from a psychiatric support service affirming the emotional and support value of the service have as much weight as statistics that show clients still have regular housing crises?

There is some concern also that focusing too much on having evidence can mean it is not seen as acceptable to develop new or innovative approaches—because there is no evidence! The difficult issue of addressing underlying causes can also be ignored—it may be that the most appropriate outcome in a particular situation would be new legislation or a major policy change in a government department, but this does not fit the evidence-based approach and is not likely to become part of a funding agreement. On the other hand, the research that is available may not give consistent results, for example, or may not identify the significant processes clearly enough for implementation elsewhere.

Other difficulties for practitioners can be practical—that is, first finding the time to consider the literature and second, to assess the findings. Partly this is about having a different orientation to research and evaluation. As Reason and Bradbury (2001:12) put it, 'research can be thought of not as an *interruption* of work, but as a means for *furthering and developing* the work we are already engaged in'. Ideally, research and/or evaluation are built into practice—as they are into training—rather than being an optional extra. However, it is also a realistic concern, given the pressures of work we identified earlier in this chapter, that organisations do not always build in time for practitioner research or evaluation. It also takes time for practitioners to work out what approaches fit in a given situation and to become confident in being able to carry them out. This relates to the debate about insider and outsider researchers/evaluators—is it more realistic or more effective in terms of knowledge, time, and resources to have evaluators come from outside the organisations and/or be separately funded or is it more effective to have practitioners involved in the process? Organisations need to make conscious decisions about these issues and allocate time and other resources accordingly.

Summary

In this chapter, we have identified:

- Background changes to human service organisations cause tensions for workers, particularly the pressure for organisations to be more businesslike rather than operating according to a more professional or community-oriented approach.
- Key frustrations for workers that relate to these changes are the limits and frustrations of funding, the pressure to work according to established routines and procedures, increased complexity of work, and the fear of risk.
- Possible prospects for change are some signs of hope for a more connected, broader approach to working in human service organisations, such as the increased interest in community, moves towards partnerships with other organisations, and interest in critical reflection and reflective practice.
- The changing nature of being a professional and new developments in research and evaluation can be seen both as a source of tension and an opportunity for change. Some myths about professionals have been identified as have more creative ways of looking at what it means to be a professional. We have begun to tease out what a different view of being a professional in a human organisation might look like. We have also identified new approaches to research and the possibilities and potential tensions they bring to practice. Some possible tools for research and evaluation will be identified in Chapter 9.

Reflective practice

What do you see as current tensions for workers?

- How do you relate to the ones identified here—that is, the limits and frustrations of funding; increased complexity of issues; pressure to link to established routine and procedures; and fear of risk?
- How might an organisation deal with these?
- How might you manage these as a worker in a human service organisation?

What changes are you aware of in the current climate that do or might affect human service organisations?

- What is your reaction to those mentioned here?
- How might these apply to organisations that you know?

Think about your experience of a human service professional, either as a worker or as a client.

- What was important to you about the worker?
- What did you see as professional behaviour?
- What would you have liked their professional behaviour to be, if different?
- If you could develop a code of practice for professionals—that is, your expectations of how they would be—what would you include?

What is your experience of/training in research and evaluation?

- What do you see as the current possibilities and tensions for research and evaluation in human service organisations?

2

Thinking about Organisations: Some Useful Theory

We can talk no more of *the* organization than we can talk of *the* mammal, no more describe one best way to run all organizations than prescribe one pair of glasses for all people....Too much effort has been wasted in trying to treat all organizations alike—governments that require the same procedures of all their ministries, conglomerates that do the same with their many divisions, consulting firms that seek to impose the latest technique on all their clients. (Mintzberg 1989:95)

In Chapter 1 we looked at some of the current tensions for workers in human service organisations. We identified that one way of looking at what happens for workers is that they feel caught between competing expectations: the organisation expects them to operate in a business-like way with an emphasis on efficiency and effectiveness; in contrast, their professional training creates expectations of a focus on quality of service delivery, independent work, and, for some at least, community orientation and empowerment of clients.

How then can we manage these tensions in working effectively in human service organisations? A first step is being able to stand back from the organisation to look at it critically and creatively. It helps with this is to have an understanding of how human service organisations work; to think about how we define a human service organisation, how such organisations operate, what background ideas influence their management, and what new thinking is affecting them.

On this basis, this chapter explores current theory or thinking related to human service organisations. We will begin with theory that focuses on writing about human service organisations specifically, but then will include writing from the business literature too. There are two reasons for this: first the distinction between human service organisations and businesses is less clear than it used to be so it makes sense to look at current thinking in both areas. Second, some of the writing, particularly from the USA, is about organisations in general, not making any distinction between human service and business-oriented organisations. Some of this literature is also relevant to thinking about human service organisations. In fact, ironically, some of this literature is more helpful in generating debate about some of the current tensions in working in human service organisations.

One of the debates is whether it is legitimate to talk about an organisation as if it had a life or existence of its own independent of its workers. While in one sense it is obviously true that an organisation cannot exist without workers, it is equally fair to say that organisations develop a momentum and culture that we experience as belonging to the organisation—that is, the organisation as a whole is distinct from the sum of its parts. Partly what I mean by this is that organisations often have a particular feeling about them—it may be easier to think of this in terms of businesses you have dealt with: some feel instantly friendly and welcoming, in others the consumer feels like an intruder. You wonder sometimes what has made the difference, as individually most of the staff seem approachable, but generally the atmosphere makes you reluctant to use the business again. Liddell's definition of an organisation suggests you need to think about both the organisation as a unit and the individual workers:

> An organisation consists of individuals and groups of people who come together to pursue particular goals and objectives....It has identifiable boundaries—that is, you can distinguish it from its environment and from other organisations it relates to. The organisation has stability in the sense that it is in existence over a period of time, and it maintains relationships with and responds to individuals, groups and organisations in its environment. (Liddell 2003:7).

I am going to assume here that we can talk about the organisation as both an entity in itself and a collection of individual workers and their interactions.

What is a human service organisation?

Human service organisation is the term most commonly used for health, welfare, and educational organisations, broadly defined as organisations whose focus is on providing some kind of service for people individually or in communities. They can be large or small, government, or nongovernment. Some examples include: schools, hospitals, drug and alcohol centres, income support agencies, family and children's services agencies, and correctional services. Using this term suggests that there is 'a class of organisations that is involved in a distinctive set of activities with similar characteristics'(Jones and May 1992:82–3). Jackson and Donovan (1991:xi) see the common characteristic as 'the prime product is a service that is designed to optimise the welfare of the client', however client and welfare are defined. Liddell (2003:7) says 'Human service organisations have some particular characteristics, which derive from the fact that they are dealing with people and the complexities of human life'. Such definitions aim to distinguish human service organisations from businesses; sometimes human service organisations are called voluntary organisation or not-for-profit organisations to make this clear. However, some businesses obviously also deal with people. We will explore in the next section what is distinctive about human service organisations.

What distinguishes a human service organisation?

There is some debate about what characteristics distinguish human service organisations—what is it that makes them similar to each other and different from businesses? As human service organisations have become more business-oriented, the lines have become more blurred. I am going to use Jones and May's (1992) three categories to identify human service organisations—purpose, technology (the nature of the work), and auspice.

Purpose

In theory, you would expect purpose to be relatively consistent across human service organisations in its broadest sense—for example, 'to meet the needs and contribute to the well-being of their consumers, and to contribute to overall social welfare' (Jones and May 1992:84). The overall goals or vision of a human service organisation generally reflect an overall purpose like this (see the boxed examples following). It is important that the overall vision does express the broad hopes of the organisation, its best expectations, if you like. If there is no vision as a starting-point, it will be difficult ever to get close to such an ideal. However, the vision or overall purpose needs also to acknowledge the complexity of its purposes. As you can see from the examples in the box, organisations vary in how explicit they are about their purpose and their underlying values. It is useful with each statement to ask what the underlying values might be.

Examples Mission or vision statements

1 Commonwealth Government of Australia: Department of Family and Community Services

Our vision—what we want to achieve
A fair and cohesive Australia society.

Our purpose—what we are here to do
FaCS takes the lead and works with others to help families, communities and individuals build their self-reliance and make choices through:

- economic and social participation
- prevention and early intervention
- a responsive and sustainable safety net.

Our three outcomes—the difference we will make
FaCS has as its focus the following three key social policy outcomes:

- Outcome 1—Families are Strong
- Outcome 2—Communities are Strong
- Outcome 3—Individuals Reach Their Potential

(Family and Community Services Department 2004)

2 St Vincent's Health Mission & Values

Our mission is to bring the healing ministry of Christ to all we serve. Our concern for others, especially those in need, permeates every aspect of the life and work of our services.

We are dedicated to providing the best possible health care, drawing on the talents and creativity of our people and others who share our vision.

We express our mission through our daily work in hospitals, ambulatory services and multi-disciplinary clinics, research institutes, aged care services, hospices, outreach activities and in the home.

The values of the Sisters of Charity are the foundation of our mission. We will be guided by these values in our relationships with the people we serve and our partners. In all our activities we strive to demonstrate:

Compassion
Accepting people as they are, bringing to each the love and tenderness of Christ.

Justice
Acting with integrity and respecting the rights of all.

Human Dignity
Respecting the uniqueness of each person created in the image and likeness of God.

Excellence
Excelling in all aspects of our healing ministry.

Unity
Creating a community characterised by harmony and collaboration.

(St Vincent's Health 2004)

3 Berry Street Victoria

Our vision for Berry Street Victoria is that it continues to be responsive in working with children, young people, their families and the community to increase life opportunities and choices.

There are ten **Principles** that underpin our organisation, and we have also worked hard to articulate our **Values**.

Values Statement

The way we go about our work and how we treat each other is important. We have, therefore, articulated the key values, which are at the core of all our work.

The five values are:

- Courage
- Integrity
- Respect
- Accountability
- Working Together

All people who work for Berry Street Victoria are expected to carry out these values in the way they work, with their clients, team members, colleagues, business associates and the community.

Our Principles

Berry Street has ten principles underpinning the work that we do. We believe that:

1   Families generally provide the best opportunity to nurture children.
2   Children have a right to grow up in a consistent and nurturing family setting which is free of violence, abuse and neglect.
3   Where children and young people are unable to live with their families, they have a right to maintain positive family and community relationships.
4   Regardless of their point of entry to our services, our primary focus is on building on strengths to prevent further disadvantage.
5   Recognising and building on people's strengths is the most effective way to achieve change.
6   The best outcomes will be achieved by the active participation of all the key participants.
7   Continuous improvement will be achieved by encouraging feedback, creativity and the willingness to try new things.
8   A person's life opportunities and choices are affected by structural factors in society.
9   Service users have certain rights and responsibilities which together with Berry Street Victoria's rights and responsibilities, will guide the way we work together.
10 We have a responsibility to use our practice experiences and work with others to identify barriers, advocate for change and improve relevant social policies.

(Berry St. 2004)

Reflective practice

These are three quite different organisations: FaCS is a national family and community services government department based in a politically conservative liberal climate; St Vincent 's Health is a large hospital underpinned by Christian values; Berry Street is a family and children's services agency operating in a major city and in regional areas.

Think about your response to each of these. What does and doesn't appeal to you and why? What values are expressed and how do these fit with the values you would want to express as a professional?

In practice, the purpose is often complicated by the variety of expectations both within the organisation and from outside it. Hasenfeld (1992:3) talks about the inbuilt contradictions of human service organisations: 'To the general public these organisations...are viewed as symbols of the caring society, a manifestation of the societal obligation to the welfare and well-being of its citizens. But they are also viewed as wasteful, fostering dependency, obtrusive and controlling ...Public assistance (income support), for example, serves both to alleviate misery and to deter "undeserving" poor'. Some of the tensions experienced by workers come from these contradictory views, which are shared with clients and which workers have often internalised themselves. This is particularly difficult in a culture where we expect clear answers rather than living with contradictions (see also the discussion on modernism and postmodernism in Chapter 3).

Part of this complexity is looking at the underlying purposes of human service organisations where social control or maintaining current social values and attitudes can be implicit in agency processes. Hasenfeld (1992) talks about the moral nature of work in such organisations, by which he means that decisions are constantly based on values. These may be implicit or explicit, subtle or blatant. Workers too may be more or less conscious of their own biases and preferences. For example, an income support worker confronted with two clients whose benefit has not arrived may be more sympathetic to a client who is perceived as neatly dressed and looks worried than one who is perceived as aggressive and messy. This is sometimes talked about as workers being expected to operate as agents of social control, of upholding standards of social behaviour, which is more explicit in some positions than others.

An obvious example of this is in child protection agencies where staff are expected both to create caring and nurturing relationships with clients but also to monitor them for reasonable standards of care of their children. The community expects workers both to keep children safe but also not to intrude 'too much' on the lives of families. Even talking about the community as if there is a unified view is unrealistic; community members will vary in how interventionist they expect workers to be. The politicians to whom the workers are answerable will have their own sensitivities—reactions to child deaths in various countries show that the political response is often significant in terms of policy change (Scott 1995; Markiewicz 1996). Workers can feel torn—should they listen to their own professional judgment, the client's perspective, the organisation's expectations, the community's views, or the politics of the situation?

Obviously all organisations can have value tensions and the distinction between generating income and providing services is not always clear. More businesses are aiming to show social responsibility and talking about generating social or spiritual capital, expressing deeper values about their relationship to the community as well as making a profit (Zohar and Marshall 2004). Some voluntary organisations aim to generate income so that they can have some independence about how they operate. However, in commercial organisations, Weiner (1990:11) points out 'there is a clear, dominant value—making a profit'; otherwise organisations would not survive. In comparison, in 'public and private human service agencies...there are usually a number of conflicting values and...they all are equally viable'. He gives an example of a long-term facility for the elderly that changed its focus to traumatic brain-injured rehabilitation because it was more profitable and, presumably, equally needed. Some agencies have stopped providing services because the level of government funding meant they could not provide services of a quality they were happy with. Wrestling with diverse purposes and their related values is clearly part of working in human service organisations. Remembering to keep asking the question—what are we here for?—may be as important as naming the current answer.

The nature of the work

A clear distinction between human service and other organisations is in the nature of the work—that is, human service organisations work with people rather than inanimate objects. How this is done is what some writers describe as the 'technology' of the organisation. The nature of this work varies immensely and it is often hard to define clearly. Central to the work is the relationship between the workers and the clients, whether the aim is to enable families to manage conflict more effectively or to provide information about how to stay healthy. However, individual workers and agencies will use a variety of approaches or tools as part of developing a relationship with clients and working on their issues. Some of these will be broad approaches, such as a solution-focused (Elliott et al. 2000), psychoanalytic (Nathan 2002), or cognitive behaviour approach, while others may be specific to the particular field of practice, such as using a risk framework in child protection.

What is actually used will vary over time, depending on what is seen as useful, the preferences of individual workers and agencies, and what is seen as effective. Liddell (2003) points out that the theory or approaches in favour shift over time, not necessarily for logical reasons. We need to be 'considering what we lose when we prematurely or inappropriately abandon perspectives which may have served us well, in part and considering what this might mean for the perspectives we could or should apply to the social phenomena we research or evaluate' (Liddell 2003:28).

Hasenfeld (1992) talks about people as the 'raw material', where the 'core activities of the organization are structured to process, sustain or change people who come under its jurisdiction' and that they are subjected to a 'transformation process'. His language suggests a passive client, though he would say that the client can react to or participate in the process. It is certainly fair to say that clients often feel they are subjected to a process and a set of procedures rather than being active participants.

Case scenario

Tracy, an Aboriginal woman, contacted her local community health centre to ask about activities for her 13-year-old, Tony, who was starting to truant from school. The worker was concerned about whether Tony was being adequately cared for and contacted child protection and the school. Tracy was astonished and angry to receive phone calls from both child protection and the school welfare officer later in the day. She felt confident that she had worked out why Tony was truanting—he needed more help with school work and she had already organised tutoring. She also thought he needed more structured activities, which is why she had contacted the community health centre for ideas. From the worker's response, Tracy felt assumptions had been made about her that as an Aboriginal parent she was not capable; she felt patronised and criticised rather than being seen as an active and caring parent who could have been involved in discussion.

A second problem with Hasenfeld's focus is that it tends to assume that the clients are always the ones who need to change, rather than the community or organisation they are connected to. Some organisations or parts of organisations aim to work in ways that enable clients to generate change in the organisation: the example of the New

Fulford Family Centre in Bristol is one where clients form the Board of Management and have a significant influence in policy making (see Chapter 7). The Brotherhood of St Laurence Family Centre also demonstrates how clients can become participants in running organisations and sharing power over resources, relationships, information, and decision-making (Gilley 1990). Almost all participants agreed that participating in decision-making was important in terms of learning, receiving better-quality services, and more awareness of their own rights.

Given that the nature of the work is focused on people, human service organisations must take into account the current community norms about how people should be treated. Community views about what is reasonable change over time. This is often complicated for professional workers due to their own professional values, which may well differ from community norms. Another complication can be the conflict between the organisation's values and individuals in the community. Some issues are relatively clear—for example, while some parents would still advocate corporal punishment, general community and agency standards would now be in agreement that this is not acceptable. However, others are less clear: the community may be concerned about young children that seem to be out late at night but, on its own, that is not likely to be a cause for major concern for child protection. The aged care system and the community may consider that an older person should be in nursing home care, but that person may value their independence more than their safety. The key for human service organisations is that having the debate about issues remains central rather than settling for routines and rules. Workers and the organisation need to continue to wrestle with asking what is the fairest, most empowering approach given the individual and the community context.

A critical issue for human service organisations is being able to show that they are effective. This is not easy to do, partly because it is often difficult to agree on what being effective means. This relates to the tension workers can feel when pressured to work to established routines and procedures (discussed in Chapter 1). There is a lot of debate around what to measure and how to measure it. Sometimes the emphasis seems to be on relatively easy to measure information—how many clients have been seen at a community health centre, how many young people completed school in a given year, how many patients have been discharged from hospital within a prescribed number of days from an operation. Longer-term and qualitative measures of what has happened are more difficult to evaluate. What does it mean to say that 80 per cent of clients expressed satisfaction with a service or that 70 per cent saw the client–worker relationship as significant in their recovery? It is often not clear what exactly it is that makes a difference in human services work. Workers, clients, and the organisation all have their views, and these are not necessarily the same.

Clearly, it is important to check effectiveness. We can have an intuitive sense of what works but not necessarily be right. Organisations vary in how they evaluate their work and tools for evaluation will be considered in more depth in Chapter 9.

Reflective practice

Josie works in a community-based service supporting older people to remain in their own homes. She has just had a phone call from Jane Brown whose mother Maisie Brown is 90 years old. Jane and her family are about to move interstate because of her husband's work and she says she will be constantly worried about her mother unless she moves into a hostel. Maisie does have some chronic health issues but has been able to live on her own with support from aged care services and her daughter visiting regularly. Josie has already had an agitated phone call from Maisie saying what's most important to her is continuing to live independently at home. Two days later, Maisie has a fall and breaks her hip; Jane is confirmed in her views, but Maisie is still adamant she wants to live at home. How then is the decision to be made? How can both voices be heard? What impact does the worker's personal experience have? What might the general views in the community be? What might Maisie's community think? How would you evaluate effective intervention in this case?

Auspice

Auspice is about how organisations are mandated, which generally connects with how they are funded. Human service organisations are generally, though not always, publicly funded. What they are called and how they are differentiated varies depending on the country. Some human service organisations are government departments, whose employees are required to work according to legislation and government-influenced procedures. These are at different levels—national, state, and regional. Government organisations are often expected to be responsive to changes in political parties and their policies. Being a government department can mean that there is a higher expectation of responding to community concerns, although this is not always the case. Workers can find it either a positive or negative experience, depending on the particular situation and their own values. It may be, for example, that a media report about a nursing home results in quick closure when workers on the ground have been expressing concern for some time. Alternatively, workers may be frustrated by rapid changes in income security policy that limit benefits because of media debate about fraud.

Many other human service organisations are also funded by government, but are auspiced or managed by another agency. These may be called voluntary agencies, nongovernment agencies, or community-based agencies. Depending partly on history, they may be church-based agencies, belong to local communities or regional communities, they may have developed in response to a specific issue, or be an off-shoot of an existing organisation. They will generally have some kind of board or committee of management to oversee the organisation, which will work with the senior worker in the organisation, usually called something like an executive director, director, coordinator, or manager. Legally, every agency must have a constitution that will spell out its structure and the allocation of responsibility. It can be useful to look at this to be clear about how the auspice works. There are some organisations where this is quite complicated—some church organisations, for example, have loyalty to their church organisation, while others are relatively independent.

Examples Agencies

- St Luke's, an Anglican nongovernment agency in regional Victoria, has a Board of Management. Of the Board's eight members, three are appointed by the local Anglican Bishop, one is appointed by the Uniting Church Presbytery, and four are community members. This represents the history of the organisation, as it began as a part of the Anglican church in Victoria in cooperation with the Uniting Church.

- Centacare, an Australia-wide nongovernment agency auspiced by the Catholic Church, also has a Board of Management for local branches. Its local Board has eight members, all of whom have to be approved by the local bishop.
- Bendigo Community House, a locally focused service, is funded by the State Government and supplemented by other grants. The house has a volunteer Committee of Management made up of interested people from the local area. The Committee is voted in (if voting is needed) by members at its Annual General Meeting.

Although these agencies operate at arms-length from government they have of course, to be answerable for their funding. Currently, governments, in the Western world at least, seem to be favouring funding nongovernment organisations often through some kind of tendering or competitive process. Depending on their philosophy, some governments argue that this is a more efficient way of delivering services, as it requires agencies to justify why they should receive funding, and that it allows the market to determine which agencies survive. Others consider that there is a conflict of interest in both funding a service and running it and that nongovernment agencies can be closer to the community and so to the consumer. Liddell (2003:42) suggests that this is doubtful in practice and adds that being privatised has led to nongovernment agencies 'being more controlled than before'. A tendering process can mean that agencies have to agree to provide services in predetermined ways that do not necessarily suit the context they are working in. Sometimes, where there is room for negotiation, this means considerable time is needed to reach an agreement about what will be funded, how services are to be delivered, and how the agency will be accountable. This can also create tensions in various ways. The agency and funding body do not always agree about what most needs to be funded. Agencies may feel that if they argue too much, the funding body can always look elsewhere. For some programs, agencies must compete with other agencies to run services. This creates a sense of uncertainty that means agencies feel less confident about challenging the system. It can also create a division in the community as agencies are aware they will be competing with each other. However, it is important to remember that agencies are made up of individuals who can form cooperative working relationships.

Case scenario

This is a 'catch 22' that I have experienced in various forms: suppose for example that an agency has been providing accommodation for young people under the age of 16 who have left their families because of conflict with their parents. The agency works hard with young people and their families to resolve conflict and so less alternative accommodation is needed; instead the funding is used for counselling or mediation. The agency could argue that it is achieving what both it and the funding agency really want—that is, that young people are safely looked after and their family relationships are intact. However, the agency is no longer living up to the initial agreement and the funding body may then reduce the funding, which will in turn mean the agency is no longer able to provide counselling and mediation. Ideally, of course the agency and funding body will negotiate and resolve this issue, but it is surprising how much effort it can take to resolve such a difference.

The other implication of being publicly funded is that human service organisations are likely to be affected by political processes. A change of government, for example, may signal a change in approach to funding. There have been quite dramatic examples over the last 20 years of changes in government policy impacting on human service organisations. I have experienced one government deciding to stop funding consumer advocacy groups, while another moved to zero tolerance for drug use rather than harm minimisation. More subtle changes might reflect government policy about the place of family—for example, a change from more services supporting young people to be independent to more services supporting young people to stay at home. Specific events can also have an impact: the death of a child was significant in the introduction of mandatory reporting of suspected child abuse in Victoria. Workers often have mixed feelings about the impact of the political process: on the one hand, it reinforces that this is an active democracy, on the other it can mean that professional views are made to feel redundant.

Most human professional organisations do employ professional workers as a major part of the workforce. This again can create tensions within the organisation between those who believe they have a right to use their professional knowledge in a relatively autonomous way and those who believe that they must work within the processes and procedures of the organisation. We will look at this issue in more detail in the next section, when we think about bureaucracies.

Essentially, human service organisations are generally defined as:

- providing services for people and/or their communities
- having a focus on services for people, rather than goods
- having relationships between clients and workers central to the work of the organisation
- making a profit or generating income is not a primary aim
- being at least partly publicly funded in general, with implications for being affected by political decision-making
- employing people trained in working with people more often—that is, professional workers
- having a significant value base to their work
- doing work that is diverse, complex, and flexible.

It is the combination of these that is important in defining human service organisations. Obviously, some of these factors relate to other organisations too. Dentists and naturopaths provide services for people; human service organisations may employ carpenters and gardeners. There are complications with others. For example, although human service organisations are not aiming to make a profit, some would certainly aim to generate an income, perhaps to maintain some independence from public funding or to be able to develop innovative programs. Agencies may want to work according to values but experience the tension of having to run programs within government funding limits. Agreement about the importance of a value base does not mean that it is easy to reach consensus about what those values should be.

Organisational structures

How an organisation is structured affects its workers and clients. The structure often implies a set of values and beliefs about roles and responsibilities, how decisions should be made and standards maintained. Writers about organisations have tended in the past to suggest that 'there was one best way to manage and to organise' (Trompenaars and Hampden-Turner 1998). The best structure was seen as one 'with a rigid hierarchy of authority, spans of control no greater than six, heavy use of strategic planning, and so on' (Mintzberg 1989:110). Mintzberg suggests that the older and larger an organisation the more likely it is to have a formal and centralised structure, partly because this is the most obvious way to control an organisation. This kind of organisation is what Mintzberg would call a 'machine' organisation, essentially a bureaucracy—that is, an organisation where there is a 'pull to *rationalize*, ideally through the standardization of work processes, encouraging only limited horizontal decentralization...need for routine efficiency'(Mintzberg 1989:111). He contrasts this with a professional configuration where there is a 'pull to *professionalise* in order to mini-mise the influence that others, colleagues as well as line and techno-cratic administrators have over their work...(this has) full horizontal and vertical decentralization of power to the operating core, with coordinating achieved largely through the standardization of know-ledge and skills'. Some organisations, of course, try to combine the two —which may give rise to the tensions we have already articulated between the organisation's desire for a more business-oriented, efficient approach and the worker/professional's desire for a more flexible, value-based approach. We will return to Mintzberg's configurations later in the chapter, but given that most human service workers are in bureaucracies we will start with exploring the nature of bureaucracies.

The nature of bureaucracies

The vast majority of human service organisations are bureaucracies. This is a statement about the structure of the organisation; rather than making a value judgment about it. Not only government departments are bureaucratic, but also many large agencies, whether they are pri-vate or public, headed by a committee of management, a board, or a department head. Size is what often determines an organisation taking on a bureaucratic structure (Mintzberg 1989). As small organisations grow, they generally seem to take on a more hierarchical and bureau-cratic structure. This is not necessarily so, however, and other possible structures will be considered later in the chapter. It would be extremely unusual to find a human services worker who has not at some point worked in an organisation structured along bureaucratic lines, or who has not had considerable contact with bureaucratic organisations in the course of their work. Bureaucracies are very much part of our culture and, to be an effective worker, we need to be able to find ways to work within and/or with them. However, bureaucracies do differ, and like other organisations, can be open to influence and change. Individuals and teams within bureaucracies can develop their own culture for managing their work.

We tend to think of bureaucracies as large, inflexible, and un-yielding organisations that are likely to be a constant struggle to work in. It is important to balance this picture (which is undoubtedly often true), with acknowledging that bureaucracies can also be open to change, respond to pressure, and allow freedom to operate. My own experience of working in bureaucracies reflects this mixture: I have experienced many of the frustrations, from realising that you can not move a piece of furniture without filling in a form to endless wrestling with rules about program guidelines that did not quite fit the situation of particular clients. However, I have also experienced times within bureaucracies where new ideas were welcomed, I had considerable freedom to operate within broad role guidelines, and I could influence program development. Matheson's article on organisational structures in the Australian Public Service, for example, confirms that within certain areas of the public service:

> it is possible to locate organic structures which survive within the inter-stices of the formal structure. Where organic structures do exist, then it is usually for those reasons that have been identified as favouring such structures generally, namely that the work is non-routine, employ-ees are highly qualified and projects are of a relatively short duration. In addition, collaborative structures are suitable where there exists a high level of uncertainty concerning future organisational activity and high levels of dependency on other organisations. (Matheson 1996)

These are common conditions for public sector organisations.

The German sociologist, Max Weber (1964), named the concept of bureaucracy. He was interested in looking at forms of organisation, based on power and authority and particularly in what makes people follow instructions. He explored the difference between charismatic authority, traditional power (from a hereditary position), and author-ity with a rational-legal basis. This third type of authority forms the basis for bureaucracies where 'conformity comes from following for-malised rules and procedures, and working within clear-cut structures' (Coulshed and Mullender 2001:29). Importantly, the structure is made up of specific positions, rather than individuals. Weber defined bureau-cracies as having a clear-cut division of labour, duties allocated through formal administrative hierarchy (i.e. each worker supervised by the worker above), a prescribed system of rules and procedures, exclusion of personal considerations from conduct of business, and employees having technical qualifications and experience related to job des-cription and requirements.

One of the tensions of working in human service organisations often relates to the underlying bureaucratic structure. Using a bureau-cratic model suggests a certain mindset or belief system. For example, there is an underlying assumption that rules and procedures are needed, that a more fluid approach would not be effective. Many of the rules of the bureaucracy are about keeping control, about having power over people who should be kept in check in some way—both workers and clients. Discretion is seen as negative, whereas rules mean that there will be consistency and fairness. Many of the rules about income security distribution, for example, are based on assumptions about people wanting to exploit the system, rather than assuming people will and can ask for what they need. These values are not generally ones that workers in human service organisations agree with and are likely to be different from the explicit values of the organisation. This underlying clash of assumptions can also cause conflict: the structure implies that a more senior manager will have more knowledge, experience, and certainly decision-making capacity. Staff further down the hierarchy may feel they know more about what is happening on the ground and how policy is impacting on people in the community, but find it hard to have this form of knowledge recognised.

Another clear implication of a bureaucratic structure is that the more levels you have, the further it is between the worker on the ground and the senior manager of the organisation. Just like on a mountain, as you go higher your perspective changes. Senior managers are often more aware of the wider political agenda, they need to be abreast of the current issues, opportunities for funding, and agency development and innovation. A good senior manager is likely to be an able networker making sure they are conscious of what is happening internally and externally. They also are under pressure to ensure, for example, that nothing goes wrong that will be seen negatively politically, and that the agency is accountable for expenditure and effective service delivery. From high up the mountain, the needs and issues for clients can seem very distant compared to the staff working directly with them. Direct service, or on-the-ground, staff are more likely to be conscious of both the rewards and difficulties of client work, the gaps in funding, and the need for different processes and relationships with other organisations. Middle managers often feel caught in the middle, that they are the 'meat in the sandwich'; from part of the way up the mountain, they are aware of the issues for clients and workers, but also have a clearer idea of the issues concerning more senior managers. Often they end up trying to communicate across the two levels. This is partly because the nature of the bureaucratic structure is to encourage people to think in levels, and that staff have to work up through the levels.

Case scenario

Jane had been working in a community health agency for several years as a generalist counsellor. She noticed that she seemed to be having more older men as clients, often men who had been made redundant or had to leave work early for health reasons and were now feeling depressed and somewhat isolated. She suggested to her manager, John, that the health centre should run a group so that the men could meet with others in similar situations. Her manager felt this was outside the funding guidelines for their service, so initially refused, suggesting Jane talk to the local community house. The community house worker did not feel she had the skills to run group sessions but was happy to offer a venue. Jane wrote a proposal outlining how she felt a group would fit the program guidelines, be a more effective way of using her resources, and build links with the community centre. She sent this to her manager with a copy to the centre's program director, Fred. Eventually she was able to develop the group. Jane concluded that she needed to be persistent in order to gain more flexibility in her work role and to build an argument that would appeal to managers.

In some organisations, this is reinforced by informal rules. All organisations have informal rules as well as formal ones. As Coulshed and Mullender (2001:33) say, 'organisations are living entities, imbued with the characteristics and inter-relationships of the staff who people them'. People inevitably express their views about how things should be done in ways that become expectations of each other or informal rules. A formal rule would be that workers are responsible to a specific line manger. In some organisations, the informal rules would support this —people would share stories about the negative impact of breaking this rule. In other organisations, the informal rules are more flexible and people communicate more freely across levels. There are clear advantages of this in terms of information flow. It can also mean that people at all levels of the organisation can share perspectives—the equivalent of travelling regularly up and down the mountain. Senior managers then stay more in touch with client issues, and direct service workers are more conscious of the broader political context they are operating in.

Some key attributes of bureaucracies are:

- hierarchical structure, with the number of levels varying depending generally on the size of the organisation

- each level has specified levels of responsibility and decision-making
- positions are created, with job descriptions that workers then apply to fill
- work is based on accepted rules and procedures
- a high degree of division of labour/specialisation
- emphasis on precision and reliability—consistency of decision-making
- recruitment on the basis of ability and knowledge/qualification.

What does bureaucracy mean for working in human service organisations?

There are obvious limitations for human service workers in bureaucracies, particularly in the traditional sense. First, bureaucracies were initially seen as appropriate forms of management for routine tasks that needed to be performed in a consistent manner. While clearly some human service tasks fit this criteria, most do not. This also disregards the importance of the process, that how something is done can be as important as achieving a task. Given that most work in human service organisations involves workers and clients relating in some way, this is a major issue.

A second major limitation is the tension within the bureaucratic structure when the organisation wants workers to focus on fairly narrow functions in a work environment dealing with complexity. Cowley (1999:11) says, for example, 'The expectation that people can be relied on to carry out only single predictable functions does little to improve flexibility within a rapidly changing world: it also creates the task focus and fragmentation that offends many nurses... the holistic nature of nursing is rendered "invisible and devalued within the system".' This links to the question of professional independence; the capacity for trained workers to be able to exercise judgments on the basis of their specialised knowledge and experience.

Human service organisations with a bureaucratic structure deal in various ways with the tension between the desire for control and consistency, and the complex world of clients. Coulshed and Mullender (2001:31) say, 'There is a debate as to how far managerialism has superseded professional work by imposing centralised control, or whether professional autonomy is retained at the point at which social workers and care managers continue to make individual judgments in complex cases and perhaps to find other space in which to manoeuvre'. Interestingly, critical reflection is beginning to be seen as a way to enable professionals to look more critically at the context in which they work as well as their assumptions and values about practice. This may be one of the tools for professionals to use to manage these tensions. Tools for critical reflection will be explored in more detail in Chapter 9.

A related issue here is the division that can emerge in bureaucratic human service organisations between those who are seen as the professional workers—often, though not always those providing direct services—and those who administer the services. I am not talking about managers here so much as the administrative staff—for example, receptionists, workers in finance, and personnel. Sometimes this becomes divisive; a 'them and us' mentality develops, with professionals seeing themselves as upholding the vision of the organisation to care for clients and the administrators as those more concerned with efficiency and control of resources. Administrators may resent what they see as the relative freedom of the professional staff to plan their work, or feel that the client work is more interesting and valued. Professional staff may envy the relative predictability of life for administrators—for example, that they will be able to go home at five o'clock and resent what they see as 'nit-picking' about details.

Part of this is the vexed issue of discretion; should professional workers be able to exercise discretion and if so how much? Lipsky's explorations of worker discretion raise difficult questions. Front-line workers value their ability to use discretion and partly have it 'because society does not want computerized public service and rigid application of standards at the expense of responsiveness to the individual situation'(Lipsky 1980:23). However, this responsiveness can work well or badly. While workers generally use discretion to support and advocate for clients, some may use discretion to control client behaviour in negative ways—for example, by neglecting clients or requiring them to come in to the office unnecessarily. Because the worker has the power to use their discretion, the client is unlikely to feel able to question the need for the visit or to complain about how they are treated. Management may devise regulations to limit the potential for negative discretion or unfair treatment, but this can again cause conflict between professionals and the administrative staff who are expected to carry out the rules.

This polarisation is an unhealthy one, often limiting the capacity of both groups to work together. It is also an artificial distinction in many ways: there is a sense in which all staff are likely to be professional in their attitude to their work—that is, seeing their work as skilled and requiring training, and wanting it to be of a high standard. Organisations can manage this well: developing goals together helps so that everyone is committed to the same overall plan. Sharing information is key to this, so that each group in the organisation understands the pressures on the other. It helps receptionist staff to know where you are and when you might be back, so that they do not end up with disgruntled clients being angry with them. It is also important to recognise that both sets of functions are needed in the organisation: direct service workers need support staff (e.g. for cars to be able to visit clients); we all want to be paid for our work. Without the professionals there would be no need for administrators.

Case scenario

Jane was becoming increasingly frustrated with Dennis, the budget officer in her section who always refused her submissions for extra funding for clients. One day she decided that she would talk to him about the particular family she was working with. As she talked, Dennis was clearly moved by the client's story. He explained that the way she had written the application made it difficult for him to approve it, but that if she added part of what she had told him, the application would fit the guidelines. Jane left, pleased that she had gained the funding for her client but also thinking that she had learnt an important lesson about how to work within her organisation. She realised that Dennis, like her, had to work to restrictions and rules and that they could jointly find a compromise.

Another aspect of this in human service organisations is about who the senior managers are in terms of their background and interests. In some organisations, the managers will have similar backgrounds to direct service. 'Having been there' managers are likely to have experience and knowledge that helps them understand the issues for staff quickly. The other side of this is that managers may therefore assume that the strategies that worked for them will work for their workers, even though the current context and culture may be different. In some organisations, managers will not have had similar or even related work experience to those 'on the ground'. This fits with the managerial model that would say that management skills are transferable across all organisations. While this is true to a degree, it is also true that this model expects managers to make what are sometimes major shifts that mean staff feel they are constantly educating their manager about the complexity of issues. It can also meant that staff feel that decisions are made without a real understanding of their and the client's perspective. Educating the manager can become a daunting but necessary task.

Senior managers also have to contend with other limitations of the bureaucratic model. They too may feel 'sandwiched' like middle managers. They need to be aware of and balance the competing expectations of groups in the environment. In theory, in a bureaucratic model, managers are simply responsible to their employing body. In practice, they often have to manage the competing demands of other interested parties: depending on the organisation, these could include: other organisations providing similar or related services, some of which may be competing for funding; consumer groups; advocacy groups, including peak bodies, unions, employer organisations, and professional associations. They are likely to also have to be sensitive to changing political preferences.

Teams in human service organisations

One of the positive aspects of working in human service organisations is working in teams: small work groups organised around a shared purpose with a team leader who generally provides the supervision and organisational management for the team. Depending on the particular organisation and team leader, the team can operate relatively flexibly within the organisation. From a management perspective, what is usually important is that the team achieves its objectives. If this is the case, then the team can have some degree of decision-making about how this is done (see the section following, on non-hierarchical structures). The team might agree, for example, that one person diversify their workload in a particular way to see if a different approach works. Team members often get to know each other well, and they may have a form of group or peer supervision that fosters this (see Chapter 4). The culture of the team is important (again, see Chapter 4): a positive, supportive team environment will encourage effective work.

Other organisational structures

Clearly not all human service organisations are large hierarchical bureaucracies. First, there are still some small organisations and relatively new organisations that are able to operate more flexibly. Mintzberg (1989) has a useful way of thinking about organisational structure. From studying a wide range of organisations, he suggests that each can be thought about in terms of six elements, which together make up different configurations. The six elements are:

1 Operating core—people who perform the basic work of providing services.
2 Strategic apex—senior manager/s, those with overall responsibility who may also generate a vision for the agency.
3 Middle line—middle managers.
4 Technostructure—analysts/administrators who aim to plan and control formally the work of others.
5 Support staff—those who provide services like public relations, counselling to staff, services to staff.
6 Ideology—the 'traditions and beliefs of an organization that distinguish it from other organizations and infuse a certain life into the skeleton of its structure' (Mintzberg 1989:113).

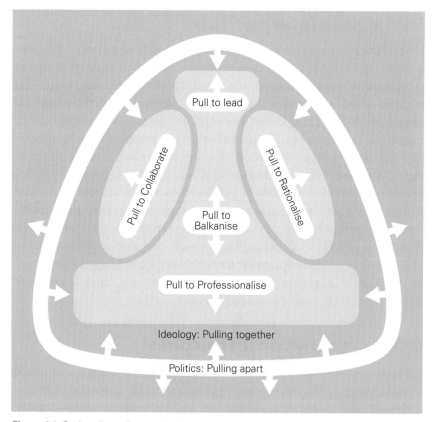

Figure 2.1 Basic pulls on the organisation

Source: Mintzberg (1989:111)

Depending on where the energy is in the organisation, one or more of these elements will have more power and this can alter the structure. If, for example, the operating core is professionals with a strong sense of autonomy and professional decision-making, the structure is likely to be flatter with more decision-making at the bottom. If the manager has a strong desire to control and direct the workings of the organisation to particular goals, it is likely to be more steeply hierarchical. If ideology or culture is the dominating force, the organisation is likely to have a flat structure—there is a higher degree of confidence that goals will be shared.

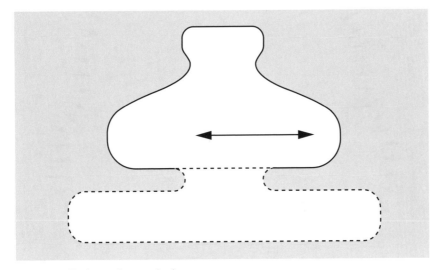

Figure 2.2 The innovative organisation   Source: Mintzberg (1989:114)

Mintzberg (1989) would suggest that all organisations have the six basic elements of his configurations to some degree, although in small organisations these roles may not be as differentiated. It might be more accurate to think of these as functions that will be taken on either by the organisation as a whole or by particular individuals. For example, the manager may also have a caseload; the administrator may organise publicity. It is useful to think about Mintzberg's elements in exploring how varied organisational structures can be and how change in the organisation can come from any of the six elements. In some organisations, for example, it feels as if there is significant power in the 'technostructure'—that is, the administrative arm of the organisation.

Professionals feel restrained by the rules and procedures imposed by the administrators.

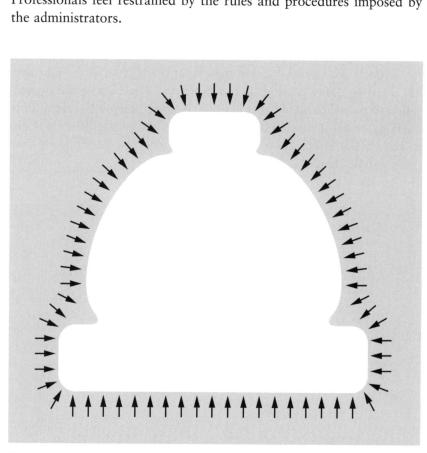

Figure 2.3 The missionary organisation

Source: Mintzberg (1989:114)

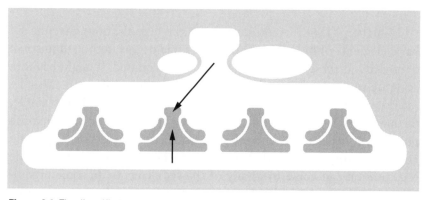

Figure 2.4 The diversified organisation

Source: Mintzberg (1989:113)

Non-hierarchical structures/approaches

This section will particularly consider non-heirarchical structures—the opposite, you could say, of bureaucracies. I am going to start by exploring a feminist approach to working in organisations because this approach has had a considerable impact in thinking about how to work in non-heirarchical structures. This also makes a useful link between this chapter and Chapter 3, where we will look at how to use a variety of theories to encourage different thinking about organisations and how they operate. Feminist thinking is also a useful example here because it makes explicit how an ideology can be applied to organisational practices.

It is daunting to try to define feminism briefly given the diversity of views and writing about it (for ideas about further reading see the end of Chapter 3). Essentially feminism raises awareness of how dominant social structures define gender in ways that are oppressive, restricting choices particularly for women. Feminist practice works in ways that encourage greater choice and equality generally, but again focuses on providing ways for women to be able to operate more powerfully. For example, Dominelli (2002) defines feminist social work as 'a form of social work practice which takes gendered inequality and its elimination as the starting point for working with women...to promote women's well-being as women define it....It also seeks to ensure that feminist insights are used to improve the well-being of children and men'.

In terms of working in organisations, feminists have advocated for at least some women-run services for women on the basis that this allows women greater opportunities to find their own voice. Such services have generally been run on non-hierarchical lines, partly as a way of finding an alternative to a bureaucratic model seen as representing a more patriarchal form of organisation. Weeks (1994:134), writing about lessons from feminist women's services, says that the 'philosophy of collectivity is the central expression of women's historical and social processes. It is conscious political action to develop an alternative to the hierarchy of patriarchal relationships...trying to put into practice the feminist vision of democratic process in social relationships'. The organisation then becomes a place for people to experience relating in a new, cooperative, mutually empowering way, rather than in the more competitive, disempowering form of most modern organisations. The aim is that this experience would translate into other spheres to generate broader social change.

So how might this translate into principles for working in women's organisations? These are likely to include:

- acknowledging the centrality of women's experiences as a form of knowledge
- ensuring the voices of all women involved are heard, particularly those who have been least heard
- making connections between personal experience and social issues
- working collectively using participatory decision-making processes
- seeking social change by operating in an alternative way from the dominant culture and working towards a more inclusive and less oppressive society.

How do these principles translate into practice? And how does that compare with other groups, such as environmental groups and housing cooperatives, who work collectively? These groups all generally have a flatter structure partly because, in Mintzberg's terms, they share an ideology, so the need for control from above is reduced. The structure may also reflect a desire, as it has in the women's movement, to try to live out an ideology about the sharing of power and decision-making. Language is important here; such organisations have often made their way of operating explicit by being called something like a collective or a cooperative.

The flat structure has implications for the organisation in terms of how labour is divided, leadership shared, and having participatory models of service delivery. Ideally each worker and/or committee member has equal decision-making power and responsibility. Individuals may take on particular roles for a period of time, for example, being the spokesperson for the organisation or being the coordinator. However, generally the underlying philosophy is that all tasks could be shared and that each person should have the opportunity to learn all of the skills needed in the organisation. This can also be the approach in small organisations with a committee of management and one or two staff. Although they may not see themselves as a collective in the same way, the committee and staff member/s may agree that tasks need to be shared and come to a mutual agreement about how this will be done.

Some agencies trying to operate as a collective do end up with a staff member designated as a manager or coordinator. Often this is a condition of funding from organisations that find it difficult to deal with organisations that have a flat structure. This can cause tensions within the organisation, especially if it means that some staff are paid more than others. Some organisations decide that in a society where having a coordinator is the norm it is easier to have one, while aiming to maintain a sense of shared decision-making. This can create tensions in itself, particularly for the coordinator. Weeks (1994) compared how coordinators in women's services saw their roles with women managers in the public service. She found that the women's service coordinators emphasised a 'group centred model of leadership' (Weeks 1994:169); seeing their role as facilitating, empowering, and encouraging cooperative working relationships and shared decision-making. In comparison, the public service managers talked about being 'out in front', active, initiating, being senior in terms of hierarchy (Weeks 1994:170). Notice the differences in language here, even in naming the roles. Weeks points out that both models have advantages and disadvantages. Collectives can concentrate so much on getting the process right that tasks are never accomplished. Too much consultation can become frustrating.

Collective agencies—and small agencies run by committees of management—generally prefer consensus decision-making—that is, making decisions that all those involved accept as reasonable. 'Consensus requires a group that is willing to work together and trust there is a solution, as well as patience and perseverance. It requires us to come to meetings with our minds not fixed on a particular solution or position; in the light of hearing all the possible positions we may modify ours' (Shields 1991:97). Making decisions by consensus can be a slow process but has the advantage that once the decision is made everyone is highly likely to support it. This can contrast with a decision made by a majority vote that leaves 40 per cent of the voters unhappy and potentially interested in undermining the decision that has been made. Consensus decision-making often gets a bad press; people see it as both very slow and meaning that everyone has to be totally happy with the decision. More accurately, the aim is to make sure that everyone's views are heard, that all options are explored so that everyone is reasonably happy with the decision. Speed is relative too; you need to compare the time you spend in coming to the decision with the time spent after a vote when you have to deal with a series of disgruntled people.

An issue that needs to be addressed in non-hierarchical organisations is that of power. Part of the aim of being non-hierarchical is to remove the power differences between people. However, as we will discuss (see Chapter 4), power comes in many forms. Individuals can be intimidating in their passion for a particular view; it can feel as if there is no space to articulate a perspective that does not fit with the espoused philosophy of the organisation. In practice, decisions may be made between meetings by those who are confident to do so. The power of being the longest-staying worker, or the one with the most history can be significant too.

Case scenario

Josie was a staff member of a women's health collective. She was becoming increasingly uncomfortable about the collective's policy of not providing individual counselling for women. After many of the groups she was running, women would ask whether they could see her or someone else individually and she had to say no. The collective believed that individual counselling perpetuated women seeing their problems as individual rather than cultural and so the centre only offered group work and community education. In a meeting, she tried to express her views but felt that as usual the meeting was dominated by the women who had begun the collective, who had very strong views about how it should be run. She decided to ask that the next meeting be structured to more truly reflect a consensus decision-making approach: each worker was to put their point of view in turn without being interrupted by others, the pros and cons of the issue were to be considered, and options developed before a final decision was made. Eventually the meeting was held and it was agreed to explore the possibility of having individual sessions to complement attendance at a group.

Some of the principles and practices of a consensus decision-making, flatter structure can also be used within hierarchical and bureaucratic organisations. Within a team, for example, the team members, including the team leader, might agree to work to consensus. This may be a balancing act for the person seen by management as responsible for the work of the team. They have to make it clear to staff what can be dealt with in a consensus decision-making style, for example, and what will have to be done by the team leader. Operating in this way can have a number of advantages for both the team and the team leader. First, it can mean that there is a sense of shared decision-making, that all team members can influence how decisions are made. This reinforces to staff that their opinions are valued and is likely to create a greater sense of energy in the team. It also means for the team leader that there are more views and ideas about issues expressed and that decisions are more likely to be adhered to.

Committees of management can also work in this way, particularly in small organisations where there is a very close working relationship between the staff and the management committee. This can mean there is a blurring of roles between the committee members and the staff—are committee members to be involved in all decisions, and, if not, when should they be involved? Often the agreement is that the committee will be involved in policy and/or major decisions about such issues as overall direction or funding. In practice, it can be hard to work out what the day-to-day decisions are and what are the more major ones. Partly, these are issues of trust and mutual respect, which often are resolved with time.

Influence of size

I want to finish this chapter by looking briefly at the issue of size. Often it seems that size has a major influence on organisational life. What is possible in a small organisation in terms of informal communication and shared decision-making becomes much more complex as soon as the organisation grows. Because of this, workers will often talk longingly of the early days of an organisation when it was easy for everyone to know what was happening, to feel they shared more actively, and in a more equal way, in the organisation's development and decision-making. Part of the appeal of smaller organisations is that it is easier for structures to be less hierarchical and systems less bureaucratic. As organisations get larger, it becomes harder to manage this, more formal structures develop with separate teams to manage different work areas, and communication is generally formalised.

Some people would suggest keeping organisations small and there would clearly be some benefits in this. However, this does not necessarily mean that smaller organisations always work better. If people do not agree or do not get on well together, conflict can be ever-present, as workers can not avoid each other. Sometimes sharing decisions can simply become a laborious process; particularly about nonessential issues. A small organisation can have a bureaucratically minded coordinator. Larger organisations can have some benefits in terms of choice of workers for clients, possibly offering a wider range of services, and more diversity for workers and clients. The answer may be to think about the size of organisation needed for a particular community or service, rather than to assume that one size is always better.

Summary

In this chapter, we have explored:

- What a human service organisation is, acknowledging that while we think of human service organisations as those that focus on work with people, there is a blurring of this role with businesses.
- How to think about what distinguishes a human service organisation, which can be in terms of:
  - purpose—the overall mission or vision and how this relates to more specific goals and the implicit or explicit values expressed in these
  - technology—how the organisation carries out its work
  - auspice—the organisation's mandate and funding, whether it is a government department, for example, or a voluntary agency auspiced by a church.

- The nature of bureaucracy and what that means for human service workers. Most human service workers work in large organisations that tend then to be bureaucratic. This usually means having a hierarchical structure with clear lines of responsibility; work is divided according to roles, carried out by trained workers whose work is controlled by rules. While we tend to think of government departments as bureaucracies, large voluntary agencies also operate in bureaucratic ways because of their size.
- Other organisational structures, such as collectives, and how these operate with their emphasis on a flatter structure, consensus decision-making, and greater sharing of roles. This approach can also sometimes be used by teams within larger, bureaucratic organisations.

Reflective practice

Think about a human service organisation you have had contact with as a worker, student, or client.

- How did the organisation come across?
- What seemed to be its public purpose?
- What other purposes did it seem to have, and did these seem to be in conflict?
- What tools or frameworks did the staff use?
- How did they relate to and work with clients?
- How did you feel about the organisation?
- What would it be like to be a client or a worker there?

Use the following example to think about how you might respond to working in a human service organisation. Jo is a team leader in a family and children's services agency. The agency is very large with several departments, each with more than one team. Although the agency tends to work in a bureaucratic way, Jo prefers to share decision-making wherever possible. Mostly, this works well and the team is seen as having better working relationships than many others in the agency. At present, Jo's manager is putting pressure on her to make team members finish their monthly statistics within a week of the end of the month. Jo is reluctant to bring this up with the team because she knows some people at least will think she should just say no. What issues does this raise for Jo in terms of her values and beliefs about how to work best in the organisation? How might these be similar to or different from those of her manager or her staff team? What do you think about Jo's approach? How might you react if you were Jo?

3

Parallel Processes: Using Practice Approaches to Explore Organisational Issues

Professionals practise in an uncertain and ever-changing world and ...they need to develop creative, innovative and proactive approaches to professional practice. (Higgs and Titchen 2001:288)

We often talk about organisations as if we think about them in completely different ways from how we think about work with clients. Workers, who are very effective with complex, disturbing, and possibly dangerous family dynamics, are somehow unnerved and feel powerless in dealing with their organisation. This seems to be because so much energy goes into working with clients that workers lose their capacity to think critically and creatively about how to work with their organisation. Sometimes too workers feel they lack perspectives that can help illuminate the organisational dynamics so that they can work with them. This chapter explores how the practice approaches workers use with clients can also be used to consider how to work with organisations. This, like Chapter 2, is part of thinking about how to stand back from the organisation in order to see how to work more effectively within it, to see how to take the action needed for change.

What I mean by practice approaches here is the theoretical perspectives that underlie working with clients. What these are will vary depending on the organisation, the professional discipline, and the interests of the worker. Some organisations prefer workers to use a particular approach such as systems theory or a solution-focused approach. Others expect workers to select the theory or theories they see as most appropriate to a given situation. This linking of the approaches used with clients to working with organisations is often talked about as using 'parallel processes'. The idea is to think about how what is happening at one level of the organisation is mirrored at another level. A simple example might be that a worker is working with a client who feels relatively powerless and who responds to the worker by saying 'yes, but...' to every suggestion. In supervision, the worker finds themselves saying 'yes, but...' to every suggestion made by their supervisor. This can enable the worker to experience how the client feels and to try a different approach—from her own experience with her supervisor, she and her client would prefer to be listened to rather than have to respond to suggestions. At an organisational level in a child protection agency, for example, the senior management might develop a 'siege' mentality—that is, a fear of being attacked, criticised, or judged negatively—again paralleling the experience of clients who fear they will be found lacking as parents. Recognising the parallels can be helpful in looking at both levels and starting to recognise where change is needed.

Once you start to apply practice perspectives or theories to organisations you will see that you can use many approaches, perhaps any approach, to deepen your understanding of what is happening in your organisation. It is a bit like having a kaleidoscope—as you turn it, you see the same basic components expressed in different patterns. Alternatively, you could think of it as taking photographs with different lenses that will provide varying angles or shades of the same picture. Part of what is helpful about doing this is that it encourages you to stand back from the organisation (you have to do that to take a photograph) and to be able to look at it a little more analytically. Rather than being overwhelmed by how it operates, you can begin to see a variety of influences and possibilities.

This is a useful way to think about theory and how theory is used. Essentially, a theory is an idea or perspective that someone (or more often many people over time) has developed about what works. Often theory is talked about as if it is separate from practice; students wrestle with how to integrate the two. Schon makes a useful distinction between 'knowing that' and 'knowing how' to acknowledge that there are two kinds of theory (Schon 1983). Knowing that is theory in the sense of ideas about what to do, knowing how is the experience of trying out these ideas, making the ideas part of how you practice. This might then become your own version of the original ideas, which can then become new theory. Ideally, these two kinds of knowing would connect in a cycle, so that a worker would try out a theory in practice, then add to it or refine it. Alternatively, a worker might reflect on their practice with its built-in theory and develop new theory—perhaps because of the limitations of old theory. Solution-focused approaches, for example, partly developed from workers being frustrated with what they saw as problem-saturated approaches. Their experience or practice demonstrated the value of focusing on what people could do rather than what they could not. This experience then led to the development of new theory.

In practice, of course, no theory or perspective develops in complete isolation from other theories (Liddell 2003). Theories often seem to develop in reaction to others—people become frustrated about a particular aspect of a theory, or a theory taken to an extreme, and decide to develop something different. Sometimes, workers find a theory just does not fit with their current context. Theories then are often adaptations from previous experience—a new theory might adapt old theory rather than developing something completely new. It is important to recognise though, that theories have underlying assumptions and values, which are articulated with varying degrees of clarity. A structural approach (Fook 1993; Mullaly 1997), for example, has assumptions about the need to change the social system to be more equitable and socially just, whereas a psychoanalytic approach would have assumptions about the influence of the unconscious on the behaviour of individuals. Each approach also tends to have its own distinct language, which reflects the assumptions and values being expressed.

I have chosen to use three perspectives here for fairly idiosyncratic reasons—that is, I could have chosen others. The three I will consider are:

- a psychodynamic approach because I have found it particularly useful myself and there is a growing literature about connections to organisations
- a narrative approach because it is a relatively new approach that I think has a lot to offer in terms of thinking about organisations
- a systems approach because it is one where the connections are relatively clear—it connects the health and welfare literature with management/organisational thinking and because people have often found it useful in thinking about organisations.

However, I will explore two general theories as important background theory first: postmodernism and critical theory. While these are not practice theories in the same sense as the others, both reflect important developments in theory for practice in human service organisations. Postmodernism is also part of often unarticulated changes in our culture in general that have an impact on organisational life.

Please note that I am presenting a brief summary of each approach that does not do justice to the diversity of views within each of them. For those interested in reading more, there is a reading list at the end of the chapter.

Modernism/postmodernism

Modernism and postmodernism are easier to understand in relation to each other. Both are complex, with writers defining or explaining them in quite different ways. I initially found postmodernism hard to grasp. I first came across a close relation (poststructuralism in relation to art) in such complicated language that I found it quite incomprehensible. Eventually, when I started teaching, I decided I really needed to understand postmodernism and was relieved to find that beneath the complicated language, there were ideas and concepts that were very useful, naming aspects of my own experience of practice and also how our culture generally has changed over the last 30 years. I also recognised that this approach is very helpful for working in the human services: it creates a way of working positively with some of the tensions of practice, holding together apparently incompatible differences.

Modernism

Postmodernism developed in response to modernism. Berger suggests the modernist period is generally held to be between about 1900 and 1960 (Berger 2003), although our culture is still strongly influenced by modernist thinking. Some writers would suggest modernism started in the eighteenth century, which helps explain why it is so embedded in our culture. Put simply, modernism relates to a more science-oriented way of thinking. It is hard for us to imagine now the liberating impact of scientific thinking in a world where people often believed that disease was caused by evil spirits or bad luck. As science demonstrated the value of, for example, sewerage, clean water, and medical advances, the new thinking became that with science, all problems had causes that could, in time, be found and resolved. In modernist society, people were more likely to believe in the same overall views about what is important and how to live; these are called meta-narratives. Parton and

O'Byrne (2000:19) suggest that distinguishing features of modernity are:

> the understanding of history as having a definite and progressive direction, the attempt to develop universal categories of experience, the idea that reason can provide a basis for all activities and that the nation state could coordinate and advance such developments for the whole society. The guiding principle of modernity is the research to establish reliable foundations for knowledge. It aims to identify the central truths about the world but also assumes that truth does not reside on the surface of things.

Given the impact of scientific achievement, modernist thinkers advocated applying scientific thinking to research and professional development. The emphasis was on training experts with specialised knowledge that had been established with clear cause and effect. This suggested the need for research that was seen as rigorous and objective, able to be verified across research studies, and with statistically significant data. From this perspective, language needed to be seen as a consistent and unambiguous way to communicate. The general expectation was that societies would continue to grow and improve with advances in scientific knowledge.

In summary then, modernist thinking includes:

- a search for logical connections (i.e. cause and effect, scientific explanation)
- finding the 'right' answer to each question; sometimes the right answer might be a new theory that was expected to apply to all situations
- a belief in absolute truth and knowledge
- the need for objective and value-free research
- emphasis on proof, establishing validity
- the centrality of experts and expert knowledge
- valuing certainty and clear answers
- a preference for linear thinking, an expectation of continuing improvement and progress
- the view that language is common and has a shared, objective meaning.

What might this mean for human service organisations?

Early human service organisations were influenced by a modernist approach and we can still see the impact now. The development of bureaucracies, as discussed in Chapter 2, reflects a modernist perspective with a desire for a rational, scientifically based organisation with clear rules, structure, and boundaries. The desire for the 'right' answer is still all too clear, with organisations developing a new program or new approach assuming that it will solve a given set of problems. This often assumes that a group of clients defined by a problem, such as drug and alcohol issues, will fit into the same box in terms of resolution. Even expecting resolution is part of a modernist approach, wanting every-thing to be 'fixed' forever rather than finding ways to live with difficult experiences. Modern organisations still tend to rely on expert know-ledge, often in the form of outside consultants rather than valuing input from users of services. Often we desire certainty and act as if it is possible even when we know we work in areas of constant change. We look for proof in research when it is more realistic to explore possible meanings. So modernism continues to influence us, but perhaps now balanced by postmodernism to some degree.

Postmodernism

Contrary to the singular 'truth' of modernist scientific explanations, postmodernism acknowledges multiple interpretations and that there is 'no one truth'. In its broadest sense, postmodernism is critical of what are called the 'totalising theories'; theories that suggest there is one truth or try to make sense of the world using one approach. How-ever, postmodernism's critique of 'totalising theories' also makes us aware of their power. Our culture operates according to 'meta-narratives' —that is, general expectations about how society should be ordered, who has power and influence, and how people should act. These are expressed as 'dominant discourses', or 'ways in which we make mean-ing of and construct our world through the language we use (verbal and non-verbal) to communicate about it' (Fook 2002:63). Dominant discourses express ideas that are often taken for granted and apply to all aspects of social life from expectations about gender roles, to views about the importance of paid employment or what people with dis-abilities are able to do. The dominant discourses operate to maintain existing power relationships, with the emphasis on power over others, rather than seeing power as shared.

To a greater or lesser degree, we internalise, or take into ourselves, these beliefs and the perceptions of who is powerful because they are so much part of how our culture operates. Often, it is going outside our own culture that helps us see what the dominant discourses are— travelling to a different country, for example, or having a friend from another culture, makes us see that we have taken certain things for granted. We might start to question why, for example, we have assumed that work is viewed in a particular way or that some groups of people are seen as more deserving of income tax benefits than others. Postmodernism encourages questioning of such assumptions, partly through 'deconstruction'; the process of 'taking apart' what we are saying so that we can see what is implicit in it. Reaching these implicit assumptions enables us to see how we are being influenced by what is taken for granted so that we can make more conscious decisions about how to operate. We can then see that there are many ways of seeing the same situation and a variety of causes for particular actions. This opens up possibilities for acting in different ways, for people to exercise their own power and choice rather than fitting with dominant thinking.

Because culture is reflected in the language we use, deconstructing speech and communication is an important part of postmodernism. There is much written about the construction of language and its meaning. A simple example is that we make assumptions all the time about shared meaning and every so often are shocked to realise we have been operating from quite different perspectives. It is not unusual in organisations to find that participants in a meeting have left with quite different impressions of what has been decided. Taylor and White (2000) use a form of discourse analysis to look at the conversations between professionals and clients, and between professionals; they explore how decisions are made to focus on a particular area of work, which means ignoring others, or how a particular view of a situation is perpetuated.

Case scenario

Jo recorded conversations with a client for supervision. As she listened to the tape she was startled to realise that she and the parent, the mother of twins, assumed from the beginning of the tape that the father's role was not important. As the tape went on, it was clear that both assumed that the work to be done would involve the mother and children and the father would be excluded. This reflects the cultural assumptions about parenting that have become embedded in how both the worker and client approach parenting issues. If they want fathers to become more involved they need to change both their implicit assumptions and how they operate to be more inclusive.

As well as questioning dominant discourses, postmodernism encourages the use of multidimensional approaches, the valuing of uncertainty and diversity, and an awareness of the subjectivity of our own and other's beliefs and values. A postmodernist would point out, for example, that our reactions as individuals are based on our own experience and history as well as the culture in which we live. Our culture has its own history that will also influence how we perceive and act in the world. I was lucky to migrate when the prevailing assumptions were that migration was good, bringing new skills and diversity, particularly as an English speaking migrant from Scotland—an acceptable country with historical links. Now migrants face quite different assumptions, particularly those from countries like Iraq; the prevailing views are more of suspicion and fear of difference. We need to identify the history and context to make these assumptions explicit so that they can be seen realistically.

Postmodernism also questions binary thinking or thinking in dualities, which is very much part of Western culture. We often think in pairs—for example, we are either workers or clients, teachers or students, powerful or powerless—whereas, in practice of course, we have 'multiple selves' and can be both parts of each pair at once or sequentially; we might feel quite powerful in one situation and powerless in another. FitzRoy gives an example: 'a working class woman from a Judeo-Christian background may experience discrimination within the employment market; however, within her own community she may enact a form of structural or personal racism against another working class woman who is a practising Hindu (in Pease and Fook 1999:91). Using such binaries creates a sense of 'the other', of people being different and often divided into more and less, acceptable or powerful. Deconstructing these means we can see that things are more complex and need more thoughtful responses.

The example on the next page demonstrates the importance of checking for assumptions.

Having a postmodern understanding can also help workers deal better with the contradictory nature of life in human service organisations, as Ife's four discourses demonstrated (see Chapter 1). Each of these discourses has its own set of assumptions about how the organisation should operate—the managerialist discourse, for example, assumes that workers will provide specific, focused, measurable services to change client behaviour compared to the community discourse where the assumption would be that worker and client together decide what needs to be considered and how.

Example

In past practice in Victoria, it was assumed and legislated that it was better for adopted children never to have contact with their biological parents. This was based on what sounded like logical premises:

- Children will settle into a new family more easily if they are not in contact with their biological family.

- Children can only cope with one family at a time.
- If biological parents can not care for their children, they should not be allowed to be involved with them at all—perhaps they do not deserve contact.
- Contact will be confusing for biological parents, they need to get on with their lives.

Now, of course, current practice assumes that where children are adopted they will maintain contact with their biological parents wherever possible and that this will be beneficial for all parties. New legislation reflects this new discourse.

In Chapter 2, we identified some of the difficulties of conflicting expectations of workers—for example, that workers have to be both caring and controlling, build nurturing relationships and take clients to court. From a postmodern perspective, we could talk about the multiple stories or views about what is happening; that in a postmodern world we do not expect there to be only one story—of either care or control —rather, the complexity is built in. This also encourages us to look for different views, to ask users of services for their perspectives with their own particular knowledge of the organisation. Asking who is marginalised—that is, whose voice is not being heard—can provide surprising answers: it may be children or young people that no one has remembered to talk to, or it might be that middle managers feel their views are never heard.

Like modernism, postmodernism is seen as having limitations and, of course, is used in practice in different ways. Perhaps the major issue that postmodernists wrestle with is whether there is still a need for some over-arching beliefs or meta-narratives. Ife (1999), for example, advocates for a discourse on human rights and needs that differentiates between the universal vision and specific action in a particular context.

Some postmodernists would be more likely to argue that such rights are too limiting and need to be seen in the context of culture. Other writers are concerned that postmodernism can be seen as giving permission for justifying inequities and oppressive practices or can immobilise workers—how do you decide which stories are not acceptable? Most writers, however, affirm that postmodernism is congruent with making value choices and arguing that some choices are better than others. Rolfe (2000), for example, manages to balance the quest for 'one truth' with a more relativist position: 'which recognises the futility of attempting to uncover a single truth, but which nevertheless argues that it is possible to commit oneself to a moral and epistemological stance with integrity and good faith. I attempt to argue, in effect, that although we can never be certain of what is true, we are still able to make choices'. The following section on critical theory suggests that combining critical theory with postmodernism offers a balance: a meta-narrative that is compatible with values of human service workers with an approach that respects subjective experience.

Rosenau (1992) is critical of postmodernist inconsistencies, such as the tendency to devalue building theory while suggesting that postmodernism has useful ideas or theories to offer. Postmodernists also tend to stress the need for creativity and intuition rather than logic or reason, but using logic is an important part of deconstructing theory or practice. However, it is important to remember that postmodernism developed in reaction to modernism and is likely to stress the opposite to reinforce the need for balance.

In summary then, postmodernist thinking:

- acknowledges that we experience the world subjectively—that is, influenced by our own experience, history, and personality as well as the culture we live in—rather than objectively
- states that what is seen as 'truth' will depend on the situation/context
- sees power as complex, able to be exercised in various ways
- values diversity, uncertainty, and the contradictory
- acknowledges that language is embedded in culture and needs to be deconstructed—that is, we need to be aware of the assumptions we make that are hidden in the language we use
- sees people as complex with 'multiple selves'—that is, people will be seen differently in different contexts—for example, a client may see themselves as a competent worker and a struggling parent
- is concerned about marginal perspectives, asks whose voice is not being heard

- prefers research that acknowledges the influence of values and the need to hear a range of voices, and is more interested in exploration and illumination than proof.

What might this mean for human service organisations?

Clearly, postmodern thinking has and is having an impact on human service organisations. The 'learning organisation' approach (see Chapter 4) enables workers in human service organisations to use post-modern thinking. There is growing interest in multiskilling rather than seeing each worker as having only one role. Interdisciplinary approaches are starting to look at what is common across professions. There is more openness to the idea of 'other voices'—that is, to taking into account user views in the development and reviewing of services (Frances 1997). A greater diversity of approaches to research and evaluation has become acceptable, particularly research that values exploring issues and perspectives rather than seeking one unified view.

A more important question might be what *could* this mean. Postmodernism has the potential to provide the background thinking to deeper questioning of assumptions within human service organisations and how they operate. Bacchi (1999), for example, uses such thinking to ask about social policy issues—what is the problem represented to be? How has the problem been chosen to be a problem? Why this one? Why now? Similarly, we could generate questions for human service organisations, such as:

- How is language used in this organisation? How is the meaning of language checked with workers and clients?
- How does the organisation acknowledge and value diversity?
- How is uncertainty experienced and managed?
- How did this issue come to be seen as an issue?
- What happens when things go wrong? Are many views explored rather than seeking the answer?
- What are the possible ways to act here? How are these influenced by our assumptions and values?

Critical theory

Critical theory is a meta-narrative that critiques the way society is structured and how power is distributed within these structures, particularly how some groups are advantaged and others disadvantaged. One of the major benefits of this perspective is that individuals are seen in terms of a broader context; rather than blaming individuals for not 'succeeding', the general social constraints and restrictions are under-stood. A critical worker then would always see individual issues in their social context; a worker with young men who are gay would be con-scious of potential discrimination and what that might mean for them at school or work.

Writers using structural analysis in critical theory often talk in term of binaries, such as advantaged and disadvantaged, oppressor and oppressed, in order to make the analysis clear. A feminist critical analy-sis, for example, focuses on how social and economic structures affect women and gender relationships in terms of access to status, power, and resources (Dominelli 2002). We talked in Chapter 2 about how feminist analysis has influenced how women's organisations in partic-ular, but also others, are run. Marxism concentrates on the economic distribution of resources and power, the differences between those who own the means of production and those who provide the labour. Anti-oppressive practice looks more broadly at how discrimination and oppression are embedded in the social context in relation to issues of gender, age, sexuality, religion, ethnicity, ability, and class (Thompson 2001). Radical and structural social work theories also provide this kind of analysis (Mullaly 1997), again focusing on those who have power and those who do not. While such binaries usefully sharpen awareness of the divisions caused by social structures, they can mean that some of the complexities of power and social life are missed. For example, an able woman from a wealthy background is likely to be more power-ful than a male with a disability from a working-class background.

Critical theory also articulates how social differences influenced by social structure become accepted as given; 'thinking and acting criti-cally...needs to be placed within analyses of how the limitations of social divisions such as class, gender and social assumptions about disability, sexuality and ethnic origin are created within social ideas that appear rational and that we take for granted, but are also change-able and changing' (Payne et al. 2002:10). The role of history is important here, both as part of the analysis and in recognising how social divisions vary over time, and are therefore not absolutely fixed. Awareness of history adds complexity to the analysis—for example, seeking to understand the process of colonisation deepens awareness of how social division is created and maintained. For Australians, it makes sense that Aboriginal families whose grandparents were part of the Stolen Generation will be wary of contact with government officials.

Critical theory also assumes that change is desirable and possible. This is change in the sense of what Fook (2002) calls 'transformation' and Ife (1997) calls 'liberation' or 'emancipation'. Such change is about the development of a socially just and inclusive society. According to Ife, 'Many critical theorists use the term "emancipatory" thereby underlining the importance of notions of freedom and liberation, whether from the structures of patriarchy, the oppression of class, the denial of human rights, the cultural invasions of colonialism, or from some more complex interaction of these oppressive forces' (Ife 1997:133). Such values and vision are usually compatible with the values of human service workers, but how to achieve such change becomes an issue. Sometimes the analysis presents the issues of power and the need for broad social change so starkly that workers are immobilised; they cannot see how to link this to their work in organisations. Others use this perspective to maintain a sense of what could be possible by, for example, encouraging clients to make their views known or advocacy for clients not able to argue for themselves.

Combining a postmodern and critical theory approach can suggest ways forward. Postmodern critical theory:

> is primarily concerned with practising in ways which further a society without domination, exploitation and oppression. It will focus on how structures dominate, but also on how people construct and are constructed by changing social structures and relations. Such an understanding of social relations and structures can be used to disrupt dominant understandings and structures, and as a basis for changing these so that they are more inclusive of different interest groups (Fook 2002:18).

Here, the meta-narrative of structural advantage and disadvantage is held in creative tension with an understanding of subjective experience that allows for difference. Critical theory, like postmodernism, suggests that an 'interpretive' or more subjective view is important—that is, identifying the meaning that people give their actions, rather than making assumptions as a worker about what the meaning might be or that an action will have the same meaning for all clients or indeed for one client all the time.

The idea of internalising external views is important here: people may take on board society's negative view so that this becomes their view of themselves. For example, two people who are made redundant because of an economic downturn may react differently: one may take the view that people made redundant must have been less able workers and blame themselves and become depressed, so less able to seek work—confirming the negative social view—the other worker may see the government as responsible for the redundancy due to policy decisions and thus remain more able to seek work. The question might then be how can we understand what is happening personally and politically, so that the experience becomes enlightening rather than limiting. Critical theory is helpful here in providing a framework for understanding the broader political and power issues, combined with seeing how each person has given meaning to these in their own situation with their own experiences and personality.

In terms of research, 'critical theory specifically rejects the positivist paradigm of objectivity, empirical measurement and the quest for universal laws' (Ife 1997:130). This relates again to some of the issues we talked about in modernism—the hope for general 'truths' that can be independently and statistically validated. Instead, critical theory emphasises research that acknowledges the subjective with a post-modern approach of asking what various meanings there might be at any point. This suggests the need for a variety of kinds of research and evaluation, as discussed in Chapter 1, which can help elucidate the range of possible meanings. Specific examples of research approaches will be explored in Chapter 9.

Case scenario

Jo has a disability that means she has to be in a wheelchair. She decided that she would like to study on campus for a university degree, though she had already internalised some doubts about her ability to do this from family and social attitudes. On arriving at university, she received many external messages that strengthened her doubts—there were few lifts, many buildings were difficult or impossible to access, doors were heavy and hard to open, the library shelves hard to reach. However, over time, she met other students with disabilities who needed to use wheelchairs, and they shared stories of frustration, while acknowledging that they did also have different experiences—depending on their past history of education, their levels of encouragement from family and friends, the attitudes of other students in their classes. This enabled them to be clearer about what was personal and what was structural. They decided that they would take action together about the structural issues that were frustrating for all of them. Initially, they met with staff they thought might be sympathetic, and once they started to gather support, they organised petitions, lobbied senior management, and arranged publicity through a local newspaper. Eventually, it was agreed that a substantial budget would be allocated to improving conditions and a coordinating committee was formed with student representation.

The key features of critical theory are:

- the value of having a framework for analysing social structures in terms of power and advantage and disadvantage
- the importance of seeing individual issues in the context of social structures
- understanding how individuals internalise prevailing social views, so that they take on the external perception of who they are
- recognising subjectivity; that people will experience similar situations differently and assign their own meaning to them
- the need to be aware of the assumptions we make—what we take for granted about the world, an awareness that history shows that assumptions are socially constructed and can change
- the view that change is possible and desirable in ways that will contribute to a transformative process—that is, liberating and socially just change both structurally and for individuals
- workers can actively contribute to change.

What might this mean for human service organisations?

First, it suggests that workers need to have an awareness of the context they are working in; what the social and political structures are, and what impact they have on clients, individually and collectively. This is relevant in any human service area of work. In an aged care facility such as a nursing home, for example, it might be related to who is able to have what kind of care depending on their financial situation and government funding. We might also become conscious of our culture's view of older people and how they should be treated. There may be a clash between these—for example, how older people see themselves and our expectations of them. It might then become necessary to challenge our own beliefs as well as those of the older people themselves and the institutions they are involved in.

Second, critical theory can enable workers to maintain a broad structural perspective on what they are aiming to do, in that they are interested in social change towards a more just and equitable society. All practice is political in nature; workers and clients can also have some forms of power and so influence change. How we negotiate with clients and with the organisation says something about what we believe about how things should be. A critically oriented worker would pay attention to how the organisation or social structures need to change, rather than focusing only on the clients. Workers would also be interested in the views of those who are less powerful and what change they might want. Paying attention to the service user can mean seeing the organisation and what it offers from a different perspective. Seeing the client's experiences as a valid form of knowledge can be enlightening for both worker and client. An income support worker, for example, might see a range of clients receiving the same benefit type. All have problems with continuing on the benefit because of one of the criteria, which she considers minor. As a critical worker rather than trying to make the clients fit, she might document the difficulties and advocate for a change in the criteria.

A danger with critical practice is that workers may 'may attempt to impose unifying perspectives and analyses on a diversity of activities that defy homogenisation. There can be no simple checklist of items that constitute critical practice' (Adams 2002:92). Adams suggests that workers tend to seek unifying perspectives to deal with the complexity and uncertainties of working in human service organisations, but instead they need to find ways of coping with tensions. Critical reflection is an important tool for enabling workers to grapple with the dilemmas of practice. This will be discussed further in Chapter 9.

Psychoanalytic approach

Psychoanalysis may seem a strange approach to thinking about human service organisations. Much of the thinking of a psychoanalytic approach is now so much part of our culture that we take it for granted. We assume, for example, that our behaviour is influenced by unconscious feelings and thoughts, that slips of the tongue are likely to mean something, that we react defensively, and that our personal history will have an impact on our expectations and reactions. Using a psychoanalytic approach has been criticised as too great a focus on the person and not enough on the context (Wood 2001), though there are writers who acknowledge both (Nathan 2002), including from a feminist perspective (Mitchell 2000). However, there are many aspects of a psychoanalytic approach that can usefully be applied to organisations as a whole as well as to the reactions and relationships of workers in them. The field of psychoanalytic thinking is vast, and I am not planning to cover here the range of approaches within it. This approach was initially articulated by Sigmund Freud, closely followed by Carl Jung. A huge number of writers and practitioners have now linked aspects of psychoanalysis to other approaches. What I want to do is to extract reasonably common themes in thinking about work with individuals that can be also be helpful in thinking about human service organisations and the organisations within them.

Essentially, psychoanalytic theory has three parts—Payne describes it as 'a theory of human development, of personality and abnormal psychology and of treatment' with two underlying ideas:

1 Psychic determinism—the principle that actions or behaviour arise from people's thought processes rather than just happening;
2 The unconscious—the idea that some thinking and mental activity are hidden from our knowledge (Payne 1997:72).

There are three aspects of the personality—the ego or the conscious self (that we present to the world), the id (the needs and drives that may or may not be expressed consciously), and the superego (our conscience or general sense of what is right and wrong). Personality in a more general sense is about how we express ourselves, how we prefer to relate to others, how we like to go about our life and work. How our personality is expressed consciously will be affected by our unconscious—for example, a person may want to come across as confident and assertive, but be undermined by unconscious doubts from past experiences.

The unconscious is said to hold thoughts, feelings, and experiences that are not acceptable to us and these are repressed through a series of what Freud called defence mechanisms—that is, ways of preventing us from having conscious knowledge or awareness that we do not want to have. Freud identified a range of defences, including:

- rationalising—justifying an action or thought—for example, instead of saying I want to go on holiday, saying my partner would like me to go
- repression or denial—not allowing conflicting ideas or unwanted thoughts into consciousness—for example, I do not really like Jane, but everyone else does, so I will too
- sublimation—directing energy from unwanted activities to more acceptable activities—for example, instead of asking for emotional support, I will eat special food I like
- splitting—defining people or ideas in terms of opposites—for example, you are either right or wrong, good or bad
- projection—attributing parts of yourself you do not want to acknowledge to someone else—for example, I am not angry, Fred is.

Johnson (1986:5) suggests that 'most people, however, do not approach the unconscious voluntarily. They only become aware of the unconscious when they get into trouble with it'. When people are tired or stressed, their capacity to keep withholding unconscious material becomes less—often these are the times when people react in unusual ways for them, such as outbursts of anger or tears, being hypercritical, not being able to remember details, or becoming overly focused on details. We need then to ask what is happening for that person, or that organisation. This means not just looking at the surface behaviour but asking what lies underneath, what is or are the causes. A psycho-analytic approach would suggest that working only on the surface behaviour will not be a successful strategy in the long run—the underlying issues will emerge again in some other way.

The importance of bringing unconscious thoughts and feelings to the surface is a major aspect of this approach. Unearthing feelings and significant historical events is often seen as cathartic, generating change in itself: repressed feelings are seen as often causing damage to the person and possibly also to their environment. Psychoanalysis is often criticised for being too interested in the past, and not enough in the present. However, this use of the past can be usefully focused. 'Psycho-analysis is concerned with the way that the past is actively present and constantly interfering with the realization of a fuller current potential' (Nathan 2002). There is also a strong focus on using current relation-ships, particularly between client and worker, to enable such repressed feelings to emerge. For this to happen, clients need to feel they are able to trust the worker with deeply held and often painful feelings. The workers reaction to the client can be used to unearth these. For exam-ple, Yalom (2000) would raise with clients the feelings and thoughts they evoke in him as well as asking himself how these affect his ability to work with the client. This can provide real, direct interactions to work with and to look at what might be typical patterns and interactions. There is clearly a potential parallel here for supervisors and workers.

Finally, it is useful to acknowledge here Jung's work on the collec-tive unconscious. Jung (1964) talked about the shared beliefs and social assumptions held by people across a particular society as part of what he called the collective unconscious. These beliefs and values then were both part of what the individual takes for granted about culture (because they are not conscious) and shared between individuals. To change social values then requires making such assumptions conscious. This is another way of looking at what in critical theory is identified as internalising social values. Both approaches acknowledge the need to make what is unconscious conscious for both individual and social change. A psychoanalytic approach more often focuses on the individual and their relationships with others, though some writing also takes into account social context; postmodernism would focus on how the individual and broader social issues interact.

In summary, key themes of psychodynamic approaches are:

- interest in the influence of history or past stories
- belief in the influence of unconscious feelings and thoughts
- naming of strategies of the unconscious such as defence mechanisms, including transference and counter-transference
- suggesting the complexity of working with people and relationships, not just focusing on behaviour or actions
- acknowledging and releasing deeply hidden feelings
- recognising that the perceived problem may not be the 'real' issue
- using of the current interactions, including the worker's sense of self
- acknowledging how the worker's reactions affect the interaction with the client
- now acknowledging the importance of culture and its place in the conscious and unconscious.

How is this useful in thinking about human service organisations?

First it is helpful to recognise that not all behaviour is conscious; people may react in ways that are unexpected and surprising to them as well as to other people. Second, a psychodynamic approach affirms the importance of paying attention to feelings, both of individuals and of organisations. Psychodynamic approaches help you to stop and think about what is really happening in a given situation. Organisations interested in change, for example, need to recognise the contradictory emotions experienced (Vince 2002). Unexpressed emotions in an agency can also mean that conflict is not expressed and so not able to be resolved, or at least worked with. It can also help to recognise the influence of history—our own, the organisation's, and cultural history —that means that at an unconscious level we make assumptions about how things should be.

The naming of defence mechanisms is helpful in this approach. In thinking about change in organisations, Vince (2002:1194) argues that

'A key insight provided by psychodynamic studies is that people in organizations desire and encourage change whilst also avoiding and resisting it...A psychodynamic approach provides ways of thinking about and enquiring into this gap especially the anxieties and defences that provoke it'. You can see individuals and organisations defending themselves in various ways. Organisations' managers frequently 'rationalise' changed decisions, finding acceptable ways to justify their decisions. Workers and organisations 'split'; a manager might, for example, label one division as good and another bad, and whatever they do fits into this framework. Individuals may repress the parts of the organisation's way of working that they do not find acceptable.

One of the aspects of psychodynamic theory that is particularly useful in thinking about organisations is the defence mechanism of projection. Projection is essentially where unwanted or unrecognised parts of the person's experience or self are attributed to another person or group. These are usually thought of as negative projections, but can be positive. Robert Johnson talks about the 'gold' in the unconscious (Johnson 1993). Jung uses the analogy of a 'hook', the object on which the projector hangs projections. For example, children who have experienced their father as authoritarian (whether he really was or not) may tend to project being authoritarian onto all 'fatherly' authorities—for example, boss, doctor, teacher. That which is projected is the authoritarian tendency of the person himself or herself—they may behave quite tyrannically without noticing it, but believe they are constantly encountering tyrants in the outer world (Von Franz 1993). Note that there may be some truth in the perception of the other person as well as in the projection—in this example, the authority figure may indeed be authoritarian, as well as having authoritarianism projected onto them. Withdrawing the projection, though, removes some of the power of the interaction, so that the authoritarian behaviour can be dealt with more easily.

This is a useful concept in thinking both about the behaviour of some individuals within organisations and organisations themselves. A small community-based organisation may perceive other similar organisations as competitive and aggressive, labelling their own competitiveness as a necessary response to the other. Similarly, a worker might talk very positively about their supervisor's warmth and acceptance but not be able to recognise these qualities in themselves. Projections prevent the person or the organisation being seen in a more whole way.

Case scenario

The Smithtown Family Agency was seen by its funding government department as consistently difficult. 'Why can't they just provide the services they are paid to do, instead of arguing about how things should be done?' was a regular question from their liaison worker, John. 'They are always uncooperative, say they need to be flexible to respond to community demand, then play by the rules when we want them to be flexible.' When a colleague said to John 'That sounds just like us, we think we should be able to decide when things should be flexible and when people should follow the rules', John started to disagree but then had to admit his colleague was right. He decided to have a more open discussion with the agency and they began to work together more effectively.

The psychoanalytic notions of transference and counter-transference take this further. Transference is a form of projection where a client transfers their feelings about their own relationships onto the worker. Counter-transference is simply the reverse: the worker's conscious and unconscious feelings are transferred to the client. The worker is limited in their degree of helpfulness by their awareness of how their own unconscious reactions affect them. A young, inexperienced supervisor, for example, might see her older, more experienced supervisor as having echoes of her mother and react on that basis; this would be transference. If the supervisor then reacted back in a parental way influenced by her experience of her own children, that would be counter-transference. Soon they would be dealing with a much more complex relationship than a standard supervisory one and if they did not sort out what is happening, it would become very difficult for them both. The following example shows how transference can impact on inter-organisational relationships.

Case scenario

Marie, who is in her 50s, is the head of a large government department that has had disagreements with a small community-based agency about how it was using its funding. Derek, the new, mid-20s, head of the community-based agency, thought the funding guidelines were too narrow and so had broadened them in practice. Marie decided to meet with him and found herself getting more and more angry. Eventually, with supervision she realised that she was reacting partly to Derek's similarity to her youngest son, who had just left home and rejected all his parents' suggestions about possible plans. Derek, too, after discussion with a colleague realised that he was expecting Marie to dismiss all his ideas as his parents did, so was not open to hearing what she was saying. Once they had become aware of these rejections they were able to set them aside; at a second meeting, the issue was resolved.

Narrative approach

The narrative approach was partly developed in reaction to frustrations with a classic psychoanalytic approach that was seen as disempowering clients, engaging them in long and not always fruitful analysis, where the analyst was seen as the expert and there was a tendency to see the person as the problem. Workers looked to other frameworks like anthropology, philosophy, education, philosophy, ethics, and literature and particularly to postmodern thinking.

Geertz (1973), an anthropologist, for example, talked about the difference between thick and thin approaches to learning about a community. A thin description would be a relatively superficial understanding of the community, quick observations, maybe one person's perspective at one time. Overall, this would be a singular, coherent, and closed-ended way of looking at things. In comparison, a thick description would mean looking at all the complexities of the community, identifying differing points of view, talking to lots of people, looking for a myriad of causes and effects and influences, expecting an intricate web of relationships. A narrative approach reflects this search for thick descriptions with an individual and/or a family, a search for multiple stories in order to develop a picture of the richness of the person's life.

A narrative approach has some similarities to solution-focused, strength-based work and brief therapy. All of these approaches emphasise working together with the client to develop a picture of the client as a whole person, seeing their strengths and resources as well as the issues they want to work on. Part of seeing the person as a whole is exploring the multiple stories that make up their lives. This clearly reflects a postmodern approach; rather than a person's life being seen as having 'a truth', many stories illustrate the complexity of a person's life. We all know this from our own experience; we are not one dimensional, we have stories as workers, friends, family members, volunteers in community organisations. How we tell the 'story' of who we are will depend on who has asked the question, our mood, the context, and the other people involved. If we are seeing a counsellor, the presenting story is likely to be about a problem, if we are seeing the bank manager the story may be more about having well-paid work. The particular story may be linear and clear or complicated and confusing.

History is important in a narrative approach, but focused on understanding where negative stories have come from and how they have gained power. This can make it easier to see how other stories have become dominated by a particular, problem-focused story. Once this has happened, the client can see that their life has different versions: the problem-focused version may have obscured other versions of them as a competent and resourceful person. They can then choose which is their 'preferred story' or version (usually a story that is working well) and seek support for that.

This relates to another important aspect of a narrative approach—separating the person from the problem. One of the ways this is done is by 'externalising' the problem or issue. Essentially, this means the issue or problem is described as having an independent life outside the client, rather than being part of them. Language is important here: using questions, for example, that help strengthen seeing the problem as separate. Another strategy is asking the client to name the problem in a way that is meaningful to them (see the following case scenario). Often this separation of the problem feels empowering; it is as if the problem once named as separate starts to lose its power.

Case scenario

Jenny was concerned about her cigarette smoking, which was making her chronic health problems worse. She decided to name her cigarette smoking Nadia, and described her as devious and undermining, but also someone who was always there when she was lonely or upset. After hearing herself describe Nadia in this way, Jenny decided that she was using cigarettes instead of developing relationships. Over time, she acknowledged her preferred story of herself as a sociable and friendly person. A family member and two old friends became her supporting audience reinforcing her preferred story and she was able to stop smoking.

A related aspect of a narrative approach is looking for what are called 'unique outcomes' (Payne 2000) or 'exceptions' (White and Denborough 1998), times when things are going well or the problem is not present and asking about what is different at those times. With a person who has depression, for example, rather than exploring the cause of depression, the focus would be on the impact of the depression, but also what happens when depression is absent. This is also helpful in times of crisis; questions about how the client has managed other crises or life events, reminds them that they do have a sense of competence about dealing with these and that this can be applied to the current crisis (Borden 1992).

The narrative approach is particularly careful to include awareness of context. Part of the context is what we talked about earlier in the section on postmodernism as the 'dominant discourses'—that is, the assumptions and beliefs in our society that generate expectations about how to behave. These assumptions are often restricting; we internalise them in ways that limit our choices. White and Denborough (1998) talk about developing 'everyday actions of resistance'—that is, working out how not to take on board both the old story and negative and restrictive aspects of culture. This might mean, for example, thinking about how gender stereotypes have limited how a client has seen themselves. A father might articulate frustration about not being closer to his children, then work to see how he has taken on board entrenched social expectations, and start to act in ways that will allow him to be more nurturing. An act of resistance might be taking a child to play group, or allowing his son to cry, rather than trying to stop him.

Given the strength of the cultural context, a narrative approach suggests using the person's community to help develop and/or maintain change. A client might ask other people how they see the client—that is, ask for their stories about them. They may also be involved in co-authoring new stories with the client, helping the client work out their preferred view of themselves. As well as or alternatively, they may become part of the 'audience', a group of people asked by the client to help them operate from their preferred story, either day to day or in a special celebration to mark the move to the preferred story.

In summary, key themes of a narrative approach are:

- the value of telling stories—to develop clarity, make sense of the parts of the story and look at its complexity
- focus on the whole person or family, not only the perceived problem
- stories are complex, often messy and continuing, rather than well ordered and coherent
- need to start where people are—their current view of what is happening and what it means for them
- the problem is the problem, the person is not the problem

- use of specific tools—externalising conversations, seeking exceptions or unique outcomes, to help see the problem as separate from the person
- interest in multiple stories or perspectives or alternative stories
- interest in the history and context of the situation—both personally and structurally
- focus on what is working and what will help to keep it working—use of rituals and celebrations, involving community to consolidate change
- acknowledging the political nature of the work, such as differences in power, and experience of social difference such as gender or race.

What might this mean for working in human service organisations?

Again this can be useful in thinking about the individual workers or the organisation as an entity. With either, you can ask what the multiple stories about this person or agency are. This is particularly useful when a problem or criticism has been identified and the focus is on the problem. Often, at this point, it seems as if the problem is all there is, there is only one story, if you like, or a thin description. This can be part of the culture of blame and fear that is very destructive in organisations. Instead, a narrative approach would ask: where did this story come from? What are the other stories? When does this person, this agency do well? How else have they operated? What is the broader picture? This helps restore a sense of balance and fairness, so that the problem is seen in context.

White and Denborough (1998) warn that this needs to be done carefully, validating the person's perspective first. It is important to explore the history and context of the situation and how it has made people feel negative about themselves—that is, to help people make conscious for themselves how a negative story has developed, so they can question those views. The person/agency is only then asked to start looking for exceptions or more positive perspectives of the other. The emphasis continues to be on the client's experience, rather than the worker pointing out positives. Too much or too early a focus on finding the other stories can be experienced as condescending and can set up fear of failure—that only positives are acceptable and that the worker has standards that people will be judged by. It is the client's perception of what is working that is important and the readiness of the worker to work on understanding and deepening understanding of that.

This approach can also help an organisation value its diversity, the 'thickness' of its composition rather than seeking to have only one story. It provides a framework for validating difference and complexity, emphasising that multiple stories add depth rather than confusion. It can also provide a language for organisations to use to develop a more positive identity. The community of the organisation, that is the community members, can be invited to articulate the other stories that give the organisation a different identity. Looking for unique outcomes or exceptions could be used as part of this process, for example, to notice what is happening that is working well. The use of rituals or celebrations could be used to consolidate noticing these. Again these need to fit with the culture of the organisation: food is often a popular form of celebration, others might use certificates or awards, either seriously or as fun.

Case scenario

A juvenile justice office identified a problem of negativity affecting the agency. Turnover was high, staff were defensive about their work, and the general atmosphere was alienating. When staff started to explore where negativity had come from, they identified several places: the political pressure to restrain clients and make sure there was no negative publicity, the development of a management culture around minimising risk after an incident with a client, and the lack of a place to affirm the value of the work with clients. When asked when negativity tended to be more successful and when negativity was ignored, they realised that negativity was less successful when particular staff members were around—two long-term staff members who loved to share both humour and pathos, stories about their work and the organisation. They also made space for tea breaks and encouraged other staff to join them. Staff decided that as a group they needed to develop more strategies to defeat negativity; they decided to take their concerns to managers, request regular staff meetings and case discussions that affirmed their preferred story of the value and difficulty of their work, and build in social time for mutual support.

Externalising the problem can be useful to move organisations from a culture of blame to a more positive culture. Externalising the issue means that it is distanced from the person, not in the sense of avoiding responsibility, but in terms of looking more fairly at the multiple influences of the situation. As part of this process, a narrative approach would acknowledge the political nature of the work, the power relationships implicit in differences in management levels, and the impact of cultural issues such as gender. Developing a culture of 'resistance' to the dominant ways of thinking could then be part of organisational change. Workers could list specific acts that would help change the culture and support each other to carry these out.

Systems approach

Systems theory highlights the importance of relationships and inter-connections. Much of the appeal of the systems approach is that it encourages thinking about how people and organisations are con-nected and influence each other. It fits well with postmodernism in terms of encouraging 'both/and' thinking rather than 'either/or' think-ing. Vaill (1996:109) puts it in terms of 'Systems thinking...asks its practitioner simultaneously to hold the whole in mind and to inves-tigate the interactions of the component elements of the whole...and to investigate the relation of the whole to its larger environment'. The assumption is that all the parts of the system are in a relationship so that change in one area will have an impact on others. This approach originated with thinking about biological systems like the body, for example, developed to thinking about organisations, then how to work with individuals and families, and then communities. One of the things that is interesting about the systems approach is how widely it has been seen as useful. Senge sees it as having been 'distilled over the course of the twentieth century spanning fields as diverse as the phy-sical and social sciences, engineering, and management'. He sees it as having particular relevance now in terms of the degree of complexity of issues: 'All around us are examples of "systemic breakdowns"—problems such as global warming, ozone depletion...the US trade and budget deficits—problems that have no simple local cause' (Senge 1990:69).

It is probably helpful to think about this approach first in relation to the body, then to generalise to see its advantages and limitations. In the body as a system, each part has an impact on other parts. This is particularly obvious with a major illness like a heart attack, but it is surprising how even a small change like a bruised finger affects other parts of the body. The body as a system has its own boundaries and operates across these, taking material in and out to maintain equi-librium, called homeostasis or a steady state. This seeking of a steady state is an important aspect of this approach. The body can overheat, for example, so it will sweat and cool down. The body can also change overall—children grow to adults—but as each change occurs the body will seek to reach equilibrium again. This means that no part can be considered to be totally independent of all other parts; each part of the body will have an interdependent connection with at least some other parts. You can also think of the body as a series of subsystems—for example, the circulation system, the digestive system, etc. The body then interacts with other systems across its boundaries—that is, other people and its environment—and all of these also live in interdependent relationships to varying degrees.

How then do we relate this to individuals, families, communities, and organisations? Families can be seen as discrete units with subsystems of parents and children, which have boundaries. Their boundaries may be considered to be open, closed, or permeable depending on how families interact with other families and their community. A family with closed boundaries, for example, might be seen as isolated or simply as 'keeping to themselves'. People and families will also tend to retain their equilibrium; the ability to stay essentially as they are: 'So I may eat cabbage but I do not become cabbage-like' (Payne 1997:138). The family then is seen as a reasonably distinct entity with its own boundaries, which interacts with other systems in what are called super-systems—that is, families interact in the community system with the school system, work system, and shopping systems. Families may change over time, they may grow, become more complex, but will keep adjusting to maintain themselves.

One of the positive aspects of systems theory is that it encourages us to think about the whole rather than only the parts. The ecological systems approach particularly stresses seeing the family in the context of their environment (Germain and Gitterman 1980). We need to see the family's interactions with other systems, to look at the impact of change in one part of the family on the other family members. Family workers, for example, know that one family member seeking to change is less likely to be successful if the rest of the family system is trying to keep them the same. Systems can be formal or informal, public or private. Finally, a systems approach would also talk about reciprocity or reciprocal adaptation—the idea that if one part of the system changes and develops, that change will have an effect on other systems. When people face changes, such as life stages or environmental change such as losing work, they or the environment or both may need to change to re-establish some equilibrium.

One of the criticisms of systems theory is that it can come across as value neutral—that what matters is the system's maintenance rather than growing or developing in a particular direction. Similarly, it can seem that the focus on interactions can mean that no judgments are made about specific behaviour. Some writers about domestic violence, for example, suggest that this can lead to condoning unacceptable behaviour such as physical abuse. Suppose a worker and a married couple are looking at typical interactions: the woman identifies that her husband arrives home late and has been drinking, she gets angry and criticises him, he gets angry and hits her. The worker might focus on how the couple could stop the process, rather than making explicit that some behaviour is not acceptable under any circumstance. This is not to say that looking at patterns is not a valid approach, but that it needs to be combined with clear expression of values.

Systems theory is often seen as being complementary to other approaches (Payne 1997). Wood (2001) suggests that the family therapy field, for example, which uses a systems approach, is compatible with an awareness of the broader social issues related to critical social theory. Psychoanalytic approaches are clearly compatible with a systems approach. There is a great deal of writing about systems approaches in business and organisational management literature particularly from the USA.

Key elements of a system approach are:

- thinking about the whole of a family or organisation as well as seeing how each worker or work unit operates
- seeing how each part of a system can influence other parts and be in turn influenced by them
- developing awareness of system boundaries and how they vary—that is, in being open, closed, or permeable
- exploring the connections between the person/organisation and the environment
- understanding the opposing forces of the system as both constantly active and seeking to maintain equilibrium
- suggesting that change is complex, needing to accommodate the whole rather than focusing on one part.

What might this mean for working in human service organisations?

This approach alerts workers and managers to thinking about the organisation as a complicated set of groups interacting with each other in different ways. It is particularly useful in showing how each part of an organisation will have an impact on at least some other parts. In a university system, for example, if the timetable is not accurate, more than one class of students will turn up to classrooms. If a senior manager is slow about approving new staff appointments in a welfare agency, staff and clients will feel the impact of lack of staff.

A systems approach is helpful in thinking about organisational change—what parts of the system have to be convinced about the need for change? How will a change in one area affect another? Do you need to work on all the different subsystems or does it depend on the particular change? Are there some subsystems—individuals or teams—that are significant if you want a decision made quickly? How can the proactive energy of one area be used to generate a more positive atmosphere generally? This approach also helps workers and managers see why change in large organisations is often slow; it is not enough to change the practices of one part of the organisation if other parts remain the same. Systems theory suggests that the system will tend to seek equilibrium or have a preference for staying the same—the danger can be that systems theory justifies this rather than challenging it. This approach also prompts organisations to look at their boundaries: what are their interactions with their environment. Sometimes, the energy required to maintain the organisation internally means that organisations forget about the impact they have on the environment and vice versa.

Case scenario

Rita was concerned about a negative culture in the organisation. Staff morale was low, reflected in high numbers of staff leaving. She had previously tried to change the culture by promoting the activities of a subsystem in the organisation—a small group of staff who were proactive and had done some innovative work. However, this backfired with other staff becoming more resentful of what was seen as their favoured status and this increased pressure on the small group to conform to the status quo. This time she decided to tackle the issue directly, and she ran a planning day to which all staff were invited. The day began with acknowledging the challenges of the work followed by brainstorming new strategies. Staff then divided into small mixed work groups to work on these strategies over the following two months. When the groups reported back at the second planning day, there was a much greater sense of energy in the room. It seemed that tackling the system as a whole was more effective than working only on parts.

Summary

In this chapter, we have explored a number of ways of thinking or theoretical approaches, all of which can be useful in standing back from organisations to see them through different lenses. The aim of this is to be able to engage with them more fruitfully so we can better understand the dynamic relationships within the organisation and between it and its environment.

The five approaches are as follows:

- *Postmodernism*. This approach reinforces the view that we experience the world subjectively, influenced by our own history as well as the culture we live in. This leads to valuing of diversity, the expectation of multiple perspectives on any one situation, and acknowledgment that there is no one 'truth'. Postmodernism alerts us to thinking about power as complex, able to be exercised in a variety of ways, but also to be aware of those with the least power and to ensure their perspectives are heard.
- *Critical theory*. This provides a framework for analysing social structures in terms of power; being aware of who is advantaged and disadvantaged. The individual and their issues are seen as inextricably connected with broader social structures; individuals internalise social attitudes and values in ways that fit their own subjective experience. Recognising assumptions that reflect this enables clients and workers to change. This approach values broader change that is both liberating and socially just.
- *Psychoanalytic theory*. This is particularly useful in reminding us of the influence of unconscious thoughts and feelings and how they are expressed in relationships. History (our own and cultural history) is important in the development of unconscious thoughts; making these conscious can generate more positive working relationships.
- *Narrative approaches*. These value and work with the stories that people use to describe themselves. This approach emphasises the whole person, using such tools as externalising and looking for exceptions to separating the person and their issues. Multiple stories and perspectives are encouraged, and the seeking of the 'alternative' story that will be enabling. The impact of social structures and power differences is recognised.
- *Systems theory*. This focuses on how each part of a system—a family or an organisation—is interconnected, so that change in one

part of a system will influence the other parts. The system experiences opposing forces—moving towards change and the desire to maintain equilibrium—which helps explain some of the tensions within organisations. It reminds us that change in systems is complex, we need to be aware of the whole, rather than a part, including the environment of the organisation.

Reflective practice

This example shows how you could use each approach to illuminate practice. Once you have read it, take an incident from your own organisation or an organisation or community group that you have been involved with. Write it down briefly. Now take each of the five perspectives above. What can they add to your thinking about what is happening here, and how you might respond?

Donna and Bill are disability support workers in a department, which provides specific care packages for people with disabilities, that is part of a large health care organisation. They have come from quite different working backgrounds —Donna from teaching and Bill from nursing; Donna has a nephew, now 15, who has cerebral palsy. They have been asked by their manager, Steve, to take responsibility for implementing a new program of carer education, partly aimed at carers and partly at professionals working with carers. Both were initially very excited to be

asked to do this, as they have both worked in the field for some time and are experienced workers who respect each other. However, now that they have started on the project, they are feeling stuck: they seem to disagree about almost everything: what should be a priority, what the education programs should consist of, and how they should be delivered. To make things more difficult, the professionals are saying they want the carers trained to take more responsibility rather than expecting the professionals to do everything; the carers are saying they are hoping that the professionals will start to see that carers can not do everything on their own.

How might it help Donna and Bill to stop and look at this situation from the different approaches we have considered?

- **Modernism/postmodernism**.
  First, thinking from this angle, might help Donna and Bill to start

thinking about and deconstructing their own assumptions about the project. Why did each of them assume they would approach it in a particular way, where did this come from? How does it reflect their training, history, experience, is there an influence, for example, for Donna from her nephew's experience? Next, or as part of this, they might see that they have been assuming that there is a 'right' way to implement this project, rather than many possible ways, each with their advantages and disadvantages. It would also help them to put into perspective the different views of carers and professionals, as well as encouraging Bill and Donna to look for different views—seeking multiple perspectives, rather than a predominating view from each group. They might also start asking whether there are voices not being heard and what other perspectives are there? This helps Bill and Donna see that they have more in common than it appeared, that they generally start from the same values and underlying assumptions, but have come to different conclusions about strategies.

- **Critical theory**. This would build on some of the questioning that Bill and Donna have started, and would encourage them to link analysing their own assumptions and values with those of the

broader social system. What are the attitudes in the community they work in and in society generally about people with disabilities and their carers? What assumptions are made in the organisation that reflect these attitudes and how do these translate into how people are treated? Are there structural issues that need to be addressed or at least acknowledged? Do carers feel like second-class citizens, for example, because they are not in paid employment rather than as valued members of the community? What are the different perceptions of carers, what different meanings do they give to their particular situation? What would they want in terms of training for themselves and the professionals they work with? Donna is conscious that her own experience of having a family member with a disability has affected her perceptions; her brother-in-law chose to be the carer while her sister worked as a nurse. Community and professional reactions to this were often negative because of assumptions about gender and made life harder for the family. This makes Donna particularly interested in challenging assumptions and values. Bill and Donna are already conscious of the relative power differences involved, and are aware that some of the carers are talking about forming a group to have their voice heard more effectively. Thinking from a critical perspective, they decide they should support this and see if there is a way to enable this voice to be heard through the project.

- **Psychoanalytic theory**. Here Donna and Bill could ask what is happening at an unconscious level for individuals or the organisation that is influencing how things are done. Does the organisation project an attitude that carers are needy, always looking for more resources and support, rather than acknowledging the organisation's own needs for emotional support and resources? Do carers tend to project frustration and being uncooperative onto the organisation rather than acknowledge their own anger and resentment about needing services? Remember that projection can be part of the issue, even if what is being projected is also actually happening. The question might then be how can each withdraw their projections and see the other more fully. This could lead to thinking about training that encourages each group to talk to the other, rather than Bill and Donna doing the talking. Bill is conscious too that he feels that Donna often splits—seeing the carers as good and the professionals as bad. While he agrees at times, he wonders if this is partly from her own family

history. When he raises this with Donna, she agrees she tends to do this and asks him to help her remember this is too narrow a view. She also acknowledges the strength of her feelings about her own family's experience, both positive and negative, and that she needs to be careful not to assume that is everyone else's experience. In turn, Bill asks her to help him watch his tendency to rationalise things rather than dealing with differences.

- **Narrative approach**. Like the postmodern approach, this would encourage seeing that there are multiple stories. Donna and Bill might start with their own different stories and then explore those of carers and professionals. Using a narrative approach, they would want to generate a more holistic story: including or emphasising stories of what worked or is working, as well as what is not. This might mean hearing about the joys of being a carer or professional, the rewards of working with people with disabilities as well as the difficulties. The difficulties would be clearly separated from the individuals involved and named so that they can be worked with as independent issues such as communication, getting what you need, or having cooperative working relationships. Here, too, they would be attuned to whose voice is not being heard—so far the discussion has been about carers and professionals, but what about the voice of the people with disabilities? Donna and Bill might decide then that the project needs to include hearing from them. This approach might also remind them about the positive aspects of the work, so that they are more able to convey a full picture to other people.

- **Systems approach**. Initially Donna and Bill were thinking of the project as training two separate groups of people. Thinking from a systems approach encouraged them to think about how each group related and how they were both connected to the wider organisation and to the environment. This illuminated the project in various ways, and they began to think about how they could encourage the two main groups to work together more effectively, rather than them providing separate training to each group. The people with disabilities also started to become more central, given that many interactions were either aimed at or directly involved them. It also became clear that the wider environment of the organisation would have an impact on the project, perhaps they needed to consider that first, if building better relationships was going to be undermined by senior managers, perhaps they needed to be involved too.

Finally, having looked at each approach, Donna and Bill felt they had a stronger base to work from. They were clearer about their assumptions and values, what was shared, and how these could be usefully articulated in the aims and direction of the project. They also had a shared understanding of how the broader context of community and social values impacted on the project and some ideas about what this might mean for them—in supporting and advocating a carer's group, for example. They were more conscious of their own and each other's personal defences that might affect how they worked together and the possible projections in how the carers and professionals related to each other. They were reminded of the value of seeking the multiple stories of carers and professionals, including the achievements and joys of working in the field. The systems approach prompted their thinking about the inter-relatedness of the many groups and individuals involved. They were then quickly able to generate a plan of action: starting by interviewing interested people with a disability, their carers, and professionals about what they hoped for from the project, using these to generate training that linked groups so that each heard directly from the other. In the meantime, they agreed they would also talk to senior managers to seek support and encourage the development of the carers group.

Further reading

Postmodernism

Berger, A. A. (2003). *The Portable Postmodernist*. Walnut Creek, Lanham, New York and Oxford, Altamira Press.

Pease, B. and J. Fook, Eds (1999). *Transforming Social Work Practice*. St Leonards, NSW, Allen & Unwin.

Critical theory

Allan, J., B. Pease, and L. Briskman, Eds (2003). *Critical Social Work: An Introduction to Theories and Practices*. St Leonards, NSW, Allen & Unwin.

Fook, J. (2002). *Social Work Critical Theory and Practice*. London, Thousand Oaks, New Delhi, Sage.

Payne, M., R. Adams, and L. Dominelli (2002). 'On Being Critical in Social Work'. *Critical Practice in Social Work*. R. Adams, L. A. Dominelli, and M. Payne, Eds. Hampshire, Houndmills, and New York, Palgrave.

Pease, B. and J. Fook, Eds (1999). *Transforming Social Work Practice*. St Leonards, NSW, Allen & Unwin.

Feminism—see critical theory above

Bacchi, C. (1999). *Women, Policy and Politics: The Construction of Policy Problems*. London, Thousand Oaks, California, Sage.

Dominelli, L. (2002). 'Feminist Theory'. *The Blackwell Companion to Social Work*. M. Davies. Oxford, Blackwell Publishing.

Payne, M., R. Adams, and L. Dominelli (2002). 'On Being Critical in Social Work'. *Critical Practice in Social Work*. Houndmills, Hampshire, and New York, Palgrave.

Weeks, W., Ed. (1984). *Women Working Together: Lessons from Feminist Women's Services*. Melbourne, Longman Cheshire.

Psychoanalytic approaches

Johnson, R. (1986). *Inner Work*. San Francisco, Harper and Row.

Nathan, J. (2002). 'Psychoanalytic Theory'. *The Blackwell Companion to Social Work*. M. Davies. Oxford, Blackwell Publishing.

Payne, M. (1997). *Modern Social Work Theory*. Basingstoke, Houndmills and London, Macmillan.

Talbot, A. (1990). 'The Importance of Parallel Process in De-briefing Crisis Counselors'. *Journal of Traumatic Stress* 3(2):265–77.

Von Franz, M. L. (1993). *Psychotherapy*. Massachusetts, Shambhala Publications.

Narrative approaches

Elliott, B., L. Mulroney, and D. O'Neill (2000). *Promoting Family Change: The Optimism Factor*. St Leonards, NSW, Allen & Unwin.

Payne, M. (2000). *Narrative Therapy: An Introduction for Counsellors*. London, Sage.

White, C. and D. Denborough (1998). *Introducing Narrative Therapy*. Adelaide, Dulwich Centre Publications.

Systems approaches

Gurman, A. and D. Kniskern (1981–91). *Handbook of Family Therapy*. New York, Brunner/Mazel.

Senge, P. M. (1990). *The Fifth Discipline: The Art and Practice of the Learning Organization*. New York, Doubleday Currency.

Weeks, G. and S. Treat, Eds (1992). *Couples in Treatment: Techniques and Approaches for Effective Practice*. New York, Bruner-Mazel.

Wood, A. (2001). 'The Origins of Family Systems Work: Social Workers' Contributions to the Development of Family Theory and Practice'. *Australian Social Work* 54(3):15–29.

4

Culture and Learning

A broad concept of culture helps us to see the ways of understanding our world which we share with others. People's shared culture enables them to make sense of, or even to construct, their real worlds collectively. There is a huge diversity in these collective ways of understanding the world and they do not all hold equal weight. There are many perspectives or cultures which are marginalized through the processes of disability, racism, sexism, homophobia, or ageism, for instance. (Baldwin 2004:43)

In Chapters 2 and 3, we started to tease out how, as a worker, you might stand back from the organisation, and start to look at it more critically, so that you can begin to think about how to approach change. We also explored how you might use theories from practice to look at organisations through different lenses to illuminate what happens within them. Seeing the organisation from multiple perspectives sharpens our awareness of how to act effectively.

In the next two chapters, we consider some of the angles or elements of being in human service organisations that are useful to focus on in more depth. People have been working in and debating about how human service organisations operate for many years, trying to sort out what seem to be significant angles for understanding them. Writers vary in how they talk about these, but there are some common themes. I will talk about these in two groups: the first group (this chapter) focuses on culture and learning and includes the influence of personality. The second group (see Chapter 5) focuses on becoming a change agent and includes generating change, power and authority, leadership, and risk.

As we talk about these, it is important to be conscious of the influence of background theory. How we choose to explore each topic will depend on what perspectives we use—for example, if we are using a postmodern approach, we are more likely to ask what the different ways that people experience this organisation are. If we are using a modernist approach, what is the issue and its cause? If we are using a psychoanalytic approach, to ask what is happening at an unconscious level? If using a systems approach, what are the ways people influence each other? If using a narrative approach, what is working well? And if we are using a critical approach, what are the influences of social structures and what do they mean for those involved? Clearly there are advantages in using more than one theory, in seeing the organisation through more than one lens.

Culture

When you visit organisations, whether they are human service organisations or businesses, you often gain a sense quite quickly of what it would be like to work there. Some organisations feel immediately receptive and open to new ideas; others feel frenetic, the workers are rushing around so much that there seems to be no time to stop and think. This 'sense' is about organisational culture. Sometimes it seems that this sense permeates over time, even when staff change; somehow the culture has become embedded in the organisation and it takes a significant amount of energy to change it. It can be useful to think about approaching an organisation as like visiting a foreign country and to ask yourself how things work here. What are the norms and expectations? What is the general feeling of the place? Maybe even, is it a place where I would want to be?

Jones and May (1992:229) point out that culture was originally a social anthropological term: 'culture as the way of life of a people'; it has also been described as 'the personality, climate or character' of an organisation (Jones and May 1992:228). Liddell (2003:167) defines culture as the 'sum total of all the formal and informal rules of behaviour and performance and communication, together with the distribution of power'. People in organisations are not always conscious of the culture: Kaye (1996:109), writing from a psychoanalytic approach, talks about the 'invisible culture' of the organisation—the unconscious, basic assumptions that people have about their organisation. She identifies the shadow or covert side of culture—hidden agendas such as managers encouraging conflict among their team to maintain their own power or the hazards of people whose emotional relationships are entangled negatively in their work relationships. She suggests dealing with this by being aware of it, developing a network of reliable storytellers who can check what is happening, and detecting and rejecting 'crap'.

Context of organisations

Organisational cultures are complex and much has been written about them. It is important to remember that organisations do not exist in a void. They are part of the society in which they operate and will be influenced by that society's norms and values. Workers in Japan, for example, are much less likely than workers in Italy to express being upset at work, which reflects social values (Hampden-Turner and Trompenaars 1993). In some cultures, establishing relationships is important before talking about business, in others this is seen as wasting time (Trompenaars and Hampden-Turner 1998). We have talked, for example, in Chapter 1 about the influence of economic rationalism or managerialism in our society and the impact that has had on organisations. In terms of culture, you could talk about a shift from a more values-oriented way of managing human services to a more business-oriented way with resulting changes in culture through the organisation. More concretely, workers talk about culture in terms of acceptable norms of work practice—for example, in one office workers might say that the office culture of working hard makes them feel guilty if they go home before 6 p.m.; in another workers might say they have developed a culture of self-care and that they tell anyone staying after 5 p.m. that they should go home. These differences in team culture could influence the organisation's capacity to offer after-hours or crisis services. Such norms tend to grow and develop a life of their own that needs conscious work to change.

Membership of cultures

Whitely (1995) suggests that each worker is a member of three cultures —the broader organisational culture with the overall vision and mission statement, combined with the style of management and beliefs about workers; the work-group or department culture with its own values about work and beliefs about management; and the personal culture of each of its members. Each worker has their own 'home culture', their vision for their lives, their values, and related behaviour. Individual workers will sometimes talk about their degree of comfort with their work group and/or organisational culture in relation to their own, saying, for example, how satisfied they feel to be working in this particular organisation, how well it fits with their view of themselves. The work team and organisation may have different cultures: one work team may value flexibility while the organisation prefers predictability. Each worker then will have their own experience of the culture, trying to balance the expectations of the work team and the organisation. Overall, the organisational culture will be made up of a fluid combination of many cultures (Whiteley 1995:25). Thinking about human service organisations in this way we could add a fourth culture—that of clients who, like workers have their own personal values and vision and who will have their own perspective on the organisation. Their culture will also impact on the organisation's culture. Given this combination, it is clear that culture is a dynamic, ever-changing experience in an organisation.

Generating shared culture

Jones and May (1992:231) suggest that organisational culture is about looking for 'shared meanings, which may be values, beliefs, ideology and norms. These are given expression through shared symbols, notably myths, stories, rites, language and artefacts'. Organisations can spend considerable amounts of time and energy trying to generate shared meaning. Shared meaning can be both formally and/or informally expressed. Often the vision or mission statement aims to capture the essence of what the organisation aims to do and may be an underlying unifying theme. Senge points out the importance of process here: the vision statement needs to be owned by workers across the organisation if it is to express shared meaning (Senge 1990). This may mean workers making conscious assumptions and beliefs about the workplace so that a shared vision can be developed. This reflects a potential tension in organisational culture, between a more postmodern view of valuing difference, but also wanting it to be shared, so that there can be a more modernist view of unified and shared vision.

Organisations vary in how explicit they are about values and beliefs and their underlying ideology. Sometimes all of these are implicit; at other times, workers find out about them by accident. It is useful to look at the organisation's written statements about their approach or philosophy. This will give some indication of what the organisation believes is important at some level (see the examples in Chapter 2). However, it is also important to recognise that what is written is what the organisation would hope to express or believes that it should express. Talking to workers, observing interactions in meetings, and experiencing the organisation may make other values and beliefs clearer. Argyris and Schon's (1996) identification of the difference between espoused theory and theory in use is helpful here. Organisations, like individuals, can identify the theory they would like to be, and think they are, working from. However, their 'theory in use' or what actually happens in practice may be different. One of the challenges for organisations is making their espoused theory explicit and then working out how to make this happen in practice and to maintain that practice. Sometimes this is easier to do in a new organisation or in the first enthusiasm of a new approach, but becomes harder to maintain over time as people struggle with the idea in practice.

Case scenario

Tony started working at an agency providing support services for people with a mental illness. He had been attracted to the agency by its website, which talked about the agency's philosophy as being inclusive and holistic with participatory decision-making for workers and clients. Soon after his arrival he attended a meeting with a client, Danny, his family, and workers from other agencies to coordinate services for Danny. Danny hardly spoke during the meeting, his parents were very negative about his ability to manage on his own, and the workers seemed uninterested in putting a different perspective. He expressed his concern after the meeting to his colleague who said to him 'that participatory stuff is great in theory, but it just doesn't always work with parents like Danny's, it's best just to have the meeting and get it over with so you can get on with the real work'. Tony was not happy with this and talking to Danny reinforced his feeling about how damaging such meetings could be. For his next meeting with a different client, Sandra, he organised a client advocate to support her, who rehearsed beforehand with Sandra what she wanted to say. This meeting went much better, with Sandra and the workers saying how much they appreciated hearing the client's voice. Tony felt reinforced in seeking to have the agency's espoused theory also be the theory in practice.

Perhaps one of the most obvious areas where the espoused theory and theory in use are in conflict is between the organisation's espoused values about nondiscriminatory work practices and the values in action expressed by staff. As critical theory suggests, workers may unconsciously, or consciously, be affected by general social values or their own personal experience and operate in quite stereotyped ways, making assumptions about how other workers operate (Weinbach 1990). It is important, therefore, for workers to be open to questioning assumptions—both their own and those of the organisation generally.

Case scenario

John had been working in an organisation supporting people with disabilities for 10 years. Over that time, he had become increasingly convinced that he was operating from the wrong gender for him, that he was fundamentally female. After counselling at a transgender clinic, he talked with his staff team. They were initially supportive, and John decided to go ahead with treatment. However, once John changed his name to Julie and started to appear dressed as a woman with make-up, some of the staff reacted negatively, feeling too confronted by their own issues about sexuality. John/Julie was upset and decided that in the long run it would be easier for everyone if he left and started fresh elsewhere.

Organisations can consciously use rituals as well as stories, symbols, and artefacts to create culture. The use of these sometimes develops organically, as workers try out different ways of operating and different rituals, stories, and symbols develop. Rituals can form around celebrations of personal events—birthdays, babies, people arriving or leaving, or major holidays or end of year celebrations. Some organisations develop rituals to celebrate and reinforce particular work events and styles—workers being with the organisation for a certain period of time, or completing a project or work with a particularly complicated family situation. These can reinforce the values the organisation promotes. Having social events often helps generate positive culture, enabling workers to have a more whole sense of each other. Understanding, for example, the family pressures of a worker can help you react differently to them. However, people need to find their own balance for this. In some organisations the expectation of a shared social and work life becomes all-consuming and potentially damaging; people need to be able to choose when they are social with work colleagues.

Reflective practice

Take the example of a morning tea or coffee break in an organisation you have worked in. Is it open to everyone —in theory and in practice—or are there subtle encouragers for some people to attend and not others? What is talked about? Is it a time when people expect to talk about non-work activities—that is, to develop more personal relationships with each other—or does it become a de facto meeting? Are there some people who always come and some people who never do? Are there clear expectations about when it is and how long it lasts? Are these known to everyone or generated by a few? Finding the answers to these questions starts to tell you a lot about the culture, what it feels like to work in this organisation.

Kaye (1996:111) suggests, 'The way in which stories are communicated can have a powerful effect on the organisation's culture'. People tell stories all the time—past experiences, good and bad, major and minor events. These stories have an underlying theme that says something about how that person perceives the organisation and its values. When I started working with a community-based organisation with a committee of management, I decided to meet with each committee member to hear how they perceived the organisation. Each person had their own stories of significance, but there were also common themes that expressed the committee's shared values. This often happens in organisations: Having underlying assumptions made explicit like a motto or label can become an important reinforcing theme—hopefully a positive one. However, the common themes can be restricting, rather than enlivening. Two examples might be: 'this is the way we've always done it' or 'if it's working, why change it?'; you could interpret these as saying 'we have developed good practice, let's keep it', but equally this could mean 'we just don't want to change'. Articulating these can be the first step towards changing them.

As suggested in talking about postmodernism, language is also important in creating culture, both the language in the stories and in the organisation in general. The frequent changes of name for government departments suggests the importance of what language conveys—from department of social welfare to department of human services has quite a different connotation. Services for people with disabilities have changed from being named in a disability-specific way, now preferring to talk about disAbililty to emphasise the focus is on the person not on the disability (Galbally 2004). Language can also be mystifying and alienating—for example, acronyms that people are not clear about, jargon that people do not understand. Often workers who are new to organisations have a sharper awareness of how language creates outsiders, and once you have become acclimatised it is easy to forget.

Subcultures

Subcultures also develop in organisations. These are groups of people who may feel or operate differently from the rest of the organisation. There are different ways to look at this—one team or group may develop a more energetic, proactive culture that then has a positive impact on the rest of the agency. Alternatively, a group may develop a crisis culture, with staff becoming burnt out and having a negative impact. In hybrid organisations—that is, those with different streams of workers—there is often a difference in culture between what are called the administrative and professional staff or between different professional staff groups. This may be reflected in the different work expectations: in schools or universities, resentment may develop, for example, from administrative staff who see the relative flexibility of academic staff as meaning they work less. Consider the following example.

Example

I worked in an organisation where the booking of cars expressed the difference in culture: the administrative staff expected staff to book cars for an exact length of time needed and were annoyed when cars were sitting in the car park when other people had wanted a car. The client services staff tended to book cars for longer than needed because they could not always predict how long a home visit would take. They saw the administrative staff as inflexible; the administrative staff saw them as inefficient/sloppy. Having both sides articulate what was important for them helped each see the other's perspective and to be more understanding.

Reflective practice

Think about an organisation that you have worked in/been part of. What was it like to work there? How would you describe it to someone who was thinking about working in it? What would be your 'sense' of the organisation? How might it feel to clients and workers? What would you describe as its strengths? What needed to be changed?

What was it aiming to do? And how successful was it and why? What were the values expressed by the organisation?

Learning in human service organisations

I have chosen to talk about this as a separate angle or element, although you could argue that this is part of organisational culture. A relatively new way of looking at culture or at change in organisations has been the 'learning organisation'. This relates to questions about how to create an atmosphere where people remain constantly open to new information and ideas, to thinking creatively about what would make services better, and willing to implement change. Much of the early writing on this came from a business perspective. Peter Senge, one of the early advocates for example, talks about learning organisations as those 'that can truly "learn"…that can continually enhance their capacity to realize their highest aspirations' (Senge 1990:6). Coulshed and Mullender (2001:81) from a social work perspective see a learning organisation as 'a term which implies harnessing the practice wisdom and skills of the workforce within the overall mission of the agency to give the most effective response to users' and as 'an organisation that helps people to learn by constantly questioning itself' (2001:84).

There is much debate in the organisational literature about the difference between organisational learning and the learning organisation. Argyris and Schon (1996:180), for example, found that organisational learning literature divided into 'the practice-oriented, prescriptive literature of "the learning organization," promulgated mainly by consultants and practitioners, and the predominantly skeptical scholarly literature of "organizational learning" produced by academics'. They go on to say that the consultants and practitioners tend to suggest ideas about structures, processes, and conditions while the academic literature asks more questions about the complexities and difficulties of implementation. Gould (2004:3) suggests 'to make a rigid analytical distinction between them probably just reifies academic turf wars rather than making a useful analytical distinction'. He suggests that there are 'two fundamental premises' that are shared: 'First, individual learning is a necessary but not sufficient condition for organizational learning....Second, the learning experience is more pervasive and distributed than that delivered through a specific, designated training or education event; learning incorporates the broad dynamics of adaptation, change and environmental alignment of organisations, takes place across multiple levels within the organization and involves the construction and reconstruction of meanings and world views within the organization' (Gould 2004:3).

The complexity of this understanding of the learning experience suggests an awareness of the likely dynamics in the organisation, including the impact of differences in power. One of the criticisms of ideas about the learning organisation centres round whether they pay sufficient attention to issues of power and authority. In response, Argyris and Schon (1996:190), for example, say 'we insist, on the contrary, that a theory of organisational learning must take account of the interplay between the actions and interactions of individuals and the actions and interactions of higher level organisational entities such as departments, division, or groups of managers'. This is important in terms of how possible cultural change is in a learning organisation: articulating assumptions and sharing world views is likely to mean acknowledging different meanings in the workplace; managers with implicit greater power and authority need to ensure that those with less power feel able to express different views.

Why is it important to think about learning and organisations?

Significantly, the interest in learning relates to better understanding the nature of change: if organisations are faced with increasingly complex issues and environments, they need to be able to take in that knowledge and adapt quickly. Experiencing this super-complexity as conflicting frameworks can be frustrating for workers as we identified in Chapter 1, but Barnett (1999:31) suggests that these contradictions can become an opportunity for learning. 'Through such experiences, if met in a positive spirit, one can come to see both the world and oneself in a different way...Supercomplexity, accordingly, can be not just challenging but disturbing....In an age of supercomplexity, work and learning cannot be two distinct sets of activity'. You could argue that as well as this being relevant for individuals, an organisation with a learning attitude is also more likely to be able to see such contradictions as an opportunity for growth and learning. Definitions of a learning organisation generally involve the capacity to question their activities and to change in some way. Many of these ideas have developed from Schon's thinking about the need for reflection as part of work: he developed the idea of reflective learning, that people learn by reflecting on what they are doing (reflection on action), but also ideally develop the capacity to reflect while acting (reflection in action) (Schon 1983).

Revan developed the related idea of 'action-learning' in the British mining industry during World War II. Because of the lack of workers, he realised that sending people away for training courses was not realistic. He developed 'structured problem-based approaches to learning on the job'. His 'law' says that 'For an organisation to survive its rate of learning must be equal to or greater than the rate of change in its external environment' (cited in Gould 2004:3).

What is action learning?

Essentially action learning is about seeing learning from experience as a valid and important way to learn. 'The key to experience-based learning is that the individual is asked to access direct personal experience and practice in "real life" situations: this contrasts with reading about other people's experience and ideas or simply thinking about ideas in a training situation. The role of the educator is to facilitate ways in which people can create, access and reflect upon their experience' (Cherry 1999:8). Action learning, like critical reflection, uses tools such as critical incident analysis to encourage reflection: the aim is that rather than workers simply doing something, they stop and think about what they are doing, but also why—what are the underlying beliefs and values? Ultimately, the aim is that workers can reflect while doing. (Theory regarding critical reflection is considered in Chapter 1, tools in Chapter 9.)

This reflects the increasing interest in seeing work and learning as intertwined: that all of us need to be 'lifelong learners'. Tovey (in Jarvis et al. 2003:145) suggests that the nature of learning has changed. Previously, learning was seen as something you did separately—you completed professional training before you came to work and/or did specific courses to learn skills or knowledge. Now there has been a shift to using phrases like 'lifelong learning', or workplace learning to emphasise that we all need to keep learning and that much of our learning happens in the workplace as we are working.

Reflective practice

Danny had graduated from social work two years before and worked in a large city hospital. For personal reasons, he decided to move to the country and started working in a juvenile justice program. Immediately he felt challenged by the work: in the hospital clients were voluntary and grateful, in his new setting they were always involuntary and often resentful. He found himself thinking in ways that he did not like: being negative about country life, making unfavourable judgments about both clients and workers who did not seem to care about clients. Fortunately, at this point, the agency had organised a strategic planning day using a critical reflection framework. As the staff articulated their beliefs and values, Danny realised that other staff struggled with similar dilemmas: how to care for their generally vulnerable clients while being consistent about acceptable behaviour. Sharing during the exercises used helped him articulate his feelings, values, and relevant knowledge. The process of planning also meant the agency identified some new directions in working with clients that energised staff. Danny decided it was time to reread some of his old course notes about working with involuntary clients, but that he also needed to seek mentoring from a fellow worker.

Think about a time when you have felt challenged by a new experience at work. What happened for you? What were your thoughts and feelings? What assumptions and values were influencing you? How did you, or how could you, use the new experience for learning?

There are two related questions to consider here—first, how do people learn to do the work they are employed to do, and, second, how do individuals and the organisation maintain a learning attitude or environment. Learning has always been important in organisations. Much professional training does recognise the need to link and integrate learning from the training body with the experience of being in the field. Most courses include time in the field in what might be called field work placements, practicums, clinical experience etc. Fook et al. (2000) identify how social work students change: their professional training interacts with the experience of being in an organisation as a worker in training so that students start to see themselves as able workers. It is then through the process of working that they continue to gain confidence, and develop the capacity to work with complexity. Rolfe et al. (2001:136) compare the experience of being in the classroom with being confronted with patients: 'In healthcare education, ...the student is taught the facts and secondly she is taught how to apply them. However, it is only when the student is in the actual practice setting with actual practitioners and patients that the third kind of practicum is encountered'. This 'reflective practicum' acknowledges 'neither that professional knowledge fits every case nor that every problem has a right answer'. Reflection is often seen as central to this as 'a process that brings thinking and action close together (both in time and space), that it is something that transcends organisational structures, and that it incorporates holistic and intuitive thinking as well as fact-based logic' (Senge 1990:37).

Learning preferences

People have preferences for how they learn and not all training institutions or organisations understand this. Some writers would relate this to personality (see Lawrence 1993), suggesting, for example, that some people learn better in an extroverted environment like a classroom with active participation compared to others who prefer an introverted environment with time to think on their own. Similarly, Vaill (1996:193) suggests the 'primary problem is not imparting knowledge to the learner but rather helping the learner to find (the) way to the knowledge. Just because we want two learners to learn the same multiplication tables we should not assume it should be taught to them in the same way....If we take learning as a way of being seriously, we have to take the idea of multiple pathways to knowledge seriously'.

Brookfield (1987:73) connects how we learn in intimate relationships to how we learn at work, suggesting that any learning exhibits three conditions of critical reflectivity. First is understanding the influence of context, such as realising that expectations of family reflect social norms. Second is what Brookfield calls 'reflective scepticism...the questioning of beliefs, norms or advice which is supposed to carry universal truth and authority'—for example, a husband refusing to conform to expectations of 'manliness'. And third is 'imaginative speculation', 'the capacity to imagine ways of thinking and living alternative to those one currently accepts'—for example, marital partners who renegotiate roles. He suggests that workplaces need to build on or develop these conditions of critical reflectivity for learning. This again reinforces the value of seeing the person as the learner, connecting the personal and professional rather than seeing these as separate. Note the connections here to postmodernism and critical theory: the expectation is that workers will actively 'deconstruct' their assumptions about how things are done and explore other possibilities.

Reflective practice

Freda was relieved to have started her first job after graduating in an agency that seemed to accept that you still had a lot to learn. After the first week, she began the agency's orientation program for two days a week for six weeks. This began with information being given about the organisation, then moved onto more experiential learning about typical dilemmas in working with clients. Freda found it particularly helpful to have the training combined with spending time with workers on the ground who talked about how and why they worked with families in the way they did. She started to feel more confident about taking an active role in interviews, asking for feedback from her colleagues after each interview.

This 'on the job' training worked for Freda. What would work for you? What enables you to learn? Does it vary depending on the task/s and the environment? What conditions suit you? What strategies are useful?

Culture and supervision

Part of developing a learning culture is developing structures within an organisation that support learning and development. Many human service organisations have developed a system of 'supervision', although this depends to some degree on the disciplines employed and the particular organisation and its context. Social workers and psychologists, for example, generally expect supervision to be part of the workplace

(Brown and Bourne 1995); nurses and teachers are less likely to expect this, although this is changing (Rolfe et al. 2001). This is probably because supervision developed from clinical practice and particularly psychoanalysis: the belief was that if workers were engaging with the personal lives and issues of clients, they needed to ensure that their own issues were not interfering with their responses. Supervision, through talking to a more experienced and usually a more senior worker, was seen as a way of ensuring that either this did not happen or that it was constructively handled.

For some workers, supervision as a word has negative connotations of hierarchy and control, rather than support and nurture. This is reinforced in some organisations by the tensions identified in Chapter 1: supervisors can feel that their role has become primarily one of encouraging throughput, making sure rules and procedures are adhered to, and focusing work on relatively narrow outcomes. Traditionally, supervision was seen as having a broad role and still does in many organisations. Kadushin (1985) identifies three main areas that are helpful in thinking about current practices and pressures; how these would be expressed would also depend on underlying theory:

- *Support.* This would generally be seen as an important part of supervision, although sometimes lost to administration. Support could include the supervisor being encouraging, enabling, empathic, challenging the worker to look more deeply at what is happening and why. This part of supervision will more often connect the personal and professional, enabling workers and supervisors to see how personal values or current personal experiences are influencing their work. A supervisor coming from a psychoanalytic approach might see support as including exploring transference and countertransference; another from a narrative approach might ask what worked as well as hearing about what did not. This might also include another 'parallel process'—reflection on the relationship between the supervisor and worker to see if this provides useful learning about how each, though more often the worker, operates in the organisation generally.
- *Education.* This aspect of supervision tends to be more about sharing knowledge and skills, and might include practising a different approach—for example, a role play of how to use the narrative approach of externalising the problem. It might also include thinking about what other kind of professional or staff development is available in or through the organisation. Some large organisations

have their own staff development team who offer or arrange work-shops; more often workers are allocated some funds to attend professional development outside their organisation.

- *Administration.* Some writers would talk about this as management or accountability; the part of supervision that involves looking at how much work the worker has, could they do more, have the monthly statistics been done and notes completed, and so on.

There is now considerable writing about models of supervision, particularly about supervision processes. Ooijen (2000) summarises these well, including:

- the developmental approach, which assumes that supervision needs to change as the worker becomes more experienced
- the cyclical model, starting with developing a contract, through working stages of focusing, providing space, and bridging theory and practice, to review a new contract (Page and Wosket 2001)
- the Double Matrix Model, which combines exploring the worker/client relationship and the worker/supervisor relationship.

Common expectations would be that supervision would happen regularly, perhaps weekly or fortnightly, though probably less often for more experienced workers, and that the supervisor and worker would remain the same for a period of time so that a constructive working relationship is developed.

Supervision in an organisation will have its own culture, depending on the emphasis given to it. This will affect expectation about supervision too—for example, is supervision given priority so that the time is free from phone or visitor interruptions; do the worker and supervisor have an agreement or contract about how and where they will meet, how often, and for how long; who will create the agenda; and what areas can be covered? The culture of supervision may or may not reflect the organisation's culture.

Hawkins and Shohet (1989:132) suggest that 'supervision needs to be built into the very fabric of an organisation', part of every staff role, particularly if the organisation sees supervision as a way of maintaining or developing a learning culture. Here supervision would be a place where people could see current issues as useful learning, as an opportunity to stop and reflect, balancing exploration with developing options for action, and a resource for thinking about wider issues of effectiveness and development. From this perspective, critical reflection (see Chapter 1) is a useful approach in supervision, creating a culture as well as providing a process for exploring practice and moving to change (see Chapter 9). It also enables workers to make connections between their individual experience and broader structural issues.

So far I have talked about supervision in terms of one-to-one relationships. Supervision can also be carried out in groups, either with a supervisor as facilitator or as peer supervision. Group and peer supervision are generally used for Kadushin's first two aspects—support and education rather than accountability. Group or peer supervision has the advantage of greater sharing of ideas and perspectives reinforcing that workers have much wisdom to offer each other. It can also be a more empowering environment, particularly in peer supervision where workers are at the same level in the organisation. In organisations where one-to-one supervision is more about power and control, peer supervision allows freer sharing of views. Critical reflection is particularly useful in group and peer supervision as the group may find common experiences, and so begin to see them differently—as collective or organisational issues rather than or as well as personal ones (see Chapter 9). Finally, team or peer supervision can encourage the development of a team learning culture. Gould's (2000:590) research in a national child care agency showed that the team was 'a critical context for learning' with teams being able to maintain their own culture in a time of stressful organisational change in spite of changing workers.

Personality differences

Learning preferences are generally one aspect of personality differences. I want to talk briefly about personality differences in general and their impact on the culture of working in human service organisations. At one level, it is obvious to anyone who has worked in an organisation that personality makes a difference to each of us. Some of us find some people just easier to get on with than others. When people give examples of what they find both rewarding and frustrating about those they work with, often what is significant is personality.

Essentially, personality is about how we express our selves, how we prefer to relate to others, how we prefer to go about our lives and work. Personality is part of what people bring to an organisation, often without it being much acknowledged, and yet it is significant in terms of the organisation's dynamics and effectiveness. While it is true that people can change and develop to some degree, personality is usually well established and operates unconsciously most of the time. The section on the psychoanalytic approach (see Chapter 3) explored the concept of personality particularly in relation to conscious and unconscious ways that the personality is expressed. As we discussed, if people are able to bring to conscious awareness what is happening unconsciously, they can then relate more positively to other people—they can separate out what are their reactions and what are those of other people. People can also be aware of their own reactions and defences, how they are likely to react when they do not like what is happening—for example, whether they rationalise or deny what is happening.

There are various personality typologies that are used by organisations to try to work out (sometimes in advance) what a worker's strengths might be. The Myers Briggs Type Indicator, based on Jung's work, for example, identifies workers according to their preferences in terms of whether they are more oriented to the outer or inner world, how they perceive the world, and whether they make decisions according to values or logic (Dwyer 1988; Thomson 1998). In practical terms, this can be about, for example, the difference between people who prefer to work to established procedures compared to those who prefer to respond to the situation as they go or alternatively the difference between those who find it helps them work better if they can talk things out as they go compared to those who prefer to think on their own. Notice I am using the word 'prefer' here. It is not that people can not work across a range, but they will have a preference. Often personality differences are experienced as frustrations—'why aren't you doing this the "right" way', meaning in the way that I would do it? In such situations, it is helpful to name differences as being about personality, rather than about people deliberately annoying each other.

Culture of risk and safety

Before concluding this chapter I want to explore what the current 'fear of risk', which we introduced in Chapter 1, can mean for workers in human service organisations.

The consciousness of risk creates a particular kind of culture for workers. The risk is of two kinds: first, the risk to clients and the need to find procedures to protect them, and, second, the risk to workers, being the risk of violence and abuse generally from clients, but also from their organisation. Having a focus on risk creates a negative atmosphere in an organisation; the emphasis becomes what can go wrong

Case scenario

Ken is the manager of a team of home and community care workers, who provide attendant care services for people with disabilities in their homes. Ken's workers see him as a warm and caring manager always willing to talk over issues with them. Tessa, Ken's deputy, also values these qualities in Ken, but is frustrated by what she sees as his inability to deal with conflict. One of the staff has been using a work car for personal use and Tessa is concerned about this for several reasons—insurance, being a bad example to the other staff, and setting a precedent. Whenever she raises this with Ken he either changes the topic or says he will talk to the worker without anything happening. Eventually, they talk about their different styles: Ken acknowledges that he does not like dealing with conflict, preferring to maintain harmony in the workplace, and that he is not really bothered about the rules for the car. Tessa is able to say that for her it is important to have a system that everyone sticks to, so that it is seen to be fair and logical. They agree that to some degree they just see the issue differently, but that they do need to be consistent and will follow up the issue with the worker together.

and, once this starts, it is a limitless discussion. Working in human service organisations inevitably has a dimension of uncertainty; people in stressful situations will react in unpredictable ways. The issue here though is that negative expectations tend to generate negative outcomes. Fearful workers create fearful and reactive clients.

Take the risk to clients first: risk to clients is mainly seen in terms of workers acting inappropriately or making the 'wrong' decision so that a client receives services that are ineffective or harmful. Unfortunately, the fear here is not so much about lack of resources or good service provision, but more about being judged as an incompetent worker or worse. This might include being blamed for negative publicity or being the subject of official complaints, with the possibility of being disciplined or even dismissed. The culture becomes one of blame and, as Coulshed and Mullender (2001:186) suggest, this can mean that 'practitioners are scapegoated for problems and are left to feel that any shortcomings in service, together with their own emotional reactions to these, are their own fault. A blame culture is frequently also a "fear of failure" culture which blights learning, confidence and morale'. Given that this culture tends to happen in stressed and stretched organisations, this can be the last straw for workers. The attitudes of blame reflects a general culture epitomised in the media of seeking action and resolution: it is easier to find a person to blame than to look at the complexity of the social and political system and the situations of clients. The danger of such a culture is that workers are so afraid of things going wrong that they limit client choice in ways that cause other kinds of damage.

Case scenario

Zoe had been working with the Jones family as part of her child protection role for about six months. Several times she had been close to taking out an order to remove the children, but so far her concerns had been dealt with. Her role was about to finish when a colleague, Jane, was the subject of a Departmental investigation—she had been working with a family where the child was physically abused and nearly died. Zoe was alarmed at the impact on Jane; she was clearly very stressed by the investigation. Although Jane had always been supported by her supervisor and other managers while she worked with the family, she now felt very much on her own and to blame for the child's abuse. Zoe began to be concerned herself about the Jones family. She decided she would remove the children in case anything did go wrong. The family were very angry because they could not see that anything significant had changed. While they waited for a court hearing, they went to the ombudsman who supported their concern. The magistrate also agreed there were not sufficient grounds for removal. Zoe felt in the end that she had reacted from fear about what happened to Jane rather than seeing the situation with the family clearly.

The second part of the fear of risk culture is about risk to workers. The amount of violence towards workers may have increased or may simply not be as hidden as in the past (Stanley and Goddard 2002). Jones's (2001) interviews with social workers suggests that clients may be dealing with greater frustration at lack of services and that their frustration and anger makes the social work role more hazardous. A second set of potential hazards for workers is feeling abused by the organisation, often in terms of not being supported in dealing with these risks. There are clearly Occupational Health and Safety issues here; workers should be able to expect that their organisations will aim to prevent or minimise risk or to support them when incidents occur. Workers will sometimes say the issue for them is not so much being abused by clients—they can understand where their anger comes from

—but by not feeling sufficiently supported by their organisation if abuse happens. Similarly, in their work with clients they are frustrated that the organisation shifts from an approach that acknowledges the limits of what can be done, to blame when something goes wrong.

Organisations often seek to deal with these risks by increasing rules. This in itself reinforces a culture of risk and fear. If you are required to think about what protection you need before you go out on a home visit or see a client in the office, it creates a sense of vulnerability. Quality assurance—the development of standards of practice and organisational systems—is ideally a way of maintaining high standards in an organisation. Many organisations spend considerable amounts of time and resources developing such systems. The difficulty can be that such systems may focus on what is done rather than trying to identify how well it is done, partly because this is harder to define. For example, the organisation may decide that a standard will be that each worker will have a minimum of one hour of supervision fortnightly. It is easy enough to decide whether supervision has happened; it is much harder to work out whether it is effective or useful.

Managing risk is a difficult issue: workers and clients do need to be protected and good practice ensured. The question is more about how to do this in a way that means effective relationships can still be developed between workers and clients and appropriate degrees of risk taken. This may partly mean workers being trained more effectively in working with angry clients. Nathan's (2002) example from a psychoanalytic approach is useful here. He talks about visiting a woman with a psychiatric disability who appears to be potentially violent. Suddenly, he is struck by a sense of how he might react in her situation—a worker and two police arriving unexpectedly at her home. He recognises her emotion as fear and sees that he is picking up her fear and becoming fearful himself. This enables him to see her differently and to start to relate to her as a person who is fearful rather than a frightening and potentially violent woman. The situation calms down and is resolved without violence.

Perhaps a useful question is how can organisations create a culture of safety and openness rather than fear and risk? Such a culture might be realistic about building in quality assurance standards that mean staff feel well supported and trained in their work—including training in how to minimise aggression, and ensuring that safeguards are in place to maximise safety and that there are effective systems to support staff if things do go wrong. Such a culture would reflect the learning organisation attitude—how can we learn from what has happened rather than who can we blame? It would also encourage staff to look critically at what is happening in the organisation and where issues of risk come from. This might mean managers meeting with on-the-ground workers to hear about their issues of concern or identifying where a lack of resources is causing issues of safety.

This is not to avoid difficult issues of incompetence or neglect for workers or clients. In terms of promoting a culture of safety and openness, the expectation would be that workers are capable, otherwise they will not be acting safely for themselves or others. Organisations need to be able to raise and manage such issues constructively. Ideally, a culture of safety and openness would mean that workers would be receptive to examining the quality of their work and how to improve it. Supervisors would be direct and clear about standards and effective work practices, negotiating clear goals about improvement or alternative work options. Similarly there would be an expectation of working with clients about why some behaviour is not acceptable, such as abuse of workers. This would mean organisations and workers continuing to wrestle with issues of what safety means, rather than trying to safeguard every possible situation.

Summary

In this chapter, we have identified:

- The culture of organisations—the sense of what the organisation is like, the 'feel' of the organisation and how it goes about its work. Culture is never static, but changes depending on those involved in it—clients, workers, managers, and the context it operates within.
- Organisations may consciously try to generate a particular culture, through shared rituals and language, for example. Often subcultures develop particularly in large organisations where teams will operate differently from each other.
- Another way of thinking about culture relates to the organisation's attitude to learning—a 'learning organisation' is one where the organisation is made up of people who see themselves as constantly learning so that the organisation can be interacting effectively with its environment. An organisation oriented to change is more likely to encourage workers to be learning and changing themselves.
- Supervision as a way of supporting learning can also be an important part of the organisation's culture. Supervision is more embedded in

some disciplines and organisations than in others and is often thought about as offering three areas—support, education, and administration. The focus will depend partly on the culture of the organisation. Supervision may be carried out individually or in groups.

- Recognising differences in personality is important in organisational life, as people learn differently and interact in various ways depending on their personalities. This needs to be valued in organisations, so that differences can be worked with constructively rather than causing conflict.

- A culture of 'fear of risk' may develop in organisations in two forms: fear of risk to clients in terms of making 'wrong' decisions so that clients receive inadequate or harmful interventions, and fear of risk to workers usually in terms of abuse from clients and harm from lack of support from the organisation. Creating a culture of safety and openness could generate a sense of openness to learning from mistakes and building in clear expectations of acceptable behaviour in relation to abuse of all kinds.

Reflective practice

Think about an organisation with which you have had contact.

- How would you describe the culture, the initial feel of the organisation?
- How is the culture maintained—are there shared rituals—for example, how is language used to maintain culture? How do new workers become part of the culture?
- How do different parts of the organisation operate? Is the culture similar across the whole organisation or are there teams/groups with different cultures?

What is the culture's attitude to difference?

- How does the culture relate to its environment—the community of interest, social attitudes in general?
- What is the prevailing view about learning and openness to change? What other views are there?
- How are differences in personality perceived?
- What is the culture in terms of risk and safety? How does the organisation react when something goes wrong? How could the culture develop to one of safety and openness?

5

Working Actively within the Organisation

...agency implies more than simply movement, but impulsion towards some intention based on our values and ideologies. (Payne et al. 2002:10)

What does it mean to talk about working actively within the organisation? We will be concentrating in this chapter on how to be an active agent mainly for change in a human service organisation. Notice that I am saying mainly for change; there are times in human service organisations when it is equally or more important to be active about maintaining something—for example, a pilot program that does not yet have recurrent funding, a service that has been running effectively for years, but is no longer seen as sufficiently innovative. Change is not necessarily good just because it is different. However, the strategies for resisting change are very similar to those for achieving change, so I will mostly focus on change here.

How to achieve change in human service organisations is a major issue and clearly relates to issues of power and authority as well as to culture. My experience of working with staff groups in organisations is that often workers feel powerless to have their voice heard. Those who are at the bottom of large hierarchical organisations particularly feel this—the weight of expectations, of rules and regulations feels overwhelming. However, being active in either initiating or resisting change is possible, and often more possible than it is perceived. Part of what sometimes seems to happen is that workers are so focused on working with clients that they have no energy left to change or challenge the organisation. Often too, workers somehow lose the capacity to stand back from their organisation to see it more clearly, to be able to identify—as they would with an individual or community client—how it works and how change might be possible, and then to take active steps to achieve it. This chapter explores how workers can be *active* in their organisations. Much of what we will consider could apply equally to working with the organisation to seek or resist change externally.

Organisations vary in their attitudes to change, and the culture about change is different depending on their past history and context. Some organisations are enthusiastic about change, seeing new developments as exciting. In others, the prevailing view might be cynical, a view that changes have not been thought through. Again there are parallels here. Attitudes of individuals to change may also relate to past personal and/or work experience. Psychoanalytic theory suggests that family experience may be particularly significant; people whose family life has felt overwhelming and impossible to change may find it harder to seek change in their own organisation. People who have experienced and managed change well will have a more positive attitude to change. Experience of learning may also contribute; in a sense, learning is about change and managing change.

Views about change will also depend on the underlying theories or beliefs you are working from. If we take the approaches in Chapter 3, for example, each will provide particular attitudes to change and/or how to manage change. A modernist approach, for example, would look for well thought-out change, asking what evidence is there that such a change is justified? Will such a change provide the answer to a particular issue? A more postmodern view might be to say that such a change is fine for those interested, but to ask whether it allows for flexibility and diversity. A critical theory perspective would ask about the social value and benefits of the change, will it help create fairer and more satisfying services for those who need them most? A systems approach helps us see that change in any one part of the organisation will affect others; we can not think about change in isolation. The narrative approach suggests strategies for encouraging change, which again includes looking at the whole situation, particularly building on what is working. A psychoanalytic approach helps people look at their reactions to change.

We all have our own 'theories of change', which may or may not reflect broader theories. Often these theories have come from our own past experience of change, but are also affected by personality and the particular context. They may or may not be made explicit, but will affect how we respond to change. Possible theories might be: change is stimulating, providing new ways of thinking and perceiving, new possibilities for better processes, and ultimately improved services; or change is frustrating, it unsettles everyone, and no one works effectively. It is useful to acknowledge our own general attitudes to change and then to see how they might affect a particular situation.

Case scenario

Frank is the leader of a small team in a large organisation. He has just told the team about an organisational restructure that means that the team will be expected to work more closely with several other teams in the division. It is not clear yet exactly how the team and its members will be affected. He asks each team member for their immediate reactions: Jane is apprehensive, her experience is change means loss of time and resources; Fred is excited, he believes change means opportunity; Sally is resigned, she sees change like this as distraction from real work; Kate is angry, she believes teams should be consulted before such change is suggested. They ask Frank how he feels; he has a mix of all of these; he is mainly concerned though about how the team can conserve its skills and knowledge while maximising possible benefits. Having acknowledged their different responses, they decide to develop their own suggested plan that Frank will take to the next restructure meeting.

Change is possible

I do not want to imply here that seeking organisational change is easy; rather that it is more possible than it is often perceived to be. My impression is that workers often give up before they start; their belief that change is not possible defeats them. In practice, change is possible, but needs to be approached strategically. What I mean by this is that workers need to look critically at what change they are seeking and how to achieve it. Clearly, achieving change is easier if you are in a more senior position with legitimated authority that comes from that. Managers can at least try to impose change or be more directive about change. However, it is also important to recognise that there are other ways of working towards change equally available to workers—and often more effective. Kleiner (1996:x) reminds us that new ideas are initially seen as heresies: 'A heretic is someone who sees a truth that contradicts the conventional wisdom of the institution—and remains loyal to both entities, to the institution and the new truth. Heretics are not apostates; they do not want to leave the "church". Instead they want the church to change, to meet the truths that they have seen halfway'.

We all know from our own experience that change is possible—we have lived through our own many experiences of change. It can help then to identify what makes us more open to change and from that what makes it easier to achieve change in organisations. History is important—if we have had good experiences of change, we are more likely to be open to more change. Workers in organisations where there has been frequent change may be less open to change, especially if they feel cynical about the motives—workers in government departments, for example, may feel that the latest restructure is more about politics than better service delivery. Being included in the change process encourages openness to change, provided the process is a genuinely open one. Compare these two scenarios:

Case scenarios

We will consider two case scenarios. In the first, Jo has worked for a large voluntary agency for several years as part of a support team for people with psychiatric disabilities. She was disturbed at a staff meeting by a presentation by the director of the agency about a proposed restructure. The change would mean that the support team would be located in a different building with other teams focusing on crisis work. Jo was concerned on two levels—first, that the team had not been consulted about the decision; second, that their clients would have to adjust to an atmosphere that would often be stressful, which would be difficult for them. She raised these issues, but the director was not receptive: she said that there had been opportunities to contribute to discussion previously (Jo discovered later that this was a meeting for team leaders at a time when the team did not have a leader) and that the agency needed another team to move for accommodation reasons and that Jo's team had been selected. The team was moved the next week—still in a state of shock. The clients did react badly to the move and several staff resigned, angry at how the decision had been made.

In our second scenario, George worked in a small subregional office of a large voluntary organisation. The organisation was thinking about closing its suboffices due to concerns about small teams being isolated and losing sight of the organisation's goals. They decided to carry out a consultation and appointed a project officer who visited each office. George was concerned about the consultation because he felt the organisation might change service delivery in a way that made it less accessible for clients—closing his suboffice, for example, would mean travelling 70 kilometres each way. As well as giving his own views to the project officer, he organised a meeting with interested clients and community members. They also expressed concern about a possible loss of services, and were able to demonstrate that George and workers in other community organisations supported each other. The report acknowledged that workers in suboffices did respond both to their geographic community and to their employing organisation, but suggested there were benefits to this. A compromise was reached where George and the other suboffice workers agreed to regular meetings in the organisation's main office and the suboffices stayed open.

What do these examples suggest about the difference in approach between the managers of each organisation and the difference in response from workers? How might you apply this to thinking about change in an organisation?

Types of change

There are many ways to think about change and again this partly reflects beliefs about change. It can be helpful to distinguish the way or ways in which change can happen. One of the debates for workers in human service organisations can be about the need to focus on structural change—how can we improve life for people on the ground if the social system stays the same? This then creates the kind of binary position that postmodernist thinking makes us aware of—either we seek broad structural change or we do nothing. Critical theory helps us move beyond this to say that we seek both structural change as well as working with people on the ground who need resources immediately. Structural issues are also internalised by individuals and embedded in relationships, so identifying restricting attitudes and changing relationships then can also be part of broader social change. Similarly, in organisations, perhaps particularly large organisations, workers can feel that the organisation is so large and they are so powerless that they cannot achieve the kind of major change they would like. There are other ways then to look at this—first, workers can often achieve change within their own area and second, workers acting together can achieve broader change over time. It may be that the initial change is about a change in attitude, for example, from 'our voice is not important and will not be heard', to 'we have useful knowledge and can make our voice heard'.

The focus of change is important

Is the desired change internal to the organisation or external? Who else is involved in or likely to be affected by change? What are the political implications for change? Are there legislative implications? Clearly if the change is within your sphere of influence, you have more chance of being able to bring it about. If the change is external to you and your organisation, your strategies for achieving change will need to be quite different.

Impetus for change

Another important question is where is the impetus for change coming from? Some change is political and may become legislative change. Such change may be welcome—for example, recognising rights for gay and lesbian couples. Other political and legislative change may be less welcome, seen as restricting flexibility for clients and workers. This type of situation is less amenable to change, though, of course it is not impossible.

The impetus for change may come from the community or particular sections of the community. The community often seeks change through lobbying politicians who, if sufficiently impressed, will then seek change in government departments and possibly in legislation. Sometimes the community will lobby organisations directly, either to resist service change or closure or to advocate for change. Workers may find that community groups are presenting similar views outside the organisation to those they are presenting inside. Workers may initiate change—bottom up change—or change may come from the top. At times, the conflicting views about a particular issue may mean that change is being suggested or initiated or resisted from various places at once. This can create a crisis in which change is more likely to happen.

Change can happen at different rates

Stace and Dunphy (1992) suggest a continuum of types of change from fine tuning to incremental adjustments, to modular transformation and eventually corporate transformation. The first two, they suggest, are more appropriate in stable environments, the second two are more likely to work in turbulent environments. It is important to be conscious of and so able to make use of this—sometimes a time of crisis can be a useful time to advocate change that has been considered for some time. This will mean that the change is one that has been thought through but will also fit a need for something to happen in response to the current crisis. What will work will mean matching the desired change with the current context, which includes what is happening in the environment, who is involved, what the variety of opinions might be, and how the need for change can be explored and agreement reached. Binnie and Titchen (1999) recognise the fluid nature of this time of change. In seeking change in a hospital ward, they used what they called a "horticultural" model of change' that:

> assumes that both the leader of the change and other participants have a degree of initiative and control....A central notion in the horticultural analogy is the recognition that, in dealing with change in nursing practice, one is dealing with something living and dynamic....We appreciated the value of the careful planning....but like, a garden design, most of our plans related more to the general shape, colour and style of what we were trying to create....Rather than forcing the ward's development...we tried to be sensitive to prevailing conditions and to adapt our plans accordingly (Binnie and Titchen 1999:225).

Strategies for change

As workers in human service organisations, it is important to spend time thinking about the change and how to present it as well as being able to be creative and flexible in our approach. Sometimes workers feel that their point of view is so obviously right that just stating it will be effective. Managers will have other perspectives—they need to think about the overall impact of the decision on the organisation. To increase the possibility of succeeding, you need to be able to present information and a convincing and reasoned argument, often to colleagues as well as to managers.

You need also to think about the kind of approach you want to take to change. This again will depend on the kind of change you want and the time you are prepared to take. Some writers talk about the differences between a conflict or a consensus model of change. Often workers will try a consensus model first; this would mean building support and seeking agreement about the change. If this is not successful, workers might move to a conflict approach—confronting those who disagree with more direct action such as refusing to act in particular ways, taking strike action, or generating a more public campaign about change.

There are many strategies for seeking change and you need to think intentionally and tactically about what might work in your particular context. You could use some or all of the following strategies, not necessarily in this order:

- *Raising the issue*—talking to other workers and managers individually, asking what they think, what do they see as the issues about a proposed change. This will give you a sense of how much support there is and how much opposition, the reasons for both, what might be persuasive for gaining more support. This also starts to put the issue 'on the table' and people will start to think and talk about it in a way that allows them to explore different perspectives. At this stage a postmodern perspective can be helpful—rather than a right answer, you want people to be exploring the issue and possible responses. This depends, of course, on whether you have a particular change to suggest or whether you are concerned about the issue, but open to possible solutions. The advantage of exploring the issue with other people first is that they are more likely to feel involved in the process and to support it. You need to be conscious here of listening as well as advocating your point of view, of being aware of when the strength of your own conviction is putting people off rather than gaining support.
- *Gathering information.* Depending on the situation, you might do this first. This could be factual information related to the proposal —indications of the need for change, costs involved, resources needed. It could also be views of relevant people, clients, workers, community members, managers; you need to think about whose views are likely to be seen as important.
- *Presenting the case for change more formally*—at meetings, for example, or writing a memo or report and sending it to senior management. Here you need to think about where you have the legitimacy to present your case, are there some avenues where you are more likely to be heard effectively? It might be that you raise the issue first at a staff meeting, and if there is general support, you ask your team leader to raise it with senior managers. Again you need to think about who is involved and what their attitude is, what do you do if the team leader is not sympathetic? How then can you have the issue raised more broadly?
- *Building support*—looking for a network of interest. Depending on the issue, you might start to look for a broader range of people interested in the same issue and potential change. It might be that

individual staff members from various teams are interested; a client group might agree with the need for change, or there may be individual managers on side. Part of what you are doing at this point is keeping the issue alive and on the agenda, generating interest at whatever point you can. What you are hoping for is that this will generate a momentum for change or at least interest in considering your issue.

- *Actively advocating for change.* It may be that you have tried various strategies and nothing has worked. Alternatively, you may have decided from the beginning that you would need to actively pursue this change. At this point, you may decide you need to be more confrontational—note the same strategies could work for resisting change. It might be that you formally or informally refuse to do a particular task—workers, wanting to change unrealistic workloads, for example, might formally state that they cannot do part of their work. Depending on how confronting you want to be, this could be a more or less public part—for example, refusing to do court reports would be public more quickly than refusing to complete case notes. Taking this further might mean stopping work altogether—a strike by child protection workers in Victoria several years ago was productive in achieving the employment of more staff. It is important here to decide whose support you may lose and balance this with the need to make your point. Depending on who you are employed by (public servants are limited in what they can say publicly), other strategies might be making the issue more public —newspaper articles have been quite successful in helping generate a climate for change, as have visits to politicians and enlisting support from other key organisations.

You can equally apply all these if you are seeking change outside an organisation or whether you are seeking change on a smaller or larger scale. If on a larger scale, building support, for example, might mean building a coalition of organisations. The same general strategies about networking would still apply.

Change is not always possible

You do need to be realistic about change and sometimes to decide that a particular change is not going to be possible in a particular climate. It might be that you seem to be the only person interested and the scope of the change is too large. Alternatively, it may be that you are the only person who is negative about the issue. With any change, whether you want to resist or advocate for it, you need to decide on what is important at the time—ask, for example, is this important enough to me to spend time and energy on? Where is my attitude to this change coming from and what might that mean? The theories we talked about in Chapter 3 may be helpful here. Am I resisting change because it is easier to maintain the current system? Am I seeking change because of my own history and how it influences my perceptions? What are the other stories possible here?

Reflective practice

The planning and development unit of a large organisation wanted to extend their residential services. The easiest way to do this was to knock down a house that was used by a client advocacy group and move them to different premises elsewhere. The manager wrote to the client advocacy group informing them of the decision and of their new location. The group was incensed at the decision because their location was ideal for easy access to services for their clients, particularly compared to the new one. The local newspaper interviewed both staff and clients and the broader television networks picked up the issue. Eventually, local politicians became involved; the client advocacy group stayed where it was and the planners started to look elsewhere.

If you had been seeking this change, how would you have gone about it? What might have meant the client advocacy group would agree? What other ways forward might there have been?

Power and authority

In thinking about organisations and change, it is useful to think about the different ways that people express authority as well as power. Both come in many forms. Power is traditionally seen as being related to authority of position, to the place in the organisational hierarchy. We are used to thinking that those in more senior positions in organisations must be the most powerful. This is partly because they are delegated to be able to make a wider range of decisions and to be able to direct staff to take particular actions. Clearly, in bureaucratic organisations, as you go 'up the ladder' you do have the authority of a more senior position; however, this does not necessarily mean that the most senior person will be the most powerful in every situation.

Thinking about power

Perhaps because of our experience of organisations, we tend to think of power as something that one person has over another person, rather than power being shared in a more fluid way. In theory, at least, greater sharing of power is implicit in flatter structures. A 'learning organisation' is more likely to make explicit a view that power is shared with a sense of openness to whoever has the ideas. In practice, power is often seen as residing more in some groups of people than others; this often relates to the binary way of looking at the world we talked about in Chapter 3—we assume that if one group has power another does not. Examples of such binaries are between professional groups, such as doctors and nurses, or between professionals and clients. Critical theory also addresses these issues—how power differences are structured in our society and how we internalise these in a way that maintains the status quo.

Healy (2000) suggests that it is more useful to think of power in Foucault's terms:

- Power is exercised not possessed.
- Power is both repressive and productive.
- Power comes from the bottom up.

Taking the notion that power is exercised not possessed suggests that all of us can have power. These ways of looking at power are both more realistic and potentially liberating for workers in human service organisations. It suggests that power does not always belong to the same person/people and that workers can also have power they can choose to use. At a fundamental level, organisations will not be able to operate without workers and so workers also have some power by virtue of their position. Workers can also be seen as powerful by virtue of their experience as well as their professional knowledge and expertise. Think of comedies you have seen illustrating the dynamic between the experienced and assertive nurse and the unnerved trainee doctor, for example. Personality is also related to power; some people are able to exert a sense of who they are or how they operate to achieve what they want.

Case scenario

James had been working in a multicultural community health centre for 20 years. Over that time, he had seen many changes in policy and practices as well as a changing workforce. Although he could have been promoted to more senior positions, he preferred to remain a front-line worker because he wanted to work directly with clients. James's knowledge of how the system worked, his capacity to relate to angry and upset clients, and his ability to orient new staff meant that he was highly respected in the organisation and exercised a high degree of power and influence. When a new senior staff member criticised James's performance in terms of throughput of clients, she found that she was not supported by management and was in turn criticised herself.

Power and empowerment

Power is not necessarily good or bad in itself. If to feel powerful is to feel full of strength and able to be our most dynamic selves, power can be positive and productive. A group of people sharing their sense of agency, their ability to make things happen, is powerful and can generate much-needed change. In social work, there is a great deal of discussion of how to 'empower' people, where the capacity to be powerful is seen as desirable. We need to ask what we mean by empowering people. Adams suggests that empowerment is a Western concept with 'notions of individualism and self-advancement' (Adams 2003:14). However, as workers in human service organisations, we do generally want our clients to become more powerful, to recognise their current resources and skills, and to be able to develop new ones, and positively manage their lives and seek change where needed.

However, there is no doubt that power can also be repressive; there are depressing numbers of examples of this both internationally and nationally, as well as organisationally. As workers, we need to be aware of the dimensions of power and be strategic about when to challenge the way power is being used.

Bottom up power

Given what has already been said about power, clearly power can come from the bottom up as well as the top down. We need to ask here where the bottom is? We often think of this as being the front-line workers in the organisation, those employed at the levels of least authority. However, it is important to recognise that sometimes middle managers feel as if they are at the bottom and find it hard to see how they are powerful. At other times, clients, carers, and volunteers may feel as if they are the bottom level that needs to assert its power. This often feels very difficult for those at the bottom, where the whole weight of the hierarchy feels an oppressive burden. Front-line workers may feel they have more in common with clients in terms of their power. In spite of this, there are many inspiring examples of people achieving change from the bottom, including:

- foster parents negotiating successfully for fairer rates of payments for children in their care
- nurses demonstrating the need for more staff, sometimes by industrial action, sometimes by documentation
- social workers documenting case examples of how the conditions of a particular income benefit made it nearly impossible to receive, resulting in a change to the conditions
- clients requesting a human service organisation be open for later appointments.

Client perspectives

One of the ironies of writing about human service organisations is that most of the writing is about the internal workings of the organisation, rather than about the clients who the organisation exists to serve. Sadly, this is how it often feels from within an organisation; that the views of clients are not often heard. Clients have an important perspective for human service organisations. Anyone who has experienced being on the receiving end of an organisation has views about what works and what does not. A friend who works in the health system was admitted to hospital recently; the experience transformed her view about the importance of the consumer voice. She could still see why the organisation arranged rosters as they did but she could also see that the hospital was organised on the basis of convenience to staff rather than patients. Involving clients in the organisation provides important information about client and community perspectives, enabling the organisation to be better attuned to its community context.

My experience of working in an organisation called a District Health Council (now defunct) reinforced the value of the consumer voice. The aim of the council was to ensure the voice of consumers was heard in the health system, including in the development and reviewing of health services. The council was run by a committee of management and a third of the committee had to be people who had been or were significant users of the health system. Consumers were represented on all of the committees and activities of the council. What that meant was that there was always a voice to speak directly from experience in a way that focused discussion. In a meeting between consumers, obstetricians, and midwives, the consumers were able to say what it was like to be left on a hospital bed not knowing what is happening, for example, in a way that the professionals involved could hear.

One of the fears of organisations is that consumers will not be realistic about what they can do, that meetings with clients will end in stalemate because they will have huge expectations the organisation cannot meet. While this is sometimes true—as it is for meetings within the organisations—clients are generally responsive to clear information about resources and limits to decision-making. Clients often generate useful and innovative ideas about how to solve perceived problems. Braye (2000), from a review of the literature, suggests what can help is clarity about what level of involvement is being offered, involvement from the start, tangible goals for involvement, and accessible structures for dialogue.

Case scenario

The Loddon District Health Council undertook a project exploring what it was like for people with a mental illness living in rural communities. The local psychiatric services were initially nervous about this, assuming there would be increased demands on already stretched services. To their surprise, what consumers wanted was community education about mental health issues rather than a psychiatric nurse available locally.

Involving consumers also provides them with the opportunity to provide feedback, to protest, or to veto particular suggestions or decisions (Jones and May 1992:332). Having a forum for clients, workers, and managers to talk about the organisation leads to greater understanding of each perspective. Getting to know each other helps break down the binary opposition of worker/client so that more complex relationships can be developed. Involving consumers can also mean they gain new skills and knowledge.

How can clients be involved in change?

There seems to be a developing interest in knowing more about client views and part of this is finding systematic ways to have clients involved. Some agencies simply ask clients to fill in feedback forms. As part of their quality assurance programs, many health care agencies now have regular surveys of patients and a system for dealing with patient complaints. Some agencies are more energetic, seeking client representation on boards of management or setting up advisory committees made up of clients or with significant client representation. Some organisations ask clients to come to specific events—either some kind of review or feedback session or planning for the future.

Some examples of client participation are:

- forming an advisory committee to a Psychiatric Services Department consisting of clients only
- membership of a recruitment panel for new staff members
- having student representatives on course advisory committees
- having client advocates in case planning meetings
- making up committees or boards of management in community development projects
- being asked for feedback about possible new staff who have visited a community centre
- meeting politicians to argue for a particular project's funding
- carrying out research interviews.

Leadership

When workers are asked about leadership, they often see leadership as being what managers do—or what they should do. Much literature on leadership reinforces this view. Weinbach (1990), for example, talks about leadership as 'managers' conscious efforts to influence other persons within the organisation to engage willingly in those behaviours that contribute to the attainment of organisational goals'. We expect leaders/managers to provide a sense of direction, to enthuse and inspire staff to work well, to make sure the work is done. Mellors (1996), writing from a federal government perspective, on the other hand, says that the differences between leadership and management are hotly

Reflective practice

There are many issues to consider here: how genuine is the organisation about wanting client input? What does representation mean? Is it a token gesture or are reasonable numbers of clients involved? Some organisations only have one client representative, which makes it a difficult and unnerving task for most clients. Who can be considered to be a client—current? Past? If past, how long ago? If participation means meetings, when are they held, are they in venues accessible to client representatives, are there costs of attending that put it out of the question? Can the organisation pay for travel and child care to make attending more possible? Are clients provided with what they need to be able to participate—for example, are they given background information other people will have, as well as time with someone who can answer queries about it, and are they provided with training or relevant knowledge so that they feel confident enough about taking part?

debated. He suggests the difference is that 'Managers manage resources to deliver goals set by others. Leaders set goals, convince others of their worth and weld teams to achieve them' (Mellors 1996:86). Mellors goes on to explore whether leadership has different aspects in the public and private sector. He concludes that there are qualities that have particular relevance to the public sector—that is, the ability to balance the requirements of the elected government and professional integrity, and to serve the elected government irrespective of personal political beliefs, combined with the ability to understand the views of different groups within society and to build bridges between them. However, these are needed to some degree throughout the human service field.

Traditionally, there was a view that some people were born to be better leaders than others, but this has lost credibility—partly because of the difficulty of getting people to agree about what makes a good leader and partly because experience demonstrates that people surprise themselves by finding the capacity to lead given the right circumstances. Sinclair and Wilson (2002) take the view that leadership is culturally, historically, and politically determined. They interviewed thirty successful leaders of organisations and concluded that:

the current environment requires leaders who are able to see their own values in terms of personal and social history, the capacity to hear and see as valid other ways of experiencing the world, the ability to relate to multiple groups and cultures and courage to stand up to the status quo, and argue for and practice a different way of doing things (Sinclair and Wilson 2002:112).

This fits with a more postmodern view of leadership—something that any worker has the capacity for given a situation that elicits it. Coulshed and Mullender (2001) say the 'recurring aspects of a good leader, in any work setting, include particularly well developed "people skills", problem-solving abilities, and the capacity to think systematically within accepted organisational structures and channels'. They also suggest that all workers have to think like a manager or a leader, taking a broad view of the context and goals of work. Workers often need to demonstrate leadership in managing their work with clients. They need to be able to inspire, encourage, and enable people to solve problems within their organisational context. However, often workers do not see these as leadership qualities and so do not see themselves as leaders. In terms of critical theory, you could argue that workers see those with the power as those in positions of power, that workers have internalised a view of who is and is not able to be a leader. Instead, a narrative approach, for example, might ask: When is leadership something you can do? What are the conditions that encourage leadership for you? What are the times when leadership is absent?

Values are part of any leadership role whether implicit or explicit, consistent or contradictory (Jackson and Donovan 1991:362–3). The questions of what a leader is trying to do and how they are trying to do it lead to questions about underlying assumptions and values. A leader may believe in the value of cooperative working relationships as well as the importance of being efficient. The challenge then is how to reconcile these values. Bolman and Deal's (1997) structure for reframing leadership illustrates that any aspect of leadership has its effective and ineffective side. They suggest four leadership styles: a symbolic leader, for example, can be seen as a prophet who inspires and frames experience or as a fanatic who manages by mirrors. A political leader can be seen as an advocate who works by building coalitions or as a con artist or hustler who manages by manipulation. A structural leader can be seen as a social architect leading by analysis and design or as a petty tyrant managing by detail. Finally, a human resource leader can by seen as a catalyst or servant, supporting and empowering staff or as a wimp or pushover, managing by abdication.

Stace and Dunphy (1992) suggest four styles for leading change. These include being directive or coercive, but also being collaborative or consultative. Workers can at least use the last two. Change often comes about in organisations as a result of collaboration. As a worker, you can seek people with a similar perspective who are interested in working together to achieve change. This might, for example, be something relatively simple like changing a meeting time or structure. Alternatively, it might be something more complex like changing how tasks are allocated or seeking recognition of time for different ways of working. Consultation is more likely to be with people affected by an aspect of the organisation, not all of whom may be interested in change initially. Through the consultation process, workers may become more aware of the issues involved and agree to seek a new approach. If managers are presented with a group of staff with a reasoned argument who want to suggest change they are more likely to listen to them than to an isolated person.

Reflective practice

Stacey is one of seven team leaders in a large human services agency. The team leaders and their managers meet monthly to discuss general management issues. The aim was to have the chairing of the meetings rotate but over the last 12 months, people have been increasingly reluctant to volunteer saying they do not see themselves as leaders, so Stacey and a more senior manager have chaired almost all of the meetings. Stacey is now feeling caught: she does not mind chairing meetings, she thinks she does it well, better at least than the more senior manager, and there are advantages in controlling the agenda. However, in the long run she thinks this is not good for the agency; if she left, the other manager who tends to dominate discussion when she chairs would take over.

What could Stacey do? What are her values and assumptions here? What might this say about how she sees a leadership role compared to other staff?

Summary

This chapter focused on working actively for change; how to be in a human service organisation and be an active, rather than a passive worker. More specifically, the chapter explored:

- Change—change can be more possible than it seems in organisations: as workers, we need to think strategically about what can be done and how to achieve it. It can help to be aware of our usual attitudes to change and where these have come from. We can also think about what kind of change is possible in a given context, whether we are aiming for gradual or immediate change, structural, and/or individual change, and what strategies are likely to be effective in a given situation. Being clear when change is not possible can also help, focusing energy on what can be done.
- Power and authority—to understand how organisations do and can operate, we need to understand how power works. Power and authority are not simply to do with position and hierarchy; people can develop power in other ways such as personality, experience, and knowledge. Being aware of the complexity of power can mean we can be more strategic in approaching change.
- Client perspectives—clients have valid and useful forms of knowledge, including their experience of an organisation, that should be taken into account in thinking about organisations. In thinking about change, clients may be potential allies and have valuable knowledge and skills to contribute.
- Leadership—we tend to think of leaders as those who are directing activity and being the public face of the organisation. A more realistic perspective is that workers demonstrate leadership capacities in many ways, particularly in their work with clients and, more often than they realise, have the ability to be leaders in their organisations.

Reflective practice

What are your own theories or ideas about change?

- Where do they come from?
- Which help you to be active in terms of change?
- Which limit your ability to change?
- What helps you be clear about resisting change?
- What other theories about change could you develop?

Think about change you have seen happen in an organisation.

- What helped bring about the change? What sorts of strategies were used?
- Who had power and influence? What did this come from?
- Who took on leadership roles? Did this change? And if so what led to the change?
- What were the different perspectives involved? For example, if there were clients, what was their view? How were different perspectives gathered, or how were they ignored?

2

Integrating Practice

In Part One, I identified a central tension for workers in human service organisations: how to maintain a sense of their own values as professionals working with clients in an era of managerialism with fragmented service delivery. Over the last 15 to 20 years, organisations have often become larger, providing more services in response to funding bodies seeking economies of scale and a focus on outcomes. At the same time, funding bodies have required organisations to apply for funding for increasingly specific programs. Rather than having workers work across programs, organisations have generally continued to deliver services separately. This does, of course, make it easier to account for program activities to satisfy funders that money has been appropriately spent. In practice, it means that for clients, services come in relatively narrowly defined packages. Clients like Ruth (see the case scenario in the Introduction) can end up feeling that they need to fit the packages, and the services are not organised to suit them.

Current literature and developments in government funding for community capacity building suggest that there is a move towards recognising the importance of connectedness for individuals, families, and communities, and for society as a whole. The links between individual and structural issues have been clearly made and there is recognition that we need to pay attention to social capital as well as economic capital. Social inclusion is seen as a key issue that identifies the need for work with communities as well as with individuals. These changes have implications for organisations and those who work in them. Gradually, more funding has become available to organisations to explore building communities, partly with a view to improving the lives of individuals and families. This may reflect a desire for a greater sense of community combined with a questioning of strong managerialist approaches to service delivery. Care needs to be taken that community capacity building does not simply become another way of imposing a particular model on communities. In some organisations, at least, there seems to be interest in different structures, and more flexibility and responsiveness to clients and communities.

What then might be the role of workers wanting to work actively, effectively, and in a way that fits with their professional values? How might organisations be structured to encourage flexibility and responsiveness to clients and communities? In Part Two, we will start by articulating principles for what I will call an integrated approach to working in organisations. These principles articulate values likely to be shared by workers and organisations in this field and reflect the theoretical approaches of critical social theory and postmodernism that we explored in Chapter 3. The combination of these suggests that we need to have principles or values to work from in organisations that help us to, for example:

- see individuals in the context of their communities
- make links between personal and structural issues
- look for a variety of perspectives, particularly those that are marginalised, such as the voice of clients
- understand the importance of processes as well as outcomes
- explore the complexities of power.

In considering how might we work in our organisations in ways that are responsive and community-oriented, we could start by asking questions. Two sets of questions need to be asked; first, what would suit clients like Ruth? How would Ruth have wanted to interact with the service system? What would we want if we were involved with human service organisations? Ruth's preference—and I suspect this would be true for most of us most of the time—would have been to develop a relationship with one worker, who could work collaboratively with her on a range of issues, with specialist knowledge, in the form of other workers or some kind of training used as needed. Inherent in this, for Ruth, would be being seen as a whole person, with her own capacities and resources as well as having issues to deal with. Ruth, though an involuntary client, did not see herself as being unwilling. She understood that she had acted in ways that put her child at risk and wanted to deal with the issues that had influenced her. She was aware of the potential difficulties of building trust with workers when they had considerable power over areas of her life. Her preference was to talk about and bring such tensions into the open. Ruth also wanted workers who understood and helped her work within the context in which she lived: her family, the community she lived in, her old and budding social networks, the community attitudes that made life difficult.

The second set of questions would be similar to those asked of Ruth, but this time asked of workers in human service organisations and of the organisations themselves. What would be your preferred way of operating? How would you want services to be delivered? What would that mean about the organisation's structures and how would it relate to the community and/or broader environment? What changes to culture might need to develop? What ways of operating would feel satisfying to be part of? How might the organisation deal with funding and issues about standards? What would that mean for the clients and communities that you work with? My expectation is that at least some of the answers for workers would be similar to Ruth's answers—that is, a desire for a more holistic, flexible way of working where workers can also be involved in negotiations about context.

In Part Two then, we will explore what it might mean to think about workers and organisations operating more from these perspectives. I have called this an integrated approach to stress the value of working in a way that is connecting for clients. This sense of connecting is partly working with clients across a range of issues, and is also about workers making connections between individuals or families and the communities they live and work in. Training in the human service field generally encourages students to see connections between individuals and communities. Much of the theory and practice of social work, for example, emphasises connections, particularly the person in relation to their environment. Ideally, social workers working with individuals have an understanding of their social context, the family and community and society within which they operate (Swenson 1998). Social work is not unique in this view (Johnson 1999), which is shared by other professionals such as nurses and teachers.

Another form of connecting might be for workers with a community or social policy focus, for example, to see how this broader perspective informs the lives of individuals and families. However, much current practice still encourages workers to see individuals and families in isolation or, worse still, as problem areas to be worked with. Funding reinforces thinking in 'silos'—that is, workers work in a narrowly defined fields whether with individuals, communities, or in program or policy development.

I too am advocating here that workers in human service organisations need to have a more active approach in generating an expectation of integrated practice in their own practice. This might mean workers looking for or creating opportunities to practice in an integrated way, expecting, for example, to work with clients as whole people or recognising when they need to pay attention to seeking community or social change rather than, or as well as, individual change. Part of this might be pointing out to their human service organisation the disadvantages for clients, workers, and organisations of disconnected practice. It could also mean workers and organisations actively negotiating with governments about what effective and connected practice would look like and how funding could support rather than undermine such practice. This might mean suggesting changes to policy or advocating for a different way of structuring an organisation.

This part of this book then will focus on what an integrated approach might mean in practice. Taking this approach will give us an example of what it could mean for workers and/or organisations to start with a set of principles and apply them to thinking about how an organisation might operate.

Chapter 6 considers key principles of an integrated approach. To start thinking about how to work with integrated practice in an organisation, we need to identify what values and principles might underlie such an approach. Returning to Ruth's experience, for example, would elicit attitudes and values about how work should be done.

Chapter 7 outlines key dimensions of an integrated approach and illustrates these with examples of organisations using integrated practice in a variety of ways. The aim here is to explore what different possibilities there might be in integrated practice rather than coming up with a particular model for all situations.

Chapter 8 identifies skills and knowledge for integrated practice, focusing on what skills and knowledge might be common across all practice areas.

Chapter 9 identifies tools for workers to maintain their ability to work effectively in human service organisations, particularly in terms of integrating practice.

Chapter 10 concludes by returning to the initial aim of this book: exploring how workers can operate creatively and actively in organisations, as well as drawing together the implications of using integrated practice.

6
Principles of Integrated Practice

A holistic approach to...practice needs to provide a set of connecting principles and strategies which allows us to see how working with different methods, different groups of people and within different organisations and legislative frameworks, are all aspects of the same task. (Smale et al. 2000:17)

This chapter focuses on the key principles or values of an integrated approach. Essentially values are about what is important, what we value. Here we want to identify what we value in terms of our approach to working in organisations. Organisations often express their values in mission statements (see the boxed examples in Chapter 2). St Vincent's Health, for example, talks about its values as compassion, justice, human dignity, excellence, and unity. Some organisations translate their values into principles as a way of making the values more specific and grounded. Professional bodies also articulate the values or principles that workers should express in their practice (see boxed example below), often linking these to an ethical code of practice. What gets people interested in working in human services generally relates to their values, or core beliefs about how they want the world to be. Often the frustration workers express in their work in human service organisations is about not being able to sufficiently express these values, sometimes feeling that such values are not validated by the organisation, in spite of their mission statements.

Articulating values and principles of how we work is important. It acknowledges that values are fundamental to how we operate as workers and in communities. Values generally inspire us to think about how we would want to work at our best in the best of all possible organisations and worlds. They are often broad and inspirational, suggesting the desire to work towards a greater good in some way.

However, we also need to be realistic that these values will then need to be wrestled with in practice. Every worker might have compassion as a value, but think very differently about what that might mean in practice. For one worker, being compassionate might be about allowing a parent more time with a child before the child has to be removed; another worker might think it is more compassionate to move the child more quickly. Differences about values will vary depending on culture, the specific organisation, people involved, and their history and situation. Briskman and Noble (1999:60) argue that social work codes of ethics and values look for a 'one approach fits all' rather than acknowledging the vast diversity of experience and values. They also suggest that such codes 'are universally informed by, and place high value on, individualism, independence and homogeneity of the clients characterised by a liberal democratic philosophy'. A more postmodern approach to values would be to acknowledge how different our values can be, particularly across cultural boundaries. This suggests the need for workers to be ever-vigilant about raising and exploring values, their own and their clients. This is balanced here with a critical theory approach; recognising that there are some broad principles that are important.

Example Values

Compare these two sets of values—one for social work and one for nursing, each from different contexts. Note the similarities and differences: both talk about social justice, for example, but in quite different ways. What might this say about the similar and different underlying beliefs about the professions and/or their contexts?

According to Clark in Pierson (2002:21), four broad principles are consistently present in statements about social work values:

1 The worth and uniqueness of every person: all persons have equal value regardless of age, gender, ethnicity, physical or intellectual ability, income or social contribution. Respect for individuals is active and needs to be positively demonstrated rather than just assumed.

2 Entitlement to justice: every person is entitled to equal treatment on agreed principles of justice that recognise protection of liberties, human needs and fair distribution of resources.

3 Claim to freedom: every person and social group is entitled to their own beliefs and pursuits unless it restricts the freedom of others.

4   Community is essential: human life can only be realised interde-
     pendently in communities and much of social work aims to restore or
     improve specific communities.

The Canadian Nurses Association organises its code of ethics around
eight primary values:

Safe, competent and ethical care—Nurses value the ability to provide
safe, competent and ethical care that allows them to fulfil their ethical
and professional obligations to the people they serve.

Health and well-being—Nurses value health promotion and well-being
and assisting persons to achieve their optimum level of health in situations of normal health, illness, injury, disability or at the end of life.

Choice—Nurses respect and promote the autonomy of persons and help
them to express their health needs and values and also to obtain desired
information and services so they can make informed decisions.

Dignity—Nurses recognize and respect the inherent worth of each person
and advocate for respectful treatment of all persons

Confidentiality—Nurses safeguard information learned in the context of
a professional relationship, and ensure it is shared outside the health care
team only with the person's informed consent, or as may be legally
required, or where the failure to disclose would cause significant harm.

Justice—Nurses uphold principles of equity and fairness to assist persons
in receiving a share of health services and resources proportionate to
their needs and in promoting social justice.

Accountability—Nurses are answerable for their practice, and they act in
a manner consistent with their professional responsibilities and standards
of practice.

Quality Practice Environments—Nurses value and advocate for practice
environments that have the organizational structures and resources necessary to ensure safety, support and respect for all persons in the work setting.

Canadian Nurses Association (2004)

Given the importance of values or principles as foundations for
organisations and professional bodies, we need to tease out what principles might underlie an integrating approach to practice.

Breadth of vision—seeing the whole

An integrated approach requires a sense of vision from a human service organisation or a worker about what it is they are aiming to do. This means stepping back from day-to-day work to ask broad questions about the overall mission or vision. Generally, as we discussed in Chapter 2, when organisations do this, their language conveys a sense of hope and inspiration and an expectation of broader change and development. The question becomes then how can these broad aspirations be realised? This opens the way for thinking creatively rather than starting with the limits of what seems possible.

In some human service organisations, regular strategic planning sessions or reviews are used to enable the organisation to take time to develop or remember this sense of vision. Such sessions can be very helpful in generating a shared vision and cooperative working relationships. Depending on the organisation, they can also be an opportunity for exploring the varying perspective of individuals and teams and either reaching agreement or accepting difference. Senge, using a systems approach, talks about the importance of building shared 'pictures of the future' as part of generating cultures that 'foster genuine commitment and enrolment rather than compliance' (Senge 1990:9). Ideally, planning and review sessions (often called strategic planning) provide enough time for workers to see connections between the broad vision and how they will operate on the ground. Sometimes, particularly in large organisations, strategic planning is carried out by senior management, rather than the staff as a whole. This clearly has disadvantages, for the input of other staff with different perspectives can be lost as well as the opportunity to develop a more truly shared vision.

Seeking a just and fair society

It is remarkable how many human service organisations and professional bodies articulate a desire to change society to make it fairer for the clients and/or communities they are involved with, reflecting a critical theory approach. Maintaining this as part of their vision is important for individual workers too. Asking students and workers about why they work in this field usually leads to discussions about wanting to make a positive difference to individuals or communities, interest in creating a better and/or fairer society, or a desire to make sure that their own painful experiences do not happen to others. While there are some people who talk about money, career, or just 'needing

Case scenario

A large children and family services organisation decided to have a strategic planning day for all staff. The organisation had grown significantly since the previous plan was developed, new programs had started, and staff numbers had increased from thirty to fifty. The day began with each staff team presenting what they saw as achievements over the past three years and current issues. It quickly became clear that the staff felt fragmented, that the 'old' staff had one view of the organisation, generally different from the 'new' staff. The facilitator for the day asked staff to divide into small groups separate from their teams and to articulate what they saw as key values for the organisation. To everyone's surprise there was a high degree of consensus and a mission statement was agreed to relatively quickly. Using this as the starting point, staff were able to begin working constructively on the issues. This also confirmed the value of planning with the whole staff group rather than managers only.

a job', these are very much in the minority. Such comments from workers often indicate a degree of burnout. Generally, workers say that if they were doing this work for the money, there would be easier ways to make a living!

Again it can be hard to work out exactly what this means in practice. Organisations will vary in how explicit they are about this value and about how they implement it. As explored in Chapter 2 in relation to a feminist approach, some organisations will aim to have their structure and ways of operating reflect this value; others will separate what happens within the organisation from what they hope for outside it. For example, a voluntary organisation using a critical theory approach (see Chapter 3) might ask questions such as: who has the power in the organisation? How can a client voice be more adequately represented and power shared? Is the organisational structure one that encourages sharing of power and decision-making with marginalised groups within the organisation or its clients? The emphasis might be on how the organisation itself can demonstrate principles of justice and equity. The organisational structure, for example, might include clients in the organisation's committee of management. Alternatively, a government department carrying out government policy may see the implementation of policy as the way to achieve a more just society—for example, through the distribution of income maintenance. As an organisation, it may continue to use a bureaucratic structure, reinforcing existing forms of use of power and authority. Underlying this is more likely to be a systems approach, aiming to maintain the overall system, while incorporating and achieving incremental change leading to a fairer system.

What does this mean for workers? First, organisations and workers need to explore what they mean by a fairer and more just society. Second, how this is approached will depend on views about change (see Chapter 4)—organisations as well as individual workers will differ in how they see change being achieved. Nevertheless, for both organisations and workers, discussing and debating what this value means is important.

Working across domains

An integrated approach by definition would assume that workers would expect to be able to use their knowledge and skills across a range of domains. Such domains might reflect current training in some disciplines where students are expected to demonstrate such knowledge and skills as policy and/or program development, community-focused work, work with individuals and families, research and evaluation, and group work. From a postmodern perspective, this would mean a both/and rather than either/or approach—workers can take on multiple roles. This would not mean that all workers would actively work across all of these areas all of the time. Realistically, most workers will focus on some areas and maintain an awareness of others. However, it would mean, for example, that in a sense all family workers would be social policy analysts conscious of the effects of social policy on families and actively looking for opportunities to provide feedback that might change policy.

These domains are one way of talking about work areas, but of course not the only one. As critical theory suggests 'categories and concepts are seen as historically and culturally specific and therefore vary over time and place' (Parton and O'Byrne 2000:24). More important differences in some situations might be a focus on older people rather than younger; or families rather than young people. Smale et al. (2000), for example, talk about direct work and intervention, indirect work and intervention, service delivery activity and change organisation activity. However these areas are described or divided, the key in integrated practice is that they are interconnected with common values, skills, and knowledge.

The focus in such a model would not only move from the individual to their environment, but also, as Johnson (1999) suggests, might start with the environment and its impact on the person. Ideally, a worker would be able to initiate or respond at a variety of levels, depending on the particular issues and vision of individuals and communities at any time. Workers in rural communities, where there is often only one worker, are often already using some aspects of such a model (Briskman et al. 1999). Rural workers are more likely to operate in an area where there are few other workers and so they will take on a broader range of tasks.

The word 'perspective' is central here. Whatever particular tasks they are doing, workers need to be able to keep other areas of practice in mind. When working with individuals, for example, a worker needs to be conscious of such questions as: would group work be more effective for these clients, are there issues around how programs are offered that are affecting this client, how common are the issues that this client is raising for people coming to this organisation? A worker primarily employed to work with a community might ask, what is the impact on individuals of the community's priorities for work, are there particular groups whose views are not being heard, what are the social policy implications of what this community is saying?

Case scenario

Sadie, a community health nurse, worked in a busy provincial city. Part of her role was to raise awareness of the need for pap tests for women. She had been trying to make links with women from culturally and linguistically diverse backgrounds but with limited success. She began to realise that as well as having issues about male doctors, their priorities were quite different—their focus was on looking after grandchildren so their daughters could work, for example. After talking to some of the women, she talked with her line manager about the need for a different approach. Initially, her manager felt this was not appropriate given her job description. However, Sadie's manager raised it with her manager who was prepared to agree on a pilot basis. Sadie negotiated with other parts of the organisation for a visiting nurse and child care one day a month at the local multicultural community centre. This meant the women could come to a familiar place, the pap test could be carried out by a woman, and the grandchildren cared for. Over the next 12 months, the rates of testing went up significantly. Both managers felt the funds could be justified and Sadie's role was broadened.

Clearly there are implications here for organisations. Funding for organisations is more often provided in discrete programs and this discourages working across domains. Organisational structures, as we discussed in Chapter 4, reflect this. Structures impact on how workers relate, what program areas are seen as connected and which are seen as separate. In Chapter 7 we will look at some of the ways that organisations can support integrated practice.

Working towards wholeness

Implicit in an integrated model is an expectation of working towards wholeness or working holistically. Critical theory reinforces the centrality of the interaction between individuals and the prevailing social structures.

Working holistically suggests looking at the whole person—physically, psychologically, spiritually, and socially (McSherry 2000:49). Human service workers and their organisations tend to be more focused on the psychological and social, and may need to be reminded about the physical and spiritual. We know from our own experience, as well as that of others, of the impact of ill-health, disability, the built environment, and internalised attitudes about physical appearance. Often the effects of these are not sufficiently explored. Working conditions vary considerably and suit some workers better than others; the current emphasis on open plan offices, for example, does save space and encourage communication, but also creates an environment where it can be hard to concentrate on writing reports, particularly for introverts (see the section on personality in Chapter 4).

Part of this is organisations accepting that workers, as well as their clients, need to be treated as whole people. As Bolton says, 'We do not practise with one part of ourselves, and live a personal life with another, all the elements of ourselves are each a part of the other' (Bolton 2001:45). Workers need to be genuine and express themselves naturally in their relationships with clients. We will look at this further as a skill in Chapter 8.

There is gradually more awareness of the importance of the spiritual, which Lancaster (1997:147) sees as 'that which gives a person vitality and life, regardless of their belief system or what physical state they are in...that which gives meaning to life. It determines how one views oneself, others and the world around. It is unique to each person and gives an inner harmony and "wholeness", enabling each of us to transcend external pressures and dilemmas'. This sense of what gives life meaning underlies the work we do, but is often not articulated in this way in work with individuals, families, or communities. It is part of the breadth of vision that workers need for themselves and those they work with; asking the question of what matters.

Working towards wholeness assumes that people and communities are more than the particular issue they are working on. The narrative approach explored in Chapter 3 reinforces that there are always multiple stories or perspectives. Related to this is affirming that each person and community has strengths and resources they bring to any situation (McKnight 1997). The 'helping' relationship is more likely to be reciprocal (see the section on valuing reciprocity and shared knowledge later in the chapter). This can be an issue for workers in integrated practice, where they are more likely to be seen in a variety of roles and so more as a whole person. For some workers, this can be quite stressful, especially if they feel they must always be the 'expert'. This is not to say that workers do not have expertise to offer; they do have particular knowledge and skills. Instead it is acknowledging that everyone has something to offer.

Case scenario

Annie had just started to work as a disability support worker with Beryl, a 90-year-old woman who had recently been registered as legally blind. Annie was amazed one day to find Beryl in the garden, planting seedlings. Beryl explained that her grandson had come to visit over the weekend and planted some new fruit trees for her, but had run out of time to plant the seedlings. Annie expressed her surprise that Beryl would think it was worth planting young trees. Beryl asked her why and when Annie said she would not be able to see them grow, she smiled and said she could feel them even if she could not see them and that as she came from a family of long livers, she expected she would be benefiting from the fruit. Annie began to realise that she had made a lot of assumptions about Beryl because of her age and disability.

This also relates to accepting the nature of work in human service organisations in dealing with confusion, doubt, and helplessness. Workers have to accept that part of being whole is admitting that they do not always know what to do and that there is not one 'right' direction. Times of uncertainty are part of life for all of us and acting too quickly can mean regretting decisions made. This is particularly so for people or communities in transition, who need time to experience and acknowledge letting go of their past way of being before moving to another (Bridges 1991). Some organisational cultures deal with uncertainty and transition better than others. In some organisations, unease about uncertainty means decisions are made before the issues have been sufficiently explored. In others, the culture requires what can feel like endless discussions about issues before resolution. Issues of power, leadership, and personality can complicate the capacity to get the balance right.

Awareness of context

How to carry out an integrated approach will vary depending on the particular context of the work. As we discussed in Chapter 3, critical theory suggests the importance of context. Context must include a sense of the broader society and culture in which we live as well as a more specific community relationship. Given globalisation on many levels, often an awareness of context will include what is happening around the world. Workers in rural communities, for example, need to be conscious that a surplus of beef or wool in some parts of the world will have an impact on local farm families. War in certain parts of the world may lead to an increase in refugees in others. Large companies shutting down factories in some parts of the world to concentrate operations in others, can either be a source of extra or lost employment.

On a general social and cultural level, workers also need to be aware of context. Individuals and communities are constantly influenced by current norms and values. Expectations of what people can and should do are affected by age, gender, ability and disability, race, ethnicity, and class. As many writers have pointed out (see Chapter 3) such expectations are institutionalised in our social structures and can be hard to identify. Critical theory suggests that workers at an individual or community level may find that such expectations are internalised in a way that is destructive and needs to be deconstructed. A postmodern approach would ask what has each of these meant for individuals rather than assuming the same meaning for all.

A more specific context for thinking about integrated practice is the level of community. A range of writers have explored the question of what a community is. Some suggest that community is essentially a subjective notion, that we define community as what we experience as community (Kenny 1994). Important features of community are 'a feeling that members have of belonging, a feeling that members matter to one another and to the group and a shared faith that members' needs will be met through their commitment to be together' (Brodsky et al. 1999:661). Using these definitions, community could apply to either a community of interest or a geographical community; the context for work could be either. However, some writers see working with geographical communities as preferable. Ife (2002), for example, suggests that in geographical communities people are more likely to be seen as a whole and can relate to their environment physically and socially. The danger of functional communities is that people are only seen as occupying a narrow role; they may be defined in terms of an illness in, for example, a cancer support group. However, it is important to acknowledge that such communities can and do provide significant connectedness for some people. Some people of course inhabit temporary geographical communities, such as prisons, for functional reasons. It may be more important to maintain a sense of an integrated approach for any community rather than to decide which definition is preferable. Delgado suggests that 'The community as an arena for practice provides practitioners with sufficient flexibility to initiate various types of interventions that are informed and determined by a community's assets and needs' (Delgado 2000:4).

Some workers and some organisations would not see themselves as having a community to relate to in either sense. For integrated practice, it is essential to have some sense of the community either of a client group or the organisation. Some organisations may feel that their geographic spread is so large that it is impossible for them to have a sense of the communities their clients live in. Francis and Henderson (1992) write about this in relation to work in rural communities and how to work effectively if as a lone worker you are expected to cover a vast geographic area. They suggest organisations can continue to maintain community context by operating in three ways: working from a distance, focused indirect work, and direct community work. When working from a distance, where the worker does aim to cover a large area, key activities are centred on researching, gathering, and disseminating information, encouraging networks, and monitoring local and area-wide issues of community relevance or interest. Focused indirect work involves focusing on a limited number of selected communities, and direct community work focuses on a particular community. Even where contact is limited, workers are still expected to see a community context.

Actively articulating the importance of values

Organisations and professions acknowledge the importance of values at a broad level. In Chapter 2, we looked at the overall aim and purpose of organisations and how values are often made explicit in mission statements. However, when working in organisations, workers often feel that budgets and accountability are seen as more important than values. Often a discussion about changing how organisations operate becomes a debate about ideal practice versus practical issues. It is important to be aware that the discussion is still really about values. The values implicit in the practical issues are that funding issues and following the 'rules' are more important. Workers then need to be clear about being active and assertive in articulating their own values, but also in teasing out the values underlying discussions about organisational issues. To argue for change in organisations or for maintenance of a valued approach, it is often useful to start with a discussion about values. This acts as a reminder of the organisation's essential aims and values, focusing discussion on what will work better for individuals, families, and communities, rather than what will work better for the organisation.

Valuing reciprocity and shared knowledge

In integrated practice, the focus is on what is common in working across organisations rather than what is different. Given this, reciprocity and shared knowledge are valued. Reciprocity or mutuality is the sense that each participant has something to offer the other. In work with individuals and families, for example, workers and clients both learn about themselves and the other. White and Denborough (1998:15) talk about one of the aspects of a narrative approach being 'acknowledging the way in which the work is mutually enriching'. A systems approach stresses the impact of each part of the system on other parts. In group or community work, participants in a group generally offer each other something; depending on the group, it may be information, mutual support, or the challenge that comes from having had similar experiences, sharing of personal information that is illuminating for other people, or shared work on a project. The sense of reciprocity is important in affirming basic values around the worth and dignity of each individual. It also makes explicit the fact that there are mutual benefits in interactions, that people still have the capacity to be helpful to each other even while they are working on their own issues.

Linked to reciprocity is an understanding that all of us have the knowledge of our own experience, and that this is a valid form of knowledge to be shared. I once worked with a committee looking at birthing issues. The committee consisted of several people who were there because of their experiences of giving birth, an obstetrician, two midwives, and a paediatrician. Initially the consumers felt inhibited by the status of the professionals, but they and the professionals came to see that their inside knowledge of what it was like to experience the system as a consumer was as important as professional knowledge.

Celebrating difference

Before we can celebrate difference, we need to appreciate that we are all different, influenced by our own personal, cultural, and social history. Critical theory helps with this, making links between the structural and personal. Talking about difference or diversity often implies starting from where we are as the norm, assuming everybody else is different from us—and perhaps would like to be like us. To be able to truly work with and across difference we need to start by seeing that we are also different from other people: more accurately, the difference is *between* us. It is very hard to set aside the taken-for-granted expectations in any culture to see that they are simply what we take for granted and not 'the right way' in modernist terms; instead, we need to be able to see many ways.

It is particularly hard for us to see our differentness when we are part of the dominant culture. The predominating social expectation is that everyone will want to be wealthy, youthful but mature, culturally acceptable, well educated, and physically able. We need to work on standing aside from the dominant culture as much as we can so that we can see the world from other perspectives. This is not easy; postmodernism reminds us that difference is complex. We are rarely different from each other in only one way and some aspects seem more important at particular times. Even for workers in a relatively narrow field there will be diversity of some kind. A worker may be in an organisation focusing on work with people with an intellectual disability. Clients will still come from a range of cultural backgrounds, social experiences, and family histories.

Attitudes to difference are part of organisational culture. Some organisations are better than others at having an inclusive culture that celebrates rather than marginalises difference. Organisations are also affected by the dominant culture and prevailing norms about what kinds of differences are privileged at a particular time. Badwall et al. (2004) write from their three different perspectives about working with issues of race and class in trying to seek change in a human service organisation. Workers feeling discriminated against on the basis of colour, felt unable to have their voice heard about being badly treated by clients who were homeless and seen as being discriminated against on the basis of class.

Some organisations focus on creating a culture that celebrates a particular kind of 'being different'. This can then create the kind of binary opposition that we talked about in Chapter 3, making a division between what is and is not acceptable. There can be good reasons for this—generating pride in what has been perceived negatively, or providing a safe space for people to support each other. There are also potential disadvantages. Currently, in thinking about mental health services, for example, there has been a move away from day centres or drop-in centres for people with a psychiatric disability. While such centres create a much-needed culture of accepting and valuing people with such a disability, the danger is that they perpetuate a 'them and us' culture. Instead, some new services focus on encouraging people with psychiatric disabilities to join existing community groups, so that the focus is on common interests rather than disability.

Case scenario

David had been working with an Aboriginal cooperative for about six months. One day while he and several indigenous workers were waiting for a meeting to start, one of the workers told a story about seeing a non-indigenous worker running across red traffic lights. This started the group telling stories about what they saw as the craziness of the non-indigenous community, always in a hurry, always rushing for something. As the group roared with laughter, David felt increasingly uncomfortable, part of him felt he should be defending them—and himself—another part of him was startled to see his own culture in a different light.

Valuing connecting knowledge and skills

Much teaching in this field is done in segregated subjects, so that students can tend to see each practice area as being separate with its own set of knowledge and skills. The focus both in teaching and in practice is often on what is different rather than what is the same. This is often reflected in training in organisations where staff attend task-focused sessions for particular work areas. Problem-based learning demonstrates more effectively that there are common sets of knowledge and skills that apply across domains as well as some particular areas of knowledge. Taking a step back from specific domains or work areas can help identify what is shared. If the focus is on the essential components of tasks, common areas of skill become apparent. If workers are concentrating on common skills rather than what is different, it is much less daunting to think about working across domains. Common skills and knowledge will be explored in Chapter 8.

Acknowledging limits—the place of specialist skills and knowledge

One of the reasons some people are sceptical about a more integrated approach is the prospect of working across a range of domains. Some organisations do expect workers to work across domains. This is often called 'generic' work; workers in some organisations have done this not so much in terms of casework and social policy, but in areas as diverse as adoption and fostering to working with older people. Working across such a wide range of fields of practice can generate similar dilemmas in integrating practice. How do you develop sufficient knowledge to be able to work with a range of client groups? Part of the answer may be in focusing on common knowledge and skills rather than what is different, but there is also a valid question about how generic can a worker be. Where are the limits and when is it important to develop specialist knowledge in a particular field? If you are being generic, what kind of generic?

The use of integrated practice suggests that the starting point is with the client in the context of their environment. From this perspective, the generic focus is on being able to move from the individual to the structural, from the client's own issues and networks, to broader organisation and social issues. Because the worker is seeing the client as a whole person, the worker will work with the client's issues in general, consulting when necessary to get information from other workers. Ideally, service provision will become broader so that clients can find one organisation that will deal with their primary issues. More experienced workers would become consultants about a range of issues. Areas that are deemed to need specialist work might then work in a consultative way with a primary worker rather than clients seeing a series of workers for different issues. Returning to Ruth, for example, a family and children's services organisation might provide the primary worker able to work with Ruth on her own family issues, her care for her child, her relationships in general, the need to build supportive networks, and financial and housing issues. These should be well within the scope of a worker in such an organisation. The primary worker might then, with Ruth, have some sessions with an alcohol and drug worker for specific information about her drug-related issues.

Summary

This chapter focused on the centrality of values to work in human service organisations. Some organisations and professional bodies make the values they aim to work from explicit and express these in their mission statements and/or in specific value statements. This is not to suggest that having a clear value statement makes implementing values easy. In practice, organisations wrestle with a range of values, sometimes contradictory—the value of client-centred work, for example, may be in tension with the value of working efficiently. Even when values are agreed to in theory, people will interpret them in different ways. However, returning to a discussion of values can be helpful for both organisations and workers to have a clearer sense of direction and purpose. Linking values to principles for practice can help organisations clarify what they want to achieve and so to evaluate their programs and practices effectively.

I have identified specific principles for effective and integrated practice. These are:

- breadth of vision—seeing the whole and encouraging organisations and workers to maintain a broad vision of their overall aims and purposes
- seeking a just and fair society—organisations seeing how their particular goals fit into a broader context of creating a fair and just society
- working across domains—organisations would expect to work in a holistic and connected way across services
- working towards wholeness—individual clients, and workers, would be seen as whole people with strengths and resources as well as issues to work on
- awareness of context—organisations would maintain an awareness of how they interact with the community and the social context in which they operate

- actively articulating the importance of values
- valuing reciprocity and shared knowledge
- celebrating difference—diversity would be both known and appreciated
- valuing connecting knowledge and skills.
- acknowledging limits—the place of specialist knowledge and skills.

Reflective practice

What attracted you to working in this field? What attitudes and values were you expressing? What has happened to these values? How do you express them now?

Think about an organisation you have worked for. What did the organisation say its values were? How did this match with the values expressed in practice?

If you were developing a statement of principles, what would this look like:

- for yourself as a worker?
- for the professional group that you belong to?
- for the organisation that you work for?

7

A Model of Integrated Practice

Such challenges to fundamental frameworks call for the abandonment of one's primary way of looking at the world, or, at least, to take seriously that there can be other, quite different and legitimate ways of viewing the world. The learning challenges that we all face in and through work are increasingly of this supercomplex kind. (Barnett 1999:38)

In Chapter 6, I explored possible key elements of an integrated approach, identifying some general principles. In this chapter, I want to look at how these can be embedded in working in human service organisations, using examples of a variety of forms of integrated practice. How do you put into practice principles such as 'working across domains' given the variety of organisational settings? What is common about reactions to talking about integrated practice is an enthusiasm for the general principles outlined in Chapter 6. The aim of this book is not that everyone uses the same strategies for integrating practice. Instead, the aim is that each worker and/or organisation determines what will be an effective way to integrate their practice in their particular human service organisation and community context, and given their particular client group/s based on the principles for integrated practice. Most of this chapter consists of examples of integrated practice. These examples illustrate the variety and creativity of integrated practice as well as how organisations and/or workers have decided to use this approach. They also show how we can think of integrated practice along several dimensions, so that we can select the dimensions that fit with our current context. I have chosen them to represent different angles or approaches to integrated practice; of course there would be many others in the field. Many of them come from my experiences of organisations in Victoria, Australia; I have identified the context for the others as part of the example.

This chapter will:

- articulate possible dimensions of integrated practice in human service organisations
- give specific examples of these dimensions of practice
- encourage you to think about what your own approach to integrated practice might be in a particular organisation.

Dimensions of an integrated approach

I have identified three ways of thinking about integrating practice, but they are not mutually exclusive (see figure 7.1). Organisations and workers could choose to work with one, two, or all three. They are: community, practice, and agency dimensions.

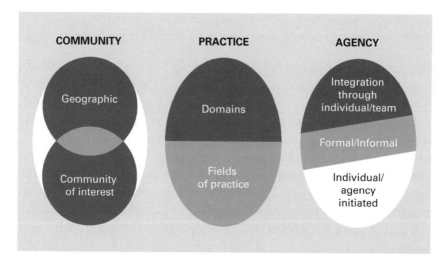

Figure 7.1 Dimensions of integrated practice

Community dimension—geographic and/or community of interest

The first dimension for thinking about integrating practice is the community orientation. I am assuming here that workers would use the fourth principle from Chapter 6, that is, 'awareness of context'. The question here is what community or combination of communities you and your organisation are working with—for example, is there a focus on a particular geographic community or on a community of interest? I am using the word focus here because you are likely to use both to varying degrees. For example, if you are an aged care worker the organisation's community of interest is older people and their families, but the organisation is still likely to restrict this to a particular geographic area. Working in geographic communities has been written about in terms of working in a 'patch' or as locality work, neighbourhood work (Twelvetrees 1991) or community social work (Smale et al. 2000); sometimes this has more of a focus on service provision or on community work or a combination.

Working in a geographic area is a relatively easy way to see how an integrated approach can work. Because of this, the first example is of a geographic patch. Generally, the idea of a 'patch' means that the organisation has decided on a structure where each worker or a team of workers is allocated to a particular area or community. The patch may be defined according to municipal boundaries or to the boundaries of the organisation. Depending on the area, its geography, and the population, a patch may be quite small and one of several within a municipality. Alternatively, a patch could cover several municipalities, a subregion, or region. Obviously what is possible will depend on the workload, the specific aims of the organisation, and the desires of the local community or communities.

Working in a patch was one major strand of community social work in the 1980s in Britain (Pierson 2002) and to a certain extent in Australia. Pierson suggests that, as a method, this was not well thought through at this time. Like locality and neighbourhood work, the aim of working in a 'patch' was to operate locally, 'developing partnerships with local people and organisations, getting to know the neighbourhood intimately, creating easy access points for the public to obtain a service' (Pierson 2002:221). Workers were placed in local offices, but still expected to carry out the processes and procedures required by the central bureaucracy. There was a tension between the expectations of the central office and the desire to involve local people in making decisions about service delivery. This suggests the need for organisations to think through implications of integrated practice. Locality and neighbourhood work have similar aims and tensions, but would generally be in an area that people would see as their neighbourhood.

Organisations and so workers will often work with a community or communities of interest, generally a particular client group. Examples could be people with a particular disability, families with children with similar issues, indigenous communities, or gay or lesbian communities. Many workers work in what can be considered to be both a geographic and a functional community; an institution of some kind that is located in a particular community often with links to that community, where people go for a particular reason or functions. Schools and hospitals are obvious examples, and prisons can also be considered in this category. A prison is a complex example of community life, with people sharing involuntarily. However, prisons, like other institutional communities can provide useful opportunities for integrated practice. Because they are relatively small and self-contained, institutional communities can feel more manageable.

Communities, like organisations, can be thought of as having their own culture as we discussed in Chapter 4. Sometimes the culture and in turn the structure of the organisation is affected by its community or communities. As we concluded in Chapter 4, the underlying theory used in organisations becomes part of the culture that interacts with the organisation's structure. These interactions will again be evident in the examples in this chapter.

Practice dimensions

Fields of practice

This relates to the range of client groups that you might work with. Depending on your training and the organisational context the potential list will vary. Often the funding will create these categories for the organisation in terms of the services clients want, or are perceived as needing. For example, in a family and children's services organisation, the client groups might be divided into people wanting family counselling, family support services, substitute care, or family mediation. In a community health setting, the services might be divided into alcohol and drug services, generalist counselling, youth services, gambling counselling, and support services. As we have already established, often in organisations, different workers will provide each of these services.

Practice domains

What I mean by practice domains here is the variety of ways a worker might be expected to or choose to operate. What these are called will vary depending on the professional discipline and the workplace. They might for example be:

- work with individuals and/or families: might be called direct work, case work, clinical work, case management

- group work, which might be activity focused, therapeutic, mutual support/self-help, educational
- community work, community development, community organisation
- program development, program management
- policy development and implementation
- research and evaluation, quality assurance.

Each of these domains has its own set of skills and knowledge, though in practice these overlap. The capacity to communicate effectively would be common across all of these, for example. Chapter 8 looks at some common skills for integrated practice.

Organisation dimensions

There are several aspects to how the organisation might approach integrated practice and one or more may be particularly significant depending on the organisation.

Individual/team

In some organisations, the individual worker is where the integration is focused, which means that each worker has an integrated role—generally in a mixture of fields of practice and practice domains. In other organisations, a team takes on the integrated role, so that some workers remain relatively specialised. For example, in one organisation each worker might offer a combination of family counselling, family mediation, and family support even though each program is separately funded. In another organisation, the whole team might be responsible for all of these, but one team member might focus on family mediation.

Formal/informal combined with individual initiated versus organisation initiated

Organisations may make a decision formally to work in an integrating way. If this is the case, the structure of the organisation will reflect the decision, work patterns will be identified, and strategies developed. The organisation might, for example, decide to have workers work across program funding areas, providing a range of services to families. Alternatively, workers may initiate a more integrated role or choose to work in an integrated way with the aim of demonstrating the value of an integrated approach over time. This might be agreed to formally with an associated aim of evaluating this as a strategy for the organisation or the organisation might accept the gradual evolution of a worker's role.

If the organisation does structure itself to offer an integrated approach, what this means exactly will depend on the specific organisation, the nature of its work (see Chapter 2), and some of the other issues we discussed in Chapters 4 and 5 related to culture, power, and leadership. In a large bureaucratic organisation, developing an integrated way of working might come from a charismatic leader who generates a vision of how a different structure might work. This would need to be linked to changes in culture to be effective. Alternatively, on-the-ground workers might start to generate a culture of looking for ways to work more cooperatively, pointing out advantages of working across program boundaries. The resulting change in culture might then lead to structural change. In a smaller, more community-based organisation, the community or environment might interact more directly with the organisation, again generating changes in culture, leading to new ways of operating.

Some organisations might consider, for example, that integration is across programs for clients, so that rather than separate teams being established for client groups such as people wanting drug and alcohol services or people wanting gambling services, one team would work across these areas. The focus then would still be on client work, but at least it would be integrated from the client's perspective. Some social service teams in Britain have covered a vast range of program areas on this basis from working with parents wanting to adopt children to supporting older people to stay at home (Barclay 1982). Other organisations might look at teamwork across casework and community work with different team members doing each kind of work; another organisation might see research and policy development as integrated. Later in the chapter, there are some examples of integrated service provision across a team that explore the benefits and challenges of this approach to integrated practice.

Figures 7.2 and 7.3 show how these dimensions combine—with core values, skills, and knowledge central to both.

Clearly there are many ways these three dimensions can interact. The next sections give a wide range of examples that demonstrate a wide variety of combinations. These examples are a mixture of work I have been involved in myself and workplaces I have had contact with. Some workplaces are clearly identified; other examples have been adapted for confidentiality. At the beginning of each example, I have identified the dimensions illustrated.

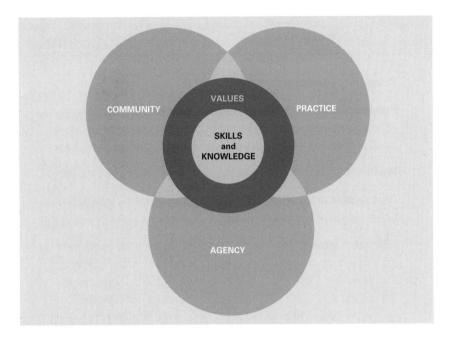

Figure 7.2 Combining dimensions of integrated practice

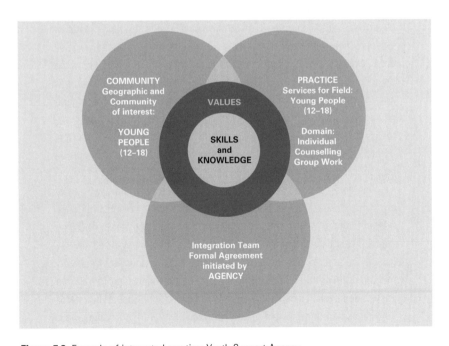

Figure 7.3 Example of integrated practice: Youth Support Agency

Example 1 Patchville

Community orientation: Geographic.

Practice orientation/fields of practice: Primarily statutory casework —families, children at risk, young people and adults on court orders as a result of offending, foster care and adoption, some generalist counselling.

Practice domains: Primarily casework and community work, some research.

Organisation orientation: Worker initiated, supported by organisation, integration through individual workers.

This example comes from my experience of a large state government department that provided a wide range of statutory and voluntary services. The department was divided into regional areas, with each region covering a large rural area. In this particular region, the workers had suggested that each worker should be allocated a particular 'patch' or part of the region to cover. The impetus for the change came partly for practical reasons: previously workers had been allocated clients as need arose. This could mean that a worker would travel up to 100 kilometres east to see one client then 200 kilometres west to see the next one. It clearly made at least practical sense to have workers see all the clients in one geographic area. Workers also felt that it would mean they would get to know the limited number of other agencies in these communities in a way that was not possible when they were all trying to cover the region. The organisation was relatively small at that time and the regional manager and team leader agreed that this way of dividing work made sense—both from a practical point of view and because they too were interested in making broader connections with the community.

I am going to concentrate here on a small rural town that was part of my 'patch'. Employment in the community was primarily in agriculture and related fields as well as small businesses such as shops and pubs. There was an established, mainly Anglo-Saxon community, many of whom had lived in the area for generations. Newcomers were obvious and frequently found it difficult to feel that they were part of the community. There were implicit and explicit community norms and expectations about what status individuals had, for example, and about reciprocity in relationships. As a rural community, there were typical issues of distance and isolation, limited choices in terms of work, leisure activity, friendship networks, or services (Briskman et al. 1999). Confidentiality was a complex issue, as people often knew a lot about each other from observation and frequent contact. Nevertheless, they did not necessarily want others to know publicly what they considered to be private issues.

I began work in the community through casework with Cath Jones and her three children. David, Cath's partner, had died about five years previously in an accident when his truck collided with a car. Cath's middle child Darren was then 15 and on a juvenile justice order, her oldest child Sue was 17 and had left school but was unable to find work, and Wayne was 12. Cath felt lonely and isolated, and that she had little or no support in the town since her mother died two years ago.

Working in this patch

1. Seeing the client/s in the context of their community.

Patchville was a relatively isolated rural community. The community had high expectations of independence and resourcefulness. Community members were expected to contribute to the well-being of the community with a dense system of mutual support and obligation. This worked well for established community members but not for newcomers or those who were seen as 'no-hopers'. Talking about choices for individuals and families also meant being realistic about what was available within their community. Employment was limited, particularly for young people, post-secondary education was not available within the community, and leisure activities concentrated on sport.

Many of the families I worked with, including the Jones family, were stigmatised in the community. Community members would remark that I had been visiting a particular family (my car was observed in the street) and suggest they would never change, they 'had always been like that'. Family perceptions of themselves were often a reflection of the community's view—in critical theory terms, the family had internalised the dominant view.

2. Seeing individuals as whole people

One of the difficulties for the Jones family was that they had become marginalised in the community. Community members implied that nothing positive could be expected from them. The family also reacted to the attitudes of the community towards them, resenting the assumptions made about their family. Darren, for example, would say, 'what's the point of trying to be good, nobody thinks you can be anyway'. Sue had left school at 16 hoping to find work and felt that the local shopkeepers were not prepared to give her and her family a fair try.

However, being involved in the life of the community meant that as a worker I could observe other dimensions of people's lives. From a narrative perspective, there were more stories about the family than the dominant negative. In McKnight's (1997:120) terms, this means stressing the 'capacities, abilities, skills and gifts of people' rather than a focus on their needs. Cath Jones, for example, had worked as a part-time cleaner at the school for four years where she was considered to be a reliable worker. She greatly enjoyed doing needlework and had thought about going to classes in the town several times. Sue looked after the children of a new teacher for two years after school. Darren had tried for the football team and went to every practice though he rarely got to play a game. Knowledge of these aspects of the family gave me a different picture of them, one I could point out to them and use in promoting more positive relationships with the community—a 'thicker' description of their lives.

3. Understanding the context

As a worker in a patch, I could do what O'Looney (1998) calls 'mapping the community'—that is, to identify resources within the community as well as the community's needs and issues. Part of this meant visiting the community regularly and being committed to visit Patchville weekly for half a day. This meant that as well as seeing established clients, I could also develop a network of people who were interested in supporting and encouraging individual and community change. Some of these people were interested in particular roles as a volunteer such as being a probation officer or an emergency care parent, but were also open to exploring how they could be involved in the community generally. This meant that I could encourage connections between individuals and families I worked with, helping to generate new networks and possible relationships.

For the Jones family, for example, I talked with a woman called Jan who was interested in what it was like for young people in the community. She was a relative newcomer but had high status, being well educated, with relative affluence. She was also, like Cath, interested in craftwork. I introduced them to each other, suggesting that Cath knew what it was like for some young people in town, and they became friendly with Jan providing support for Cath in times of crisis. More generally, I was able to call a meeting of people interested in community issues who agreed to meet on a regular basis. We decided to carry out a community survey to work out what people saw as the major issues needing to be tackled in the community and form a working group.

4. Working across domains

In Patchville, the issue of greatest concern from the survey and anecdotally was the high rate of youth unemployment. Farming was changing, fewer jobs were available in agriculture. Young people were leaving the area, or, if they stayed, were not able to find work. The working group called a public meeting which was well attended. A committee formed to look at what might be done. They identified the need for a fruit and vegetable shop in the community. The committee was successful in receiving a grant from the Federal Government and started a small business employing local young people. This also started to shift the community perceptions of unemployment; from a critical theory perspective, community members were able to define the issue as a structural one rather than personal. Jan was involved in the committee and volunteered to help with the running of the shop. Sue, who had been unemployed for over 12 months by the time the shop started, was one of the first employees.

5. Personal connection and reciprocity with the community

Effective community work in Patchville partly depended on connecting with people and being known. People were dubious about working with someone from outside the community and it required a demonstrated commitment to build relationships. Over time, I was known as more than a unidimensional worker, developing some friendships within the town. A sense of reciprocity was helped by such dramatic episodes as my car catching on fire in the main street; a bus driver coming from the opposite direction stopped and put it out with his fire extinguisher. The local garage close by came to see what they could do to help, various people gathered round and worked out who could give me a lift home and who would provide cups of tea in the meantime.

6. Acknowledging personal and community experience

As a narrative approach suggests, communities have stories that are significant in identifying their expectations, attitudes, and values. As a worker, it can be important to have a deeper sense of the stories that are important for the community. It is important too that these stories are about what the community sees as its strengths and resources as well as its issues. One of the most poignant stories for Patchville was about the simultaneous deaths of four young men who had been racing each other in two cars. This was a major source of grief for the community in general.

Although it was rarely spoken about, it informed the community's attitudes in many ways. The community was proud of how it had supported families through their grief as well as developing programs for young people about safe driving. This also influenced a desire to be more active about looking at issues for young people in the community.

What were some of the key features of integrated practice here?

What is clearest about this example is the advantages for clients of having workers who are also working more broadly with the community as a whole. Such workers can help create opportunities for clients to build broader networks and mutually supportive relationships.

Second, having an integrated approach provides important context to working with clients, understanding some of the possibilities and pressures from the client's community, as well as the wider social context. From a critical theory perspective, working effectively with the Jones family meant understanding how the dominant culture was expressed in the community's view of the family and how they internalised that view. It also meant being interested in changing the dominant culture as well as change for the Jones family. Working across domains fostered the capacity to make these links; from a postmodern perspective, many ways of working were seen as useful rather than one 'right' approach.

Third, it encouraged exploration of difference in a way that allowed different stories to be told. From a narrative perspective, you might say the community affirmed a wider variety of stories, so that people, particularly those who had been marginalised, were seen in a more whole way—and as having something to offer, being able to reciprocate in relationships.

What did this mean for the organisation?

From an organisational perspective, the work with the community and the specific clients of the department complemented each other. The department's espoused value of encouraging community support was able to work in practice. While it was difficult to compare the previous system with this one in resource terms, there was a sense of time and resources such as cars being better used. Workers were spending more time seeing people—whether clients or community members—and less time travelling. There were clear benefits in terms of clients and community feedback, that they felt better supported and resourced and actively participating in change. Depending on their background training and experience, some workers felt more challenged by this approach than others. The core work was being completed and workers generally had a sense of satisfaction about their greater sense of connection to the community. However, some workers felt they needed new skills and knowledge, particularly in working from a community perspective, and it was agreed that this needed to be provided. Issues about control and community work were also raised— what would happen if, for example, the community decided to oppose a departmental policy? It was agreed that regular supervision and communication was needed so that at least the organisation was aware of developing issues and that such questions would be dealt with as they arose. The system of allocating workers to 'patches' was formalised with an understanding that while statutory casework would need to be undertaken, workers' roles could vary depending on their patch and that time would be allocated for community work as well.

Example 2 'Prisonfarm'

Community orientation: Primarily functional.

Practice orientation/field of practice: Adult male offenders and their families.

Practice domains: Work with individuals, families and groups, community work.

Organisation orientation: Integration through individual workers, developed informally by workers, then supported by organisation.

This prison was part of a state government department. I was employed by and worked from the central, city-based office as part of a team of six social workers covering all country prisons. The team was a relatively new initiative; previously there had only been two social workers who visited all the country prisons and provided support to the workers at the city prison. With the increase in the size of the team, the senior workers debated the most effective working model. There were eight country prisons altogether and it was decided that the best use of resources would be to allocate one worker to two prisons, with back-up support from the two senior workers. This was seen to have the advantage that each worker could develop understanding of the particular culture, personalities, and power dynamics in each prison as well as developing relationships with staff.

The particular prison I am going to talk about is an open prison with, at the time, about a hundred prisoners, all adult men. I will call it 'Prison-farm'; it was located in a rural area, about 20 kilometres from a town of 25,000 people.

My job description for working in this prison was primarily about working with individual prisoners and their families, dealing with personal issues, and assessing men for special leave for things like family weddings or funerals. I was located in the city about two and a half hours drive away and visited the prison weekly, sometimes staying overnight in the nearest small town. Staff at the prison were not used to having a visiting social worker and took some time to adjust to the idea. The culture was fatalistic, there was a strong sense of everyone 'doing time'; many of the prison officers were working there because their farms were not producing enough income, so there was also a sense of staff wishing to be elsewhere. Staff were pessimistic about change in the prisoners they worked with and this permeated into the culture of the prison generally.

Over time, my role developed and grew, in response to suggestions from prisoners and families and eventually from staff. Overall, the following areas of work emerged:

- *Individual work with men and joint counselling with couples.* Talking to men individually often revealed issues in relationships or marriages. Concern about these issues often stressed the men in prison; there was a belief among officers that this stress was one of the primary reasons for prison escapes. By being available during visiting hours at some points, I could see couples who wanted counselling together, in the hope that work on issues would be at least under way before release.

- *Group work.* Talking with men individually revealed many common issues. Alcohol and drug use was one, frustration about ending up in prison again was another. I arranged to do a series of sessions on drug and alcohol use and management with a worker from the local community health centre. Another group was established to look at issues around returning to prison; the men in the group were able to be both supportive and challenging to each other, speaking directly from their own experience.

- *Community work.* All of the prison officers, but very few of the prisoners came from the local community. There was very little other contact with the community, apart from clergy from various denominations who would come if asked. One of the reasons identified in the group for returning to prison was that people often did not feel comfortable with people in the community who had not been to prison; they were not sure how to be around them, what to talk about. To try to counter this, the prison governor was initially prepared to consider some kind of team sport that could happen at the prison rather than prisoners going outside. I had been gradually establishing contact with community organisations in the nearest large town and discovered a sport and recreation worker whose area covered the prison. She was a particularly energetic worker and agreed that this was a valid part of her role. She visited the prison, established good relationships with the governor and officers, and gradually a sport program developed and flourished. Eventually it was agreed that a prison team could take part in local competitions and for a time this was able to happen. Getting something started generated other possibilities and other community groups and organisations began to visit too.

What were some of the key features of an integrated approach here?

First, as in any community, it was important to spend time getting to know the key players, in this case the governor and prison staff and some of the key prisoners. Relationships were critical: much of my time initially was spent in 'using my self'; demonstrating respect to staff as well as clients while recognising differences in values. Using a psychoanalytic approach was helpful in reminding me to be aware of my own and other people's projections, for example. The concept of reflexivity is also useful here— being aware of how I might be perceived and how I might perceive others, checking what assumptions and values we might each have, and how these affected our interactions. Both reminded me of the impact of history for all of us, the influence of our different experiences. Once I had established reasonable relationships with staff, it was then much more possible to work with them—rather than seeing me as the opposition, the culture changed so that we were more often seen as working together.

Second, it was important to look for opportunities to 'broaden the perspective', to see what might be possible across the spectrum of domains. Starting with getting a sense of what mattered for individuals led to an understanding of common issues that could be worked on jointly. This partly related to changing the culture from a passive, 'waiting' culture to a more active, 'change is possible' culture. Seeing activities begin, and interest developing from the community and prisoners, helped generate a broader perspective about what could happen for staff as well as prisoners.

Third, in a prison, as in any institution, it is important to see individuals as whole people able to contribute to the community, than solely as prisoners. Using a narrative approach, you could talk here about seeing that there are multiple stories, and avoid the binary construction of prisoners and non-prisoners. The prisoners began to be seen as people with something to offer. This was also reinforced in group work where reciprocity was demonstrated so clearly. People see that they have something to offer; they have related experiences that are a useful form of knowledge. Certainly, in the prison groups, people were able to challenge each other much more directly from their own knowledge and experience than I could as the worker.

Fourth, understanding the context of the prison and the community next to the prison was important. Perceptions here were complex; some staff and prisoners assumed that the community would not want to have anything to do with the prison. In psychoanalytic terms, they projected their own feelings about the prison onto the community. While no doubt this was true for some community members, others, including some of the visiting clergy, wanted more involvement but were not sure how to go about it. Having someone make contact was, in some cases, all that was needed.

Finally, this is a useful example of how integrated practice can work within and contribute to changing the culture in an organisation, even in a legally constrained system. A systems approach was helpful in seeing how the different groups and individuals in the prison impacted on each other; change in one area had a beginning impact, working with several aspects of the system at once was much more effective in achieving change. Clearly, the overall structure and processes of the organisation remained the same; however, the involvement of the community, development of activities, and articulating of different values helped to generate a different atmosphere. I am not suggesting that attitudes changed altogether, but interestingly, even though the changes in the prison meant more work for staff, they rarely complained. There was a sense for them, as well as for prisoners, that there was greater energy and possibility in the organisation.

What did this mean for the organisation?

This needs to be looked at in the sense of the social work team as a whole and their place in the organisation. Remember, this was a large bureaucratic government department with a relatively new service. However, the response to the expansion of the social work role was positive. The change in culture and morale at the prison was noticed and the benefits for prisoners and their families affirmed. Senior managers agreed that the social work role needed to be flexible, as long as the basic casework service continued to be provided. This led to some useful loosening of some of the procedures around use of cars and time so that workers could be more truly flexible, as well as legitimising of a broader role.

Example 3 Mental illness in rural communities

Community orientation: Primarily functional but located in several geographic communities.

Practice orientation/fields of practice: People with a mental illness living in a rural community.

Practice domains: Research, community work, and policy development.

Organisation orientation: Organisation initiated, integration through individual worker.

This example comes from the Loddon District Health Council, a small community-based organisation that aimed to encourage consumer participation in the reviewing and development of health services. Two staff were employed—a full-time executive officer and a half-time administrative officer, with funding from the State Health Department. The committee of management of twelve people was made up of equal numbers from three groups—consumers of health services, workers in health services, and interested community members. The assumption here was that the committee should reflect a variety of perspectives rather than one view—a clearly postmodern approach.

The committee of management had some members who wanted to explore in more depth what it was like for people with a mental illness living in rural communities. Their assumption was that people would have a variety of experiences and that these were likely to be different from an urban experience of having a mental illness. We (I was the executive officer) successfully applied for money for a project officer. She worked with a consultative group made up of consumers, providers, and committee members, and developed a research plan. This involved asking the local Department of Psychiatric Services to send out letters to rural consumers in their area, asking whether they would be prepared to be interviewed and if so, to contact the project officer. About twenty-five people made contact and were interviewed.

The results of the interviews clearly showed that one of the major issues was stigma: many of those interviewed had hidden their mental illness from the community from fear of people's reactions. One commented that when she had broken her leg, people readily brought food and offered help; when she had a mental illness everyone stayed away. Again, this reflected dominant social values, which had been internalised by at least some of those interviewed and their families. Other issues were around access to services, difficulty of distance, and lack of knowledge of mental illness. However, the priority generally was seen as increasing knowledge about mental illness in the community with a view to decreasing stigma and so increasing community support.

What next?

The committee decided to apply for funding for a project officer for two years to work with the six small towns covered in the project to provide information about mental illness in whatever way the community thought would be effective. Again we were successful and the project officer (the same person) was employed. The committee of management wanted the worker to approach this in an integrated way in the sense of being open to working across several domains. However, it was also clear about the limits to this—the organisation was not aiming to offer individual or family counselling, instead the domains of practice could include group work with an educational, information-sharing aspect or offer mutual support, further research, and/or community organisation of some kind. This reflected the culture of the organisation with its emphasis on working with groups and communities rather than providing ongoing support for individuals.

The project workers then met with consumers and service providers, generally in separate groups at first, then in some areas the groups combined to work on particular tasks. Each group decided on different activities, taking into account the interests and ways of operating of their particular community. The project demonstrated its value so well that after the funding finished, the local Psychiatric Services policy changed to include such work as a continuing part of its work and a new position was created.

How does this reflect integrated practice?

1 *Breath of perspective.* The committee and workers were able to work from the individual and their issues to a community perspective and back to the individual, making the links critical theory documents.

2 *Acknowledging common knowledge and skills.* The workers, especially the project worker, transferred their listening and communicating skills from research interviews to working with groups. The project worker was conscious that often her capacity to listen in informal conversations was significant in allowing the groups to work effectively. Individuals would need to debrief or vent their feelings and thoughts so that they could join group discussions. Awareness of a psychoanalytic approach was important here; awareness of where particular reactions were coming from, what was understandable defensiveness, and what might relate to fear or ignorance. Understanding the relevance of history of individuals was also significant in building working relationships.

3 *Awareness of context was central to the project.* Each community was different and wanted to plan the activities that would suit them. A worker trying to impose one approach would not have been supported.

4 *Reciprocity rather than expertise.* The knowledge and skills of each group member were valued, which created a sense of reciprocity. The experience of people with a mental illness was seen as an important form of knowledge needed to ground the activities—in narrative terms, the variety of stories about what it meant to be mentally ill was valued.

What did this mean for the organisation?

This was a small organisation and the success of the project demonstrates how powerful small organisations can be; it also is a positive example of how paid staff and voluntary committees can work together. Much of its approach to work reflected the feminist, non-hierarchical approach considered in Chapter 2. The quite different knowledge and skills brought by each committee member were recognised and valued. While the paid workers were expected to carry out the majority of the work, committee members expected to contribute, to learn new skills, and participate actively in projects. Notice that the suggestion about the project came from committee members, reflecting their own knowledge and experience; some of them formed a subcommittee to oversee the project.

The project reinforced for the organisation the value of working with a flexible and broad approach, networking actively, and building cooperative working relationships with larger and more powerful organisations.

Example 4 New Fulford Family Centre

Community orientation: Mainly geographic; emphasis on families with young children.

Practice orientation/fields of practice: Work with community with emphasis on families with young children.

Domains of practice: Counselling, group work and community development, some research and policy work.

Organisation orientation: Integration across team, some specialisation by individual workers. Counselling and community work were specialised; group work of various kinds carried out across the agency.

This is a currently operating family centre in an urban community in England, which offers a model of integrated practice. This family centre is one of many in Britain, but not all operate in the same way. Holman (1988) suggests, for example, that there are three groupings: those that use a client-focused model, those that use a neighbourhood model, and those using a community-development model. Some, like this one, aim to combine therapeutic, client-focused work with a community development approach. While the staff group as a whole aims to sustain an integrated model, staff members specialise to varying degrees.

The New Fulford Family Centre serves two outer city estates in Bristol, with a population of about 22,000. The area has few resources. Barnardo's, a large family and children's services organisation, established the family centre in 1984 partly with central government start-up funding. The centre is now financed by Barnardo's with some funding from the local authority, Bristol City Council. The aim of the centre is to facilitate opportunities for growth and development for children under 5 and their parents, and where appropriate to prevent children needing to be looked after by the local authority. More detailed objectives include: challenging abuse and violence in families, promoting children's rights, promoting self-help and aiding family functioning, enhancing individual strengths, increasing community strengths and development, and relieving isolation and stress. As this suggests 'the focus of the family centres' work encompasses the individual, the family and the community' (Stones 2001:194). The centre uses an ecological approach, looking for the connections between individuals and community.

Rather than having each worker carry out all aspects of the work of the centre, workers generally choose to focus on a particular area. Activities and services divide into four areas:

- work with individuals and families, which includes confidential individual and family counselling, play therapy and family play sessions, and a welfare rights service
- resource provision, which includes laundry facilities, the nearly new room (for clothes), holidays and outings
- groups that include social drop-in groups, a group meeting to offer each other advice and support, a unity group for black and multiracial families for social activities and support, and a parenting group
- community development, which focuses on meetings where 'information is shared, strategies developed and funding opportunities are grasped and we all have headaches trying to achieve the best we can for the area in partnership with others who work or live here (New Fulford Family Centre 2002:3.3).

While staff members focus on particular work areas, they aim to maintain an awareness of what each area means for the others, sharing information that is relevant. This partly relates to connecting structural and personal issues and awareness of the need for policy change. For example, some of the workers offering counselling heard from families that many of them had been placed two or three flights up in the council housing buildings and were struggling to carry up children and shopping. The community development team surveyed the housing area and found that this was a major issue for many families. They then raised this with the local housing authority and a policy was agreed to that meant families were placed on the ground floor.

One of the positive aspects of the family centre's integrated approach is that it allows clients to move from being recipients of services to being active participants as volunteers in activities or in the management of the centre—in narrative terms, they are seen as having multiple stories. The Parents Council, which is made up of representatives of all of the groups at the centre, meets fortnightly, once a month on its own, and once a month with staff. As the committee of management, it oversees the work of the centre. Meetings are forums for raising issues of concern in the community and exploring what the centre's role might be. In recent years, for example, the Parents Council became aware of issues of bullying and racial harassment in local schools. These were raised as concerns in the

Council meeting and it was agreed to apply for workers to focus on those areas. The racial equity worker has started a group with a parent from the Parents Council for support for black and multiracial families, which includes looking at the impact of racism and discrimination. Jenny Lewis, the current Project Leader, gives examples of clients who start by coming to the centre often for confidential family work or welfare rights help, then join groups either with a focus on their children or on their own interests or issues. From there, some become interested in a broader role in the centre; they might either join the Parents Council or start training through the centre to become a child care worker or volunteer to help with one of the centre's activities. Other people start with coming to something like a group, then may decide both to have counselling and to volunteer. The range of options means that people can start where they feel comfortable.

How does this reflect integrated practice?

Christine Stones (1994), who was the director of the centre for 17 years, sees the centre as offering an integrated model with the following key points:

- *Open door policy.* Referrals are accepted from all professional organisations and self-referrals are encouraged. People will often come because they hear about the centre from a friend or neighbour.
- *Several targets.* The centre focuses not only on issues with the individual and his/her family but also on the structural and environmental components of the risks and opportunities facing families.
- *Neighbourhood base.* The centre relates to a particular neighbourhood, thus enabling it to link with both the informal and the formal networks, encouraging people to support each other rather than becoming dependent on workers. This also facilitates recognition of particular local pressures on families.
- *Combined focus.* The centre recognises the individual needs of each family member but also addresses the family as a dynamic group.
- *Participants.* The role of families using the centre is that of participants and not recipients. Families can not only be active in deciding the nature of their involvement in the centre but are also encouraged to influence the policy and practice of the centre. In some contexts it may be possible for families to move to a role of controller.

What does this mean for the organisation?

Stones (2001:50) suggests that:

the advantages of an integrated approach are several. An open door policy counteracts the powerful process of stigmatisation which so often occurs in centres restricted to referrals from professional organisations…An open door also encourages the involvement of a range of families and with their singular contributions of strengths and vulnerabilities….Selecting several targets for intervention, recognises the reality of the risks and opportunities which families face…the problems and potential that the majority of families face are neither restricted to their family functioning nor to their environment but to both….Participation emphasizes activity rather than passivity. It can also lead to a sense of partnership both between families and between families and staff.

There are also issues in an integrated approach of this kind (Stones 2001). A potential issue is role strain—that is, families can move from being in a counsellor/client relationship to being joint committee members. Workers have to be very conscious of keeping information discussed in counselling to themselves, unless clients raise issues publicly. This requires a high degree of awareness of what information is known where; it can be very easy for a worker to slip and suggest, for example, that Jane Smith will be able to help about an issue because of her own experience. Workers need flexibility to move between roles. Some workers, initially at least, find it quite hard to move from the role of counsellor to working together with a client on a joint project. Sometimes, this can be simply the strain of coming from an interview with someone who is very distressed to a lively committee meeting where everyone is joking and laughing. Role strain is potentially an issue for clients too; some may not want others to know that they have confidential sessions; a worker might inadvertently reveal this by seeming to know them. For others, recognition that they are known is important. Articulating this issue generally deals with it; staff respect people's preferences (Stones 2001). Because most people using the centre are from the community, they are usually known in several ways anyway. From a narrative perspective, this is about acknowledging that people have multiple roles or stories—postmodernism would talk about a 'thick' description.

A second issue within the integrated team is the potential for conflict and competition. How able is the team to affirm the range of work that is done and not to value some kinds of work more than others? A danger in the integrated team is for some people to see a client group or way of working as more difficult and so more deserving of time or more important so needing more funding. A dilemma often raised is the clash between families in crisis and community development meetings about long-term change. Setting priorities for applying for funding can risk polarising people, for example. It is fair to say that these questions or debates can happen whether the team is integrated or not; it may just be different groups of staff having the discussion. Critical theory is helpful here in generating an understanding of the need to work at both levels, rather than one or the other. At the Fulford Centre, these issues have been thoroughly explored and, as a team, there is a firm belief in the need for both immediate, family-centred counselling and work on longer-term issues. This helps maintain an attitude of all areas of work being important.

The third issue Stones raises is 'reality or rhetoric—does participation really happen broadly'. Notice that what the centre is aiming to do is create a structure that lives out a particular ideology—in a similar way to the feminist organisations we talked about in Chapter 2. The structure with the community members as the decision-makers embodies a philosophy of empowerment. Stones (2001:27) points out that this empowering culture relies on the willingness of professionals to give up a status of expert, through the sharing of their expertise and knowledge. 'This requires a level of confidence and maturity….The degree to which staff can work together across some of the distinct parts of a centre's program and processes influences the extent of an integrated approach'. The current project leader at the centre agrees and says that there is a continuing need to talk with staff about working in an integrated way and to acknowledge that it needs to be worked on. Regular staff development days that look at staff issues help to reinforce the vision and ethos of integration. The staff group at the centre was very stable for a long period, which also made a difference; with newer staff, time needs to be spent in revisiting the agreed principles and the theoretical basis for the centre's approach. Part of this is recognising what community members offer. Staff readily acknowledge the insider knowledge of the community members about their community; the Parents Council can and does speak confidently about the community and its views. Staff also believe that effective support and change often comes from contact with others in similar situations as well as or instead of from professionals. Community members are also very active volunteers in the centre, providing activities that otherwise would not be possible. In doing this, they also act as role models for other community members. Some child care workers at the centre started as clients, and now through training primarily at the centre, are employed there.

Overall, the family centre is an inspiring example of how integrated practice can work. There is a genuine commitment to an integrated approach here from the staff, community, and the funding body. Integration is both for clients receiving counselling and for the staff team in providing a range of casework, group work, and community development activities, which include research, evaluation, and policy development.

Example 5 St Luke's—Integration of family work to clients

Community orientation: Primarily functional within geographic communities.

Practice orientation/fields of practice: Work with families, substitute care including foster care and residential care, and work with people with psychiatric disabilities.

Domains of practice: Working with individuals and families, some community work.

Organisation orientation: Organisation initiated, integration through individual workers.

St Luke's is a large human services organisation in Bendigo, Victoria, a provincial city with a town and surrounding population of about 92,000 people. The organisation began in 1979, auspiced by the Anglican Church and supported by the Uniting Church. At this stage, the organisation 'was a collection of inherited programs' (Scott and O'Neil 1996:43), located mainly in Bendigo. Over the next eight years other programs were added so that the organisation was providing the following services for children, young people, and families:

- residential care for children and young people
- family counselling
- youth services including a youth hostel
- foster care
- financial counselling
- a preschool program.

St Luke's also provided oversight of a neighbourhood house, a psychiatric community support program, a poverty action group, and a parent self-help group.

At this stage, findings from a review process were that:

- It was easier to focus on family weaknesses than strengths, so strengths were often not used.
- A family's needs were not always met within the confines of one program.
- Outcomes appeared to be better when services were provided close to where families lived.
- When children were placed away from their family, the chances of strengthening the family were reduced (Scott and O'Neil 1996:43).

The review highlighted a funding anomaly; the aim of the residential care and particularly the foster care programs was to keep families together, but the funding rewarded the organisation for placing children away from families. As Scott and O'Neil (1996:44) say 'the inevitable question had to be asked: was St. Luke's designed the way it was because that was the best framework to promote outcomes consistent with the organisation goals, or was its organisational structure designed to meet government funding requirements?...it was obviously program-centred in design, although in many ways the practice was client-centred'.

After a trial common intake process for six months, in the early 1990s, it was decided to remove the boundaries between programs and develop a more client-focused approach. At the same time, a suboffice structure was established, so that more workers could be located in the communities families lived in. By the mid 1990s, while the range of specific programs had increased, the organisation continued to be committed to an integrated approach.

What does this reflect about integrated practice?

Scott and O'Neil (1996) suggest that the 'lack of program boundaries enhanced both the packaging of services and the creativity used in measuring and consolidating growth. It reinforced the belief that members of a family make up a complex whole which cannot be adequately understood by focusing on its members individually'.

In the new system, for example, if a parent contacted the organisation requesting foster care, the worker would explore with the family what change was wanted and how that might be done. It would often then become clear that foster care was not necessarily the best option. If the parent was frustrated by family relationships and foster care was the only way they could see to resolve them, other options like family mediation or counselling were raised and often preferred. If foster care placements were still used, the placement would be part of a plan to address issues, rather than seen as an end in itself. Sometimes too the process of exploration meant that families would start to identify other resources of their own. The common intake process combined with a solution-focused approach also created an atmosphere in which families had a breathing space to stop and think. The sense that a range of resources was open to them lessened a sense of urgency for some families, so that they could think with the worker more creatively about how they might contribute to resolving the issue.

This experience did raise the issue in the agency about how generic a worker can be, as it was raised in the 'patch' system (see example 1). Here the question is more specifically related to working with families. In more rural areas, workers often have to be generalists as there are simply limited numbers of workers around. This may have helped to create a climate in St Luke's that made the transition to an integrated model easier. However, they do acknowledge that integration can lead to a loss of specialist expertise that is needed and/or that workers enjoy providing. Some staff did leave as a result of the change to an integrated model, feeling that their skills were no longer valued.

What did this approach mean for the organisation?

Overall, the organisation was very positive about the experience. As a large voluntary agency, it would have been easy to retain a structure that separated out each area of work. The agency demonstrated its capacity to think from a client perspective and develop a structure that worked on the ground while continuing to have separate funding sources. This highlighted some of the frustrations for the organisation with funding discussed in Chapter 1—the 'silo' culture. St Luke's received much of its funding based on single input services such as family mediation or foster care. This can disadvantage organisations working to prevent family breakdown. With foster care, for example, between the late 1980s and early 1990s, St Luke's significantly reduced the number of days that children were in foster care beds, by working more intensively with families to keep children at home. Because foster care is funded on the number of 'bed days'—that is, days children are in foster care—their funding was in danger of being reduced although they were carrying out the aim of foster care by ensuring children remained with their own family.

St Luke's did try to seek policy change in relation to categorical funding, with limited success. Rather than removing barriers between funding categories, a new category was created called Homebase, which did allow some program flexibility for a limited period of working with families. The process illustrated the difficulty of government departments making policy shifts about funding allocations, which continues to be an issue.

Example 6 Potter County Human Services Organisation, USA

Community orientation: Geographic.

Practice orientation/fields of practice: Services for older people, drug and alcohol, mental health and mental retardation.

Domains of practice: Work with individuals and families.

Emilia Martinez-Brawley (1992) carried out a research project for the Center for Rural Pennsylvania to examine ways to make the delivery of rural human services more efficient and effective. The project organised panels of rural policy-makers, human services providers, and representatives of state organisations. The panel members identified barriers to effective rural human service delivery and generated policy recommendations. They considered that what they called 'categorical'—that is, programmatic—service delivery fostered administrative duplication, treated problems separately even when they were interrelated, forced clients to shop for services from several organisations, and promoted competition among client groups for scarce resources.

The report gives an example of an organisation, Potter County Human Services Organisation, which had decided to integrate all its human services at the administrative level, while still providing services separately. Before 1987, Potter County provided ageing, drug and alcohol, and mental health and mental retardation services in cooperation with surrounding counties. The Country Commissioners decided to integrate the human services system because they had noticed that many people felt they were not receiving needed services. The organisation now has a single administrator and financial, clerical, personnel, and management operations are integrated. All services are based in the same building, with a single reception system. The intake system is the starting point for all referrals and people are then referred to a particular categorical program. Case managers from the programs meet weekly to discuss cases, establish priorities, and assign primary caseworkers to clients. The housing of the categorical programs in a single facility promotes communication and cooperation across program lines.

What does this say about an integrated approach?

The report concludes that there are many strengths of an integrated model. From a client perspective, an integrated approach shifts the burden of diagnosing service needs from clients to human service organisations. There is a clear 'understanding that people's problems are interrelated and solutions will occur only if all the problems receive attention' (Martinez-Brawley 1992:10). The primary caseworker 'coordinates the client's treatment program as a single package administered through the human services department' (Martinez-Brawley 1992:11). Typically, 'the primary caseworker is a social worker with expertise central to the client's problems. The primary caseworker coordinates a treatment plan that enlists the help of other social workers who have expertise related to the clients' other human service needs' (Martinez-Brawley 1992:11). The system encourages more staff communication and cooperation, promotes comprehensive human services planning, and reduces administrative costs. Finally, the report recognises the barriers to integrated services—that is, categorical funding streams with accompanying categorical accounting requirements, which prevent moving funds according to need. Often funding is allocated on a demographic basis that does not necessarily meet the needs of a particular county. The separate accounting requirements require more work in administration. There is also duplication of oversight of programs, with several state and federal government departments being responsible for categorical programs. Martinez-Brawley suggests that confidentiality requirements for categorical programs can also provide more problems for clients who may have to go through each organisation's intake process.

What are the implications for organisations?

I have included Potter County because it illustrates what an integrated approach could mean primarily from an administrative or organisational perspective. Even without taking client interests into account, integrating services clearly cost less and encouraged communication across the organisation. The Potter County experience also documents some of the barriers to being more efficient that come from not having an integrated model—the duplication of accountability systems, lack of flexibility to respond to particular needs, and the costs of separate accounting.

Summary

This chapter began by articulating three dimensions for thinking about integrated practice:

- First, the community dimension—may be geographical and/or a community of interest such as older people or people with a mental illness. All organisations have a community they relate to in some way, some more closely than others. A functional community may also have a geographical dimension and vice versa—for example, an organisation may focus on work with older people in a particular region.
- Second, the practice dimension—includes both the fields of practice a worker might cover in the sense of services for clients such as family counselling or alcohol and drug services, and the practice domains—the kinds of work done, such as group work or policy development.
- Third, the agency dimension—whether the integrated practice is at the individual or team level, whether it is formal or informal combined with whether it has been initiated by the worker or agency.
- These dimensions can be used to create a wide range of possible forms of integrated practice. Workers and organisations need to consider how these dimensions can operate in their particular organisation and context.
- The rest of the chapter offers a variety of examples of integrated practice to illustrate just how varied this model can be. Each example ends by considering: What does this illustrate about integrated practice' What does this say about the organisation?

Reflective practice

Think about a job you have had or an organisation you have worked in. How could you apply the dimensions of integrated practice? What would be the community orientation? What fields of practice and practice domains were involved? What was the organisation's orientation to work practice—how much could workers define their work practice?

Given your responses, how could you have approached your work in an integrated way?

8

Skills and Knowledge for Integrated Practice

The confident, effective practitioner is the one who is able to respond flexibly and creatively to a range of influences, needs and wants of clients or colleagues, and unforeseen events and forces. A practitioner who thinks they know the right answers all the time is bound to be wrong. To people willing to 'not know' all the time, all sorts of things are possible. (Bolton 2001:33)

Discussion about skills and knowledge often focuses on the ability to complete tasks. For example, we talk about skills in engaging with clients or being able to write policy documents. Knowledge is often taught and written about in discrete areas such as group work or community work. This chapter explores a different way to think about skills and knowledge, which is particularly useful for thinking about how to be an 'active agent' in a human service organisation as well as for integrated practice. The emphasis is on skills in terms of general capacities rather than being task-focused. This is partly because of the nature of human service work and particularly integrated practice: workers need to develop skills that can apply to a variety of situations. This relates to the development of both skills and knowledge; we need to make connections across areas of knowledge rather than seeing them in isolation. Knowing how to work with groups of people, for example, has similar themes whether you are working with families, staff teams, volunteers, or a community action group. Finally, looking at skills and knowledge in this way reflects the need for workers to be able to be responsive and continually open to learning, reflecting, and acting in a frequently changing world.

Skills for integrated practice

Flexibility and fluidity

Any worker needs the capacity to be flexible in their approach; to be able to work with the given client, community, or issue or in their organisation, to work out the most fitting response to a situation. Without flexibility, the danger is that you assume that a certain response is the 'right' one, which may not fit with the particular client's issues or needs. Some organisations struggle with this, trying to make established rules fit all situations, rather than creating more flexible guidelines.

Fluidity is a related dimension of flexibility, suggesting the need to be able to make transitions readily from one kind of work to another. Suppose, for example, an individual client comes to see you, initially it appears to be for emotional support about loss and grief because her mother has moved into a nursing home. As you explore her feelings, it becomes clear that she is actually very angry about the situation for both her mother and other older people in the community who, she considers, are not being sufficiently supported by community-based services. Now, your perception of your role as the worker needs to change; in postmodern terms you start to have a 'thicker picture'. Rather than seeing her simply as a grieving daughter, she has become an angry advocate for broader change. What is it then that this client wants from you? How does this relate to your knowledge of these services from other people? What do you know about how to work on the existing and possible structures? As a worker, you need to be both flexible in responding appropriately and fluid in working across domains.

Flexibility might also relate to workers seeing people in a variety of roles. A worker might, for example, be seeing someone for individual work, while at the same time participating in a community-based management committee with them. This requires another kind of adaptability or flexibility that is more likely to be needed in integrated practice. In Chapter 7, Stones (2001) identifies this as potentially a kind of 'role strain' in integrated practice that workers need to be aware of. In the family centre she describes, workers deal with this by raising it as a potential issue with clients and are then able to work out how to manage it. A postmodern understanding is helpful here: an awareness that all of us occupy a variety of roles all the time; or in narrative language, we as workers also live out multiple stories. This enables us to see that in a sense who we are essentially is common, but different aspects are highlighted at particular times.

Self-awareness and the capacity to reflect critically

Self-awareness and the ability to reflect are essential parts of good practice, but not only practice that involves contact with other people. All of us need to be conscious of our reactions to others, their reactions to us, and the impact of these reactions on our ability to work together; a psychoanalytic approach is helpful here. Such awareness is often recognised in work with individuals and clients, but is equally important in community work, social policy development, or within the organisation. A worker may, for example, react in a policy development meeting to a particular manager; on reflection they may realise that the reaction was only partly to do with disagreement about policy issues, but was also partly because the way the person communicated reminded them of a recently divorced partner.

A great deal has been written recently about the value of reflective practice, which is essentially, Taylor (2000:138) suggests, 'the systematic and thoughtful means by which practitioners can make sense of their practice as they go about their daily work'. Critical reflection (as discussed in Chapter 1) takes this a step further, linking awareness of self to awareness of the social structures we live in. Critical reflection processes enable us to articulate assumptions and beliefs from our own personal and social experience so that we can contemplate how to change our practice (see Chapter 9). This skill closely relates to the next one, use of self.

Use of self

Ivey and Ivey (1999) talk about this as 'natural style'; Ife (2002:233) talks of the importance of a worker being aware of their own personality and able 'to use it to maximum effect'. Basically, workers need to be able to acknowledge how they prefer to operate as a person and to use their own style creatively and honestly. People are very quick to pick up when workers are not being genuine and this can undermine the working relationship very quickly. There is no right personality for any kind of practice or human service organisation; it is rather a matter of being able to use your personality consciously and well. It is important not to pretend to be, for example, an exuberant, joking personality if you are actually relatively quiet. This is not to say that as workers you should never aim to develop your ability to operate more broadly. There are challenges for all of us: for the exuberant person in becoming quiet to listen, for the introverted person in becoming able to enthuse others.

Being yourself in this sense can include what in work with individuals is often called 'appropriate self disclosure'. Essentially this is about using information about yourself for the benefit of the working relationship. In work with individuals, it might be about revealing that you have had a similar experience—for example, in being a migrant, or in wrestling with your own adolescence. Similarly, within the organisation, in community work or research or evaluation, talking about some aspect of shared experience may enable you to develop relationships with the community more quickly. At one stage, I was evaluating a project run by an urban-based agency in a rural community; when people realised that I too lived and worked in a rural area, they were much more prepared to trust me and to talk more openly about the project (Gardner and Lehmann 2002). Notice the assumptions here (which may not be accurate); reflexivity helps us be conscious of when we are perceiving others and being perceived by them in particular ways.

Implied in 'using the self' is awareness of self. Particularly important in working with other people is a sense of how each is socially themselves—how each of us has been partly influenced by our social environment. For example, we may talk about how other people are different from us given their gender, culture, age, abilities etc., implying

Case scenario

Jo was working for a state government department and was responsible for managing funding of a range of residential services for culturally diverse communities. She was asked to mediate between a hostel for older people and the local Ethnic Communities Council. She discovered staff thought the Ethnic Communities Council was being unreasonable in wanting ethnically appropriate meals for residents as this would mean preparing four or five different meals each day. Jo was unnerved to realise that she too had assumed that by the time they were older, people from non-English speaking backgrounds would have adapted to 'normal' food. Because she talked about her own feelings of not having thought about this as an issue, staff felt their perspective was understood. Fortunately one staff member was more open and with Jo's support enabled staff to see that people should be eating food they enjoyed. She also pointed out that some older people were reverting to the language and culture of their original country and their diet needed to reflect this. The staff then began to think more creatively and realised that some meals could be the same for most people—for example, most people would be happy to eat curry and rice once a week. The Ethnic Communities Council agreed that there could be some flexibility and the issue was resolved.

that our way is right, rather than thinking about how we are different from each other. Awareness of critical theory can help us make assumptions explicit so that we can identify more clearly how we are similar to and different from other people. We can then use those differences more creatively.

Ability to be strategic

This skill is about being able to recognise and use power and opportunities for change effectively, either inside or outside the organisation. Workers generally have a variety of forms of power, depending on who they are and their position. A worker, for example, might have the power of their qualifications and/or experience, the power of their personality or passion, and/or the power of their position in the agency and community (see the discussion of power in Chapter 5). To be able to be an active agent for change means recognising the power you do have.

Part of the skill of being strategic is also about being able to see where there are opportunities for change (see Chapter 5) and how to use them, and how these fit with the power you have as a worker. You need to be able to assess what kind of strategies will be effective in a particular context—when, for example, you need to do more work on generating support and to work out who is likely to be helpful, what arguments are likely to be convincing to which groups, and that when the climate is right people are more likely to be supportive. Sometimes the energy for a particular change is simply not present; you need to decide whether to keep putting effort into it or 'cut your losses' for the time being.

Case scenario

Dave had been trying for over a year to change how the agency organised its rosters so that it would reflect a more family friendly policy. Senior managers thought it would complicate things unnecessarily. In January, a new senior manager was appointed who had three young children and wanted more flexibility in working hours. At the same time, two of the staff on the same level as Dave were under pressure from their partners to be more available for child care. Dave decided it was timely to raise the issue more broadly within the agency; he put it on the agenda for the staff meeting and the agency-wide meeting, and wrote a one-page proposal on how it could work and what the criteria would be. This time, there was a lot more support and it was agreed to change how the rosters were done.

Listen and communicate

These skills are relatively obvious central skills for all work with human service organisations. To be active in the organisation, workers need the ability to communicate effectively—that is, to encourage exploration of issues, acknowledgment of strengths and resources, to use questions well, to listen and reflect accurately and sensitively, and to be challenging and confronting as needed. The ability to listen and communicate well is central to all areas of work. Often it is easier to see the value of these skills in formal sessions with clients, meetings with community groups, or task-focused committees. We tend to think of work as focused, formal occasions, but in some types of work much of the work is relatively informal. Short conversations, incidental chats, tea-room discussions can be equally important. In a sense, as a worker, it may be more taxing to remember to maintain effective communication at these informal times whether they are with clients or with other workers in a human service organisation.

We can tend to assume that workers in human service organisations will be good communicators, but this is not necessarily the case. Some will have better skills than others; workers are not all equally good at listening or explaining what they think, nor does being a supervisor or manager guarantee good communication skills. Some workers will assume they do not need to be careful about communication with colleagues although they would be with clients; they may assume that colleagues will be more resilient or that they can relax and do not need to think about what they say. Managers and supervisors tend to have their own sensitive areas too—examples of projection demonstrate this and psychoanalytic theory helps awareness. Differences in communication can relate to personality: an introvert who has spent a lot of time with clients may relax back at the office and be reluctant to talk to anyone.

Case scenario

Carla had a reputation as a manager of not communicating well with staff. She realised after talking to a fellow manager that she had assumed that staff would always expect her to solve issues when they came to her office with a problem. Because she found it hard to think and respond on the spot, she tended to be aggressive before they could—as she thought—criticise her for being indecisive. Once Fred explained that he always thanked staff and said he would get back to them when he had time to think about the issue, she relaxed and listened more openly.

The culture of an organisation affects how communication is viewed: is it important that everyone be involved in conversation? Is good communication valued? Do people prefer to work on issues face-to-face or through documents and email? Some organisations are perceived in a particular way because of how they communicate: the reception desk can be an important starting point for this. Is the initial contact friendly and open? Does the organisation seem reluctant to communicate? Do people rarely return phone calls or react in a hostile way for no apparent reason?

Ability to see and generate connections

Given the nature of integrated practice, it is clearly important for workers and/or their human service organisations to be able to see the connections across the potential areas of work and to be able to generate connections. What this means in practice will vary with the nature of the work being done and the attitudes of the organisation. Some organisations would see this as an explicit part of their work—developing partnerships, networking, building cooperative working relationships. Others tend to be more inwardly focused; sometimes because they are so large that keeping up with internal shifts in their own organisation is enough.

Case scenario

Shared Action is a community development project initially funded to increase the safety and well-being of children. The particular neighbourhood was stigmatised by the broader community to the extent that neighbourhood residents were often reluctant to say where they lived. Over time, people began to see that their own attitudes to their neighbourhood had an impact on what they felt they could do as individuals. They could also see that policy decisions about housing estates impacted on their community and in turn, on their individual sense of themselves. Making these connections led to a desire to work on the physical appearance and resources in the community, to make their area a visually attractive place to live.

Part of this skill is enabling other people to make connections too; in individual work, for example, to have clients make links between their individual and broader structural issues. A young man with a baby feeling unwelcome in a play group might come to see that his lack of confidence in the group is related not only to being the only male there with his first child, but also to the general social attitudes in his community that only women should be at home caring for children, which he has also internalised. Similarly, in a community work setting, people might make connections both about their individual situation and about broader policy issues.

Making connections is also about putting people in touch with each other, and generating partnerships and cooperative ways of working. Again these connections can happen in all sorts of ways depending on the starting point for work. A worker researching the experiences of families living with a Vietnam veteran might use a snowball technique, asking families if they know of other families with a similar issue. A worker in social policy on housing might contact a tenants group to ask about its experience. A worker in a community interested in generating activities for children might work with the community to invite other interested groups, perhaps businesses and individuals, to a meeting and form a cooperative working group with representatives from each group. A systems approach can help with articulating all the parts of a particular system, thus identifying where links need to be made.

An important aspect of such connections is ensuring that a range of voices is heard, particularly the voices of those who will be affected by decisions made. Wadsworth (1998) explores the value of joint groups of workers and clients in evaluating services. She gives an example of bringing together a group of Alzheimer's nursing staff and families with a family member needing to go into nursing home care. Joint meetings enabled each to see how similar their emotions were about the people with Alzheimer's and to move on to sharing concerns and ideas for change. Not all groups are as successful and Wadsworth (1998) suggests some ways of working on this. For example, for people who are marginalised it is generally not realistic to expect them to confidently speak up with people they see as more powerful and articulate; it helps to meet separately first and explore issues then structure discussion so that both groups are able to put their views.

Sense of timing

The awareness of time and timing, and the capacity to wait are all skills in practice and work in organisations that are rarely articulated. In all areas of practice, workers need to be aware of when it is timely to, for example, talk rather than listen, make a suggestion rather than encouraging exploration, to invigorate rather than be receptive. Issues around time are often implicit in the teaching of counselling skills; when do you move on from hearing the person's story to exploring issues, at what point do you becoming more challenging or confronting, how is the decision made about finishing contact (Ivey and Ivey 1999)? There is much debate about how long you should work with a person on individual or family issues. Similar issues about time and timing obviously come up in research interviews, but also in social policy or community work—is this the right time for a change or development, are people ready, have people had enough time to consider the issues before moving to a decision? All these can also be applied to working in human service organisations—is this the right time for raising an issue, is this a useful forum to advocate for a point of view, are key people present or would it be better to wait until they are?

The capacity to wait is often important for a worker. What seems a clear and obvious decision to the worker may be the opposite for an individual or a community. Apart from the fact that the worker may be wrong, the individual or community may simply need more time to come to an understanding of what is important to them. In the current climate of limited numbers of sessions and short-term project work, it can be hard to allow or create a sense of timeliness. Workers need to remember and communicate to managers that if people feel overly rushed decisions or resolutions are less likely to last. Similarly, in research and evaluation interviews, creating a sense of time is important, especially if you are dealing with sensitive issues (Renzetti and

Case scenario

An Indigenous organisation had been receiving funding for a family support program. The funding body wanted to make changes to the program and was also concerned about receiving statistical data that was accurate and on time. Pat, the project manager from the funding body, met with the committee from the organisation several times and felt no progress was being made. She decided to issue an ultimatum—no proposal with built-in timelines by the end of May, no continued funding. She was alarmed to have a phone call the next day from a senior manager warning her that the community was thinking about going to the media. They felt their views had not been heard, the project had been rushed with insufficient time for community consultation, and that Pat was unrealistic in her expectations about the resources needed to collect data. Pat acknowledged that her ultimatum came more from frustration about progress than real deadlines and asked for help in terms of understanding the community's issues.

Lee 1993). Once-only interviews create a time pressure for covering issues; it can be more realistic to think about interviewing people several times or at least offering the possibility. When evaluating projects, interviewing people over a period of time allows the changes in both the project and their views about it to be documented. Similarly, in organisations, workers may need to be assertive about delaying decision-making until everyone can think about options, or pushing for change that might otherwise be missed.

Creativity and imagination

Integrated practice means workers need to be able to make connections, often in ways that people have not considered. At other times, new ideas and possibilities, new perspectives on existing issues are needed. A narrative approach talks about 'other stories', of different ways of looking at a person's history that helps them see new possibilities for their future. Working with individuals and families is good practice in creativity; people will often come to their own ingenious conclusions about what will work for them. At other times, workers are stretched to work creatively with families where they feel that existing strategies are not effective. Adams (2002:92) points out that 'some situations are so complex and convoluted that simple solutions to people's problems are out of the question….Critical practitioners have to develop…creative approaches to uncertainties rather than simply following prescriptions'. Creativity is equally needed in other areas: to develop a policy or program that captures a vision and gives it a practical expression, to find ways to release a community's imagination about its future, or to carry out research and evaluation in ways that encourage participation. In organisations, creativity may be needed for issues from how to make staff meetings more lively to stimulating thinking about new approaches to service provision.

The developing interest in art and music therapy is another aspect of the importance of creativity. Sometimes clients and workers can express feelings and the possibility of new developments more easily through art or music than by using words. This can be useful in community development as well as work with individuals and families. In a creative arts project in Philadelphia, for example, the work began in a disadvantaged suburb with painting a mural on the side of a house next to an empty block of land. As residents watched the mural develop, they became interested and asked to join in. Now the project has grown to an organisation running art and drama classes; the neighbourhood has been transformed and is known for its murals and art projects. Residents are actively involved in presenting an annual concert and in ongoing neighbourhood activities.

Large organisations vary in how much they encourage creativity. As we discussed in Chapter 2, sometimes the size of large organisations means they operate bureaucratically, seeking uniformity rather than innovation. However, there are some that look for workers to develop alternatives and make suggestions; in others, creativity is encouraged within teams. Sometimes creativity is valued in working with clients/communities, but not in seeking organisational change. The capacity to be creative then needs to be aligned with being strategic.

Case scenario

A university research group wanted to involve local residents in a project that would increase awareness of native species of fauna living in their area and what would protect and endanger them. A new underpass had recently been built that was likely to affect the native species. In previous work, the group had found it difficult to get the local community involved; information flyers and newsletters had little impact. This time they decided to work with a primary school class, taking the children to the site to identify species and then develop an exhibition that the community would be invited to. The children created many works with the help of a local artist and the exhibition was very well attended. Evaluation sheets showed that people's knowledge of both species and how to care for them had been significantly extended (Brockley et al. 2004).

Ability to find out what you need to know

Inevitably, workers in integrated practice will not know everything they need to know. You could argue that this would be the same for any worker in a more specialised area too. People do not come in neatly divided boxes, so that any kind of work is likely to raise issues across a wide spectrum. Working in communities is similar in that it requires workers to know a bit or a lot about many things. This sense of needing to know a lot across areas may be part of what workers find daunting about integrated practice. It is not possible to know in depth about every possible area of practice. The key is to know how to get the information that you or the community needs. Alternatively, it may be about how to find someone who has that knowledge and who is interested in being involved. This involvement might be about providing a one-off session for an individual or community sharing particular knowledge or it might become an ongoing involvement.

Organisations can support this ability by structuring ways for knowledge and skills to be shared. A worker with experience in a particular area could act as a consultant for less experienced staff until they gain confidence. Mentoring is a useful way for workers to learn new skills and can work in various ways: a new worker might observe a mentor, do some joint work, and then move to working independently with occasional sessions for discussion.

Case scenario

Shared Action was a community development project funded initially by a philanthropic trust for three years. When I asked Shared Action community members how they felt about the project finishing, they were confident about being able to manage themselves because they now knew how and where to find people who would be able to give them the knowledge, skills, and/or other resources they might need.

Ability to work with uncertainty

Uncertainty is inherent in human service organisations; people are infinitely diverse and liable to act in unpredictable ways. In Chapter 2, we considered the current context that has a high degree of complexity and uncertainty with a resulting impact on workers and organisations. The current environment also generates an expectation that we continue to learn and develop. This in itself can create a sense of loss of control and uncertainty; as Barnett (1999:35) suggests 'to admit to being a learner is to admit to being uncertain...one is in danger of losing one's authority—or one feels that that is the case'.

What is important is how uncertainty is dealt with, either by an individual or as an organisation: whether it is seen as a problem to be controlled or what makes the work dynamic and appealing. You could argue that if everyone is a learner, that we can all be learning from each other. As a worker, you need to work out your own reactions to uncertainty and how to deal with them—another part of self-awareness.

People react differently—another aspect of personality at least in part. Some people thrive on uncertainty, others find it stressful and try to create more regularity. Organisations also seem to do this and it becomes embedded in the culture. It is important to remember that this is true for clients as well as workers. You might, as a worker, be comfortable with uncertainty and be unwittingly placing clients under more pressure by leaving decisions open. Vaill (1996) uses the metaphor of white-water rafting for working in organisations, suggesting that to survive the uncertainty—or more positively to relish the experience—workers need to see learning at work as a way of being. Sharing the feelings raised by uncertainty can help—giving a sense of mutual support or seeing that there are different perspectives, as the following case scenario demonstrates.

Case scenario

Kate and Jerry were working on a community development project together. They became increasingly frustrated with each other's style of work: Kate wanted to leave things open and see what developed; Jerry wanted to clarify goals and start working on specific activities. Community members seemed to be drawn to one or the other and this was starting to create division in the community. They talked to their supervisor about it who helped them to name the differences between them: one was their capacity to live with uncertainty. Kate liked things to be uncertain, she felt too restricted if there were too many specific plans. Jerry did not like uncertainty, he felt that the project was getting out of control, there was no sense of purpose and direction. Both could see the advantages and disadvantages of their perspective, and they worked out ways to balance each other.

Sense of humour

Finally—though perhaps most importantly—workers need a sense of humour. Some people might not see this as a skill, but a sense of humour can be developed. Humour often eases work in human service organisations; it can provide a way of standing back from what is happening and seeing it differently. If something can be deemed funny instead of only exasperating, it allows you to move forward in a different way.

Humour can be used positively or negatively; what I mean here is the positive use of humour—seeing the funny side of a situation and encouraging people to laugh at it. I do not mean humour that belittles other people or sarcasm that can be disparaging. Positive humour can become part of the culture of organisations as well as being important in work with individuals and communities.

Knowledge for integrated practice

A similar process could be used to identify common areas of knowledge. Chapter 3, for example, explored how to apply theories that are used more often in work with individuals and families to working in organisations. Psychoanalytic theory in particular is an approach seen to be for individual work, but Chapter 3 demonstrates how useful it can be in thinking about how organisations relate to each other. Often an area of knowledge is seen as specific to one domain of work, when in practice it is needed across domains. Some examples where it can be useful to see the connections of areas of knowledge could be:

- Understanding the individual—that is, having an awareness of how people grow and develop in terms of their psychological, social, spiritual, and physical well-being. Psychoanalytic theory (see Chapter 3) is useful here as well as theories of human development.
- Understanding processes of change. These were discussed in Chapter 5 and can relate to work both inside organisations and negotiations outside organisations with other agencies or communities.
- The range of family systems experienced by individuals and the impact on them. The systems approach discussed in Chapter 3 is useful for thinking about this and about how organisations operate.
- The complex nature of power. This was discussed in Chapter 5 and again is useful for thinking about the dynamics between individuals, within groups, in organisations, and in organisations' negotiations with communities. An understanding of postmodern theory can also be helpful here (see Chapter 3), illustrating how differently power can be perceived and used.
- Understanding of communities and how they operate. This can be useful both for thinking about individuals and families and their relationships with their communities, as well as how organisations negotiate and relate to the communities they operate within. This would relate to critical theory (see Chapter 3) in terms of how dominant social attitudes impact on communities and are internalised by individuals and families.
- How to use research findings. Research and evaluation (see Chapters 1 and 9) relate to all aspects of work in organisations: the effective-

ness of the organisation's work, considering the organisation's processes, and identifying what else might need to be thought about.

- How policies are developed and how they impact on people and communities. Workers in organisations need to understand how their organisation's and other policies impact on them and those they work with, as well as how policy can be developed and changed.

Here are some examples of what this might mean in practice:

- A community worker is focusing on working with young people in a particular community. He becomes conscious that he needs to understand what happens for young people during adolescence and what that might mean for these young people in their community.
- A community health worker is working with a refugee family from Iran who have come to live in a very monocultural, traditional Australian community. After some hostile reactions to the family, she realises that she needs to understand how the community may react to a family who is different, what the power implications are, and how to work with both the family and the community about this.
- A researcher wants to explore why few children from Italian backgrounds are in foster care. She realises she needs to start by finding out about Italian culture and exploring the expectations of family and community and that there may be policy implications for what she discovers.
- A district health nurse is working with a young gay man with HIV/AIDS who has been living on his now limited savings. While she understands what to do in terms of his physical health care, she is uncertain what he is entitled to in terms of income support and continued access to medical services of his choice. She is also unsure about his emotional needs and her own reactions to him being gay. She decides she needs to find out more about current policy and talk about her own attitudes with her supervisor.
- A worker with families with children with attention deficit disorder has been challenged by several parents about whether new evidence shows behaviour modification could work as effectively as medication for their children. He has been feeling himself that there has been an assumption that one approach—that is, medication—will fit all the children. He decides he needs to check the latest research findings about treatment in general and assess the results.
- A community worker for a children and family services agency decides to approach the local Aboriginal cooperative to see if there would be interest in a joint after school and holiday program for

primary school children. The initial reaction is positive but later appointments and meetings are not attended. The worker starts to wonder whether she has made assumptions from the dominant culture about how to work and decides to check what is appropriate culturally before trying to go further.

Knowledge of strategies

Using an integrated approach would mean being able to use a wide range of strategies depending on the current issues. Again some of these strategies have common knowledge and skills but may be applied to different domains; others require particular knowledge. Strategies generally come from a particular theoretical approach and it is important to be aware of this, so that the strategy used is compatible with the context you are working in. However, it is also true that theories overlap; they too have connections and so some strategies are used across theories. As Payne (1997:71) says 'The relationships and oppositions between theories provide a context in which their value can be assessed against one another, and against the modern social context in which they must be used'.

Some examples of strategies that can be used across domains are as follows:

- *Negotiation and mediation.* Essentially negotiation and mediation are about a reasonably structured approach to working with people in conflict (Beer and Stief 1997). The worker uses the structure to ensure that all parties involved are able to put their point of view, and together generate possible options to resolve the conflict and come to an agreement. This approach can, for example, be used in direct work with clients in such areas as general family work, family court work, working with young people and their families. Such strategies are easily transferable to working with any groups in conflict, including between organisations or community groups or within organisations.

- *Use of narratives or telling stories.* A narrative approach affirms the value of people's stories. For example, in a community badly affected by a bushfire, local people will often bring up the impact of the fire years after it has happened. That story is a defining one for the community in terms of both its capacity to survive and the pain of the experience. There will also be alternative stories that can be explored to generate a sense of hope and possibility of change. For example, an individual might have a dominant story that is around being a victim, yet they may have an alternative story showing that they are also a survivor. An indigenous community might have a dominant story of oppression and trauma, but have an alternative story of survival and pride in their own culture. This approach strategy can be used with individuals, families, groups, and communities as well as in organisations (see Chapter 3 for more detail).

- *General problem solving approach.* This is probably the most obvious common strategy, and is a shared approach across many practice theories. Compton and Galaway (1999:82) talk about this as a 'life process' with essentially the same components of engagement, assessment, intervention, and evaluation. While writers describe parts of this differently and emphasise some parts more than others, overall this is a very common pattern of work whether it is with individuals or communities.
- *Using a group.* The experience of running a group is similar whether groups are self-help groups, task groups, networking groups, staff meetings, policy development groups, or management groups, to name only a few. There are common processes and issues: how will the group make decisions, who will facilitate, how will the group decide when its life is at an end, how will the group deal with members who dominate or do not participate?
- *Advocacy.* With this strategy, the worker speaks on behalf of a client, whether the client is an individual, a community, or an organisation. Often this will be with organisations or agencies where the client is concerned that their voice will not be heard. This is a strategy that needs to be used carefully so that the worker is not disempowering. Ife suggests that advocacy 'must be accompanied by some form of power analysis, and must always be seen as a short-term measure' (Ife 2002:248). The aim ultimately is for the individual or community to feel confident enough to argue for themselves. Workers may suggest such strategies as coaching, role plays, accompanying people to meetings, or practising in less threatening situations.

There are of course also specific strategies used more in particular domains, although they may still be used in others. Popple (1995) suggests that in community work, for example, there are a range of strategies:

- community organisation—that is, 'improving the coordination between different welfare agencies' (Popple 1995:59)—this could be broadened to include other agencies and businesses etc.

- community care—that is, encouraging social networks and voluntary services
- community development—that is, assisting groups to acquire the skills and confidence to improve the quality of the lives of its members (Popple 1995:60)
- social/community planning—that is, 'analysis of social condition, setting of goals and priorities, implementing and evaluating services and programs' (Popple 1995:56)
- community action—that is, 'Usually class based, conflict focuses direct action at local level' (Popple 1995:57).

While these are often thought about as part of a community work role, it is still important to see how they can be shared. A worker focusing on social policy might well use social/community planning as a strategy; a worker mainly working with individuals could easily take on a community care role.

Summary

This chapter aimed to articulate common skills and knowledge for workers in human service organisations interested in integrated practice:

- The skills are not specific to particular practices or fields of work, instead they are common across all work areas. They are: flexibility and fluidity, self-awareness and the capacity for critical reflection, the ability to be strategic, listening and communication skills, use of self, the ability to see and generate connections, sense of timing, creativity and imaginative ability, to find out what you need to know, to work with uncertainty, and a sense of humour.
- We have also looked at how to make connections for areas of knowledge across fields of practice. This demonstrates how it can be more useful to think about what is common, and can be applied to different fields, rather than concentrating only what is different. This leads to identifying some common strategies that develop from knowledge such as negotiation and mediation, the telling of stories, and group work skills.

Reflective practice

Think about your own work and your workplace or a workplace that you know about.

- How do you relate to the skills named above?
- What fits with your work and workplace?
- What would you add or delete?
- What fits with your approach to work—or what could you see yourself using?

- Why? What appeals to you about those particular skills?
  What about areas of knowledge?
- What is currently seen as common across parts of your work or your organisation?
- What is seen as specific to particular areas?
- What could you now identify as common and/or specific ways of working?

9

Tools and Strategies for Integrated Practice

We have to live effectively in a world which is radically uncertain. In such conditions...we will survive and prosper only by engaging in a critical way with the world....All of our frameworks of action, interpretation and self-understanding—whether on an individual or an organisational level—have to be available for perpetual scrutiny. (Barnett 1999:42)

At this stage of the book, as a worker, you will have developed:

- an understanding of current tensions and possibilities in working in human service organisations (Chapter 1)
- frameworks for thinking about organisational structures and how they impact on workers (Chapter 2)
- the ability to use general and practice theories to reflect on organisations and their processes (Chapter 3)
- an understanding of organisational culture and learning, and the influence of personality in organisations (Chapter 4)
- the ability to comprehend (and hopefully use!) ideas about change and power (Chapter 5)
- an awareness of values and principles for working in human service organisations and what these might be in integrated practice (Chapter 6)
- an understanding of a model of integrated practice and how such a model might be used in a variety of organisational contexts and structures (Chapter 7) and
- a consciousness of common and connecting skills and knowledge that are important in being an active worker in human service organisations, particularly in an integrated practice model (Chapter 8).

This chapter aims to provide practical and concrete tools and strategies to enable you to work actively and effectively within human service organisations in general and particularly in developing and maintaining an integrated perspective. Past experience of integrated practice suggests that it is difficult to maintain without concrete frameworks and tools. Workers need resources to facilitate stopping and thinking about what they are doing and why, as well as how to work in a more integrated way. The resources suggested here come from a range of fields. The use of a critical reflection framework has been used to reflect on practice in education, nursing, and a range of health and welfare fields. The background theory to this approach is in Chapter 1. The importance of seeking mutual support in various ways, which I have called networking, comes mainly from the welfare field, though also, to some degree, education, but is easily adaptable elsewhere. Compatible evaluation and research approaches can also help develop and maintain an integrated approach. What are often called participatory approaches to research are consistent with the principles and practices of integrated practice.

I have divided these tools into three areas, although they do overlap to some degree:

- Use of a critical reflection approach. This section looks at specific tools used to help develop and maintain a critically reflective approach. They are tools that could be used as part of supervision or independently. I have included here the use of a critical incident, using reflective writing and a framework for using critical reflection for integrated practice.
- Networking for effective and integrated practice. This section looks at how to build support for yourself working in a human service organisation, using, for example, peer supervision, critical friendships, or mutual support groups.
- Using research and evaluation for effective and integrated practice.

The chapter finishes with a brief section on suggested strategies for being active in human service organisations.

Use of a critical reflection approach

A number of ways of using the theory of critical reflection have developed, which can be used as part of supervision, individually or in groups, or independently. In Chapter 4, I explored the culture of supervision and how this varies depending on the organisation. In some organisations, using critical reflection would fit well into supervision, allowing exploration of a situation or a general approach to work in the agency. Critical reflection would enable workers to consider these in more depth, asking deeper questions about underlying assumptions and values, the theory used, and the meaning of a particular situation; and from there to change to, hopefully, a more active and powerful stance in the organisation. In some organisations, supervision does not allow for such an approach, as time in supervision is taken up with task-related issues. Sometimes workers can negotiate with supervisors for time for critical reflection in supervision; others may need to find a peer to work with or use the frameworks below on their own. While this may not be ideal—it is easier for assumptions to remain hidden when you are on your own—it can still be a helpful process.

Many critical reflection tools involve taking a particular experience and exploring what it means. Often this is called a critical incident, or it may be called a story, a significant learning experience, or simply an experience.

Use of critical incident

Critical incidents are often used in small groups (workshops or classes or team meetings of some kind), and they can also be used in supervision groups. The groups are usually small to allow the group to develop a sense of trust and so that each participant has time to share an incident. Having a group provides a range of people to provide mutual support and input but, of course, you can use this approach in supervision, with a colleague, or on your own, by using the questions suggested.

In the group process, participants are asked to choose a particular incident that has been significant to them in some way, often called a 'critical incident'. The incident need not be traumatic or critical in itself; it might be something a worker has continued to feel uncomfortable about over time. It is critical to the worker, rather than being a critical incident in the sense of an event requiring debriefing. In the process, each participant can be thought of as a 'critical researcher' using both reason and intuition to analyse thoughts and feelings to explore their own experience (Adams 2002). Inevitably this involves expressing emotions, often deeply felt (McDrury and Alterio 2002). The aim is to move towards change in some way: a change of understanding, perception, and/or being able to act differently.

Often a set of possible questions is provided as a starting point for discussion. The overall framework for questions is often similar, as you will see in these examples. Both sets of questions below encourage the person with the incident to start by looking at the incident more closely, particularly at their own reaction to the incident and how this might have been influenced by their own experience as well as the context. Both also encourage thinking about underlying beliefs and assumptions at a personal, but also at a social or cultural level. The sequence is important—the exploration of the incident comes first, followed by questions about what could change, the emphasis shifts to what could be done or perceived differently, and how this might happen.

Fook et al. (2000), for example, identify a three stage process:

- the identification of an incident critical to the participant
- a detailed description of the incident
- an analysis of the incident.

The analysis uses two sets of questions that are seen as 'a resource list of questions to stimulate reflective analysis and discussion' (Fook et al. 2000:227). The first set of questions focuses on 'deconstruction' or analysis of the incident, such as:

- How did I personally influence the situation through: my experience/social background; my interpretations; my actions and interactions?
- How might the situation have been interpreted differently, and how might it have been interpreted by different players in the situation?....
- What knowledge and assumptions (substantive, procedural, cultural and perceptual) are implied and used in my account? Are they relevant and appropriate to the situation at hand?

The second set of questions focuses on 'reconstruction'—that is, leading towards change, such as:

- What needs to be changed about my assumptions, theory, actions, interpretations, skills, as a result of these reflections?
- What strategies can I use to make these changes?

Similarly, Taylor (2000) uses a framework for 'emancipatory reflection', which moves through four stages of:

- *Constructing*: What was happening? When, where and why? Who was involved? What was the setting? Why were you involved? What were the outcomes of the situation?

- *Deconstruction*: What beliefs and values were you using? What were you reacting to and why? How do you feel about what happened and your reactions? What do you think about them?

- *Confronting*: Where did the theories, ideas, values you used come from? Why do you continue to use them? Whose interests do they serve? What power relationships are involved?
- *Reconstructing*: In the light of what I have discovered, how might I work differently?

The idea of using a critical incident can easily be adapted to any work scenario. The above questions are general enough for use across work contexts, but some writers and practitioners suggest more specific questions. Brookfield (1995:115), for example, suggests a 'Classroom Critical Incident Questionnaire' with questions like 'At what moment in class this week did you feel most engaged/distanced from what was happening. What action did someone take—teacher or student—that you found most affirming and helpful/most puzzling or confusing? What about the class that surprised you the most?'

Case scenario

When Donna presented her incident it seemed initially that her concern was about being physically abused by a client. As she started to explore further what the incident meant to her, it became clear that what she was really angry about was her supervisor's dismissive attitude of 'what else can you expect if you work here'. Taking this further, Donna considered that this seemed to reflect a general social attitude to violence and a passivity about seeking change. She identified her own values about actively seeking to resolve conflict rather than allowing it to escalate or fester, which had come from some painful experiences in her own life. Questions from the group helped her articulate assumptions about receiving support from her supervisor. She decided to raise the issue of how the organisation supported workers with her supervisor and her team, but also to articulate with both her concerns about how conflict was treated in the organisation and with clients.

Reflective writing

Reflective writing may have similar aims to the critical incident and could be used in a complementary way. Essentially, in reflective writing participants are asked to write about a particular experience, then explore what they have written about in a group—often in a class or workshop, but this could also work in a team. The aim is to start drawing out what is important for the writer, identifying what has influenced them both on a number of levels.

Brown and Jones (2001), for example, use this approach for student teachers. Students begin by writing about a particular experience of teaching, then they gradually build up a collection of writings and get feedback from colleagues in class. Over time, they select a piece of writing on a theme that interests them and continue to write and receive comments till they have a finished piece of research on their own practice. The aim here is for reflective writing to be 'a research instrument through which teachers hold up a self-portrait against which they check out how they feel...(and) as an instrument through which successive and alternative conceptions of practice are marked and preserved for scrutiny...Reflective writing, can, we hope, provide a way of seeing practice in a fresh way which in turn can lead to different ways of acting' (Brown and Jones 2001:181).

Bolton (2001) emphasises the value of writing in an open way, in the spirit of writing creatively rather than documenting an incident. Her view is that such writing can be, and may work better if it is, an open process without set questions. She encourages people to write in whatever way is helpful for them—such as stories, poetry, autobiographical narratives, journals, or drama. Rather than writing factually about an incident, she suggests writing about incidents as fiction. 'Writing fictionally from deep professional experience can be more dramatic, leap over the boring bits, tackle issues head on; convey multiple viewpoints; sidestep problems of confidentiality; fear of exposure, and some of the inevitable anxiety which accompanies the exploration of painful events....A fiction can be a vehicle for conveying the ambiguities, complexities and ironic relationship that inevitably exist between multiple viewpoints' (Bolton 2001:109).

In workshops with small groups, which could be a team of workers, Bolton describes a process of starting with people writing about whatever is in their minds for six minutes, just to start the process of writing. Next she would ask people to write about a time they learned something vital, writing for between 20 and 40 minutes, recreating the situation from memory, but considering it as fiction. Next each person in the group would look at their own writing, identifying connections for themselves, before sharing with the group. The group would then help each other take this further, looking at thoughts and feelings, meanings, issues raised. People might then take this further by writing about the same incident from another angle—writing the same story from someone else's perspective, for example. Note that, as Bolton points out, most of these steps can be undertaken to some degree by yourself or with one other person, though she suggests it is more helpful in terms of reflective practice to talk about writing in a group.

A journal is a particular form of reflective writing, where the writer can use the act of writing to explore and clarify thoughts, feelings, incidents, and possibilities. Students on work experience of some kind are often asked to keep a reflective journal; some courses leave how to do this up to the student, others suggest a particular structure. An often suggested structure is dividing each page into two, so that the left-hand side can be used to write about what happened, and the right-hand side can be used for reflections. One of the advantages of a journal is that it can be an uncensored place for exploring reactions and making connections—though it is important to make sure, especially as a student, that the journal is not required to be seen by staff or to be used in assessment.

Case scenario

Whenever Freda raised issues with her supervisor, she ended up feeling that she was being stupid and wasting her supervisor's time. She used this as an incident in a critical reflection workshop and part of what she realised was that she came to supervision expecting her supervisor to provide answers for her dilemmas although she usually had some half thought-through ideas herself about what she should do. She decided to try using a journal to sort out some of her initial thoughts and found that she needed to start by expressing some of her frustrations about how life was for her clients. Once she had done this she could see the issues more clearly and came to supervision with a request for specific assistance, which her supervisor responded to positively.

A journal for your own use can be developed as preferred by the worker. Given that case notes can be documents required by courts or available to clients and supervisors, a journal can provide a safe space to vent emotions or dream about what might be possible—often a helpful process for arriving at what is realistic but also creative. The journal can include whatever you want it to: focused thinking about a particular issue, a poem about something that has gone well, drawings, articles or pictures from newspapers, etc. Some workers will 'dialogue' in their journal, then use this as a beginning for talking about an issue with a colleague or a supervisor. Bolton suggests that to be effective, reflective journal writers:

- take responsibility for discovering personal learning needs, and attempt to ensure they are met
- only learn in this way by examining vulnerable areas, the cutting edge
- question, explore, analyse what you do, what you think and what you feel and also what peers feel, think and do (Bolton 2001:159).

Critical reflection framework for integrated practice

The critical reflection framework often opens up questions for workers about how they are working and why and how they might work differently. For some workers this will, in itself, lead to questions related to integrated practice. This next tool provides a framework for critical reflection that focuses on the question of integrated practice rather than on a significant or critical incident. In a sense, it is for workers to use when they want to focus on this particular model in the context of critical reflection thinking. Again two sets of questions or areas to consider are given. Do not feel limited or constrained by the lists, feel free to add questions or areas that you find helpful to include or focus on the questions that seem to be more relevant at a particular time.

Select an area of your work that you want to reflect on. This could be a part of your job you feel some dissatisfaction with, an area you feel there is potential to develop more, or you might want to consider how you are approaching your job overall.

Consider the following questions. Some may apply more than others. Use them as a starting point to consider an integrated approach to your practice.

Stage One

- What are you doing?
- Why are you working in that way?
- What theory, assumptions, values, experiences is this based on?
- What agency issues, resources, perspectives are influencing you? What theory, assumptions, experiences is this based on?
- What are or might be the different views about what you are doing? What are the views of clients/community members/workers in your own and other agencies/managers?
- What would you and those listed above think is going well with what you are doing?
- What would you and they like to be different?

Stage Two

- How could you reframe your assumptions or theories to enable you to move forward?
- How might you work differently?
- What skills, knowledge, ideas might be useful from the other domains? What other aspects of the integration framework could you be working from?
- What is stopping you from working differently—yourself, expectations and assumptions of others, agency practice, policy issues, community views, something else?
- What can you do to start working differently—being an active agent? What plans can you develop? What beginning steps can you take?

Case scenario

Mike worked as an outreach worker for people with disabilities. He became increasingly frustrated by the unwillingness of local councils to provide meals on wheels for people in relatively isolated areas. When he thought about his assumptions, he realised that he saw himself as the provider of information to individuals about services and to services about individuals, rather than as someone who could have more of a community understanding about where his clients lived. He decided that on his next visit to his more isolated clients he would talk to them about their communities and have a look around. He discovered that most clients needing meals lived close to pubs that would occasionally deliver a meal to them. He talked to the pub managers about making this regular and to the local council, which was happy to negotiate with the pub managers about meals.

Networking for effective and integrated practice

Working in a human service organisation is a mixed experience: depending on the particular team/organisation, the current context, and the nature of the work, workers can feel well connected and supported or isolated and undermined. Any worker, let alone one trying to generate a new approach, needs to be aware of how to develop and sustain their own networks within and/or outside their organisation. Usually workers are familiar with the idea of support networks for clients, but somehow they find it hard to apply the same ideas to themselves and their practice. Workers need to think consciously and be proactive to ensure they find ways of being sustained in their approach to work. For some workers, existing organisational systems will be effective—a supervisor will offer encouragement, constructive challenge, and practice wisdom, other team members will be enabling, but this may not be the case for everybody.

This is particularly likely to be so for workers wanting to develop an integrated approach to practice. Getting together with other interested workers can help generate new perspectives and ideas when you feel stuck as an individual worker. Boud et al. (2001:8) suggest that 'there is evidence to suggest that fostering critical reflection and reassessment of views more readily comes from interchange between peers, than even from well-planned discussion sessions with teachers'. Certainly my experience of working with students and workers is that small groups can be very effective. The workers not involved in the issues can often see other perspectives and possibilities, perhaps because they are less involved.

There are many ways for workers to think of networks for themselves. The first step is often becoming aware that you want a greater feeling of connection and support. This may gradually emerge or, for some workers, it is a sudden realisation. Second, you need to start thinking about what kind of support network would suit you, what is possible within your organisation, what are the options outside, what are the pros and cons of each, what mix of things you might want, what fits with the rest of your life, what is possible in terms of distance, costs, and other resources.

Working with groups

Some ideas about using small groups

- Using an existing team and team meetings to explore integrated practice. If you are in an agency that supports integrated practice, this is likely to be happening anyway. If you are not, your team may still be interested in allocating some time in team meetings to explore how else the team might work. This could be a more positive approach than having team members complain about existing arrangements, focusing discussion on how to operate more constructively instead of going over old ground.
- Use an existing peer supervision group (or initiate one) to develop a critically reflective approach that may create an environment where

an integrated approach can be explored. Peer supervision is essentially where workers meet on a regular basis to discuss aspects of their work and provide some elements of supervision for each other —providing information, education, and mutual support (Hawkins and Shohet 1989). The group usually begins by establishing what the group will do and how it will operate. Facilitation of such groups is generally shared, with workers taking it in turns to assist the group process. The group will need to clarify to what degree it can set its own agenda. In some agencies there are expectations about how such groups work—for example, that each worker will take it in turns each meeting to raise a case scenario or issue for discussion. If you want to use an integrated practice framework for your own scenario, you will need to start by introducing it to the group so that they have a sense of what questions and responses you want from them.

- Mutual support/issue-raising groups. Some workers may not feel that their agency offers a place where they can explore an integrated model. Instead, you could then gather together a small number of people interested in exploring issues together or in supporting each other to work differently. Such groups can be formal or informal, meet as requested or regularly, or wherever the group chooses. A group might form from an existing worker network or be a focus for developing networks. A group interested in considering integrated practice might arise from shared concerns about gaps in community resources or about frustration about limitations in a particular program. Such a group might then meet to use the integration framework as a group and decide on some coordinated activities within or across agencies. Alternatively, a network of workers who already meet informally for mutual support might decide to meet on a more regular basis for a time to allow each worker to consider their work or an aspect of it in turn.

In all of these groups, it is important to start by talking about group rules or expectations. These will vary to some extent, depending on what is important to the group. These might include, for example, confidentiality, being honest and open, nonjudgmental, and respectful. The group might also want to decide what it will do if there is conflict or how to make sure people all have a chance to contribute. While some of these issues sound straightforward, and hard to disagree with, they can be more complicated than they appear. Confidentiality, for example, suggests that what is said within the group should not be taken outside the group. Are there any limits to this? What happens if staff get seriously concerned about the well-being of another staff member? What if a worker becomes clearer about an issue and wants to take it up with their manager? Are they doing this for themselves or on behalf of the group? Groups and individuals will vary about some rules—for example, some people may be happy to be challenging but not to be challenged, or only to be challenged on days when they are feeling resilient. How does this get built into the group rules? Discussing group rules is also important in starting the process of the group acting as a group, seeing itself as a group.

Case scenario

Several team members in Rachel's team expressed frustration at the lack of in-depth discussion about approaches to work. Rachel suggested trying peer supervision—an hour once a fortnight when a team member would volunteer to present an issue that was of significance to them that had implications for the team. They decided to try using a critical reflection framework. Some team members were sceptical initially, but agreed to try the process. Peter presented the first issue which related to Angela, a young woman who had just told her parents she has decided to come out as a lesbian. Her parents had reacted very angrily, and were demanding the agency 'fix' her. When Peter had affirmed Angela's right to decide about her sexuality, they had left, saying they were going to complain to the local Member of Parliament about the agency. As the team explored the incident, they realised they had very mixed initial reactions, different assumptions about how to react, and from what values. Coming to a position of shared values from which to support Angela's decision consolidated a sense of how they worked well as a team. This also reinforced the worth of the group process—hearing different views enabled each to clarify their own.

Working in pairs/critical friendships

Not everyone is able or interested in accessing a group of people. Some people prefer to develop peer relationships with one or two other people, again meeting to explore work issues. Brookfield (1995:140) talks about people having 'critical conversations' where there is ' an openness to diverse perspectives and ideologies and a respectful acknowledgement of the importance of each person's contribution irrespective of seniority or status'. Such conversations can be organised on a regular or ad hoc basis; some workers prefer to plan something like monthly meetings where each can raise an issue or, using Bolton's perspective, tell a story, then be able to explore it in more depth. There are advantages in planning meetings; in the busyness of most organisations such times for reflection are often what disappears first. Building them into diaries helps make sure that they will happen. As with groups, it can help to begin exploring expectations and setting some kind of ground rules. Time is often an issue, so check whether, for example, the time will be shared equally each meeting or whether one person will share each time. People vary about how planned they want to be—for example, should a more urgent issue take precedent. What is important is that the system works for the people involved. You might, as a worker, meet with two different people separately and have quite different expectations with each.

Hawken and Worrall (2002:48) suggest a similar process called 'reciprocal mentoring supervision' which is about 'structured, reciprocal learning relationships between peers (two or three) who wish to work together, where trust, support, and challenge encourage honesty, in-depth reflection and constructive analysis on practice and related personal and contextual issues, enhancing self confidence, personal and professional learning and promoting best practice'. Participants choose who they will meet with and the expectation is that they will plan specific times to meet with the time being shared equally by all participants. The participants are all from the same level, so there is no expectation of one 'supervising' the other.

Francis (1997:170) encourages the development of critical friendships in classes with student teachers at university. Students are allocated to groups of four where they 'examine ways of giving and receiving feedback and explicitly practice skills which group members or [Francis] identify as necessary to (re) constructing "being critical" as an act of "friendship"'.

Francis suggests the following process in her work with students who are learning to be teachers:

1 Each student on their own writes a brief description of an incident from school or university experience—no analysis, just who where, when, what happened.
2 On a separate page each then reflects on the incident in terms of personal meaning given to it—for example, interpretation of intent or outcome, feelings, beliefs, application of theory, comparison with other events etc.
3 Critical friends exchange first page descriptions and provide feedback with enough detail provided to establish context for further discussion.

4 Groups of four talk about principles of critical friendship then each reads their individual incidents to the group and spends time sharing interpretations and attempting to identify the beliefs, values, and personal theory of the participants in the incident, including the writer, and are encouraged to seek multiple interpretations.

5 Each goes back to their own incident and reconstructs the meaning given to it in the light of new understandings of personal beliefs and values.

Case scenario

Kate and Sam were from the same large organisation but worked in different sections. They met at a critical reflection workshop and found each other's style of asking questions very helpful. They agreed to meet for lunch for an hour once a month and to divide the time equally. Each would email the other a brief, usually half-page description of the incident before their meeting. They then took it in turns to analyse each incident, being careful to stop the first incident after 30 minutes. Over time, they noticed that there were often patterns in the incidents and with these they focused more on what could change. Both found the process very helpful and when they reviewed their meetings at the end of the year, they agreed to keep meeting the following year.

Finally, it is useful to note that groups or critical friendships can use all of the tools described here. Small groups or pairs could use a piece of reflective writing, use a set of questions for reflection, and/or talk about specific incidents.

Using evaluation and research for effective and integrated practice

In Chapter 1, I suggested that evaluation and research could be seen either as a tension or a possibility in human service organisations. Newer approaches reinforce the value of research and evaluation as tools for organisations and workers. In a sense, research and evaluation are ways of finding out more about what is happening in practice, how practice is perceived and experienced by the different people involved, and what difference it makes. This, of course, is evident is some approaches more than others. Being critically reflective is a form of research—where the worker is researching their own practice.

Given the explosion of writing and use of such research, I am not aiming to cover the whole field of possibilities. What I want to do is to concentrate on some examples that enable workers to work in a way that is manageable, includes clients and other relevant people, and enables exploration and discovery; approaches that are compatible with the principles and values of integrated practice. To use these approaches successfully workers would need to:

- have a capacity to ask broad questions about overall purpose as well as more specific ones when needed
- see research and evaluation as part of what workers do as well as what evaluators and researchers do
- see people and communities as whole beings, with strengths and issues, rather than a problem to be researched
- be interested in the voices least heard
- retain an awareness of context and structural issues
- be aware of the influence of their own and other people's values
- see the evaluation or research process as a joint one where knowledge is shared
- acknowledge shared understandings and links
- acknowledge what the evaluation or research can and cannot do.

In broad terms, these relate to what is often called a critical approach to evaluation and social research. Everitt and Hardiker (1996:89), for example, suggest that evaluation 'is about understanding what goes on in practice ie making the implicit explicit. It seeks to answer the question, what are the meanings and interpretations of practice held by those involved in it?'. Harvey (1990:6) says that critical social research '...tries to dig beneath the surface of appearances....It is important the (research) account be located in a wider context which links the specific activities with a broader social structural and historical analysis'. These approaches link to the postmodern and critical approaches discussed in Chapter 3, focusing on:

- recognising that people will experience the same event differently and so different understandings need to be heard
- looking for meaning and processes as well as outcomes
- making connections to broader social issues
- acknowledging the subjectivity of the evaluator
- acknowledging the place of values.

More specifically, related approaches fit within what is often called participatory and/or action research, though these also have a variety of names. This would include Owen and Rogers's (1999:220) 'inter-active evaluation' and 'clarificative evaluation'—where 'evaluation efforts are influenced strongly by those who are "close to the action".' This form of evaluation has increased greatly over the last 30 years. Wadsworth (1998:12), for example, talks about the change in her role as an evaluator from 'a 1970's role as "*messenger*", to a 1980's "*go-between*", and to a 1990s "*dinner party hostess*" or "*caterer*".' They include utilisation-focused evaluation (Patton 1997), participatory/collaborative evaluation (Cousins and Earl 1992; Heron 1996), em-powerment evaluation (Fetterman 2000), as well as action research (Cherry 1999; Winter and Munn-Giddings 2001).

What these approaches share to some degree is that they see the involvement of participants as central—that is, the people who are on the receiving end of a program, whether that is workers or clients or communities. They are also all open to including both qualitative and quantitative methods of evaluation and research; what is important is matching the method to the particular project. Generally, they aim to ask questions about meaning and purpose, processes as well as outcomes. They would emphasise the value of the process being beneficial to those involved as well as results being used productively. There is gen-erally more acceptance now that evaluation is not value free and that 'the methods we choose reflect our values as evaluators and professionals' (Gardner 2003) and these approaches would reflect that. They would vary on how explicit they are about making connections to wider struc-tural issues. Some, like Herda (1999), would stress the need to articulate contradictions and biases, others like Fetterman (2000) would see evaluation as aiming to give users of services a voice for social change.

Clearly, part of the aim of carrying out evaluation and research is the expectation that results will be used. Too often reports are left on shelves rather than being actively used documents. It is important to think about this before starting, perhaps particularly in the current pressure to operate in a managerialist way with clear performance measures and outcomes as well as the move to evidence-based practice (both discussed in Chapter 1). Useful questions might be: who is the audience or audiences? Who do you want to be interested in the results? Who is likely to be able to ensure that the results are used? What kind of evidence are they likely to be interested in? It is likely that you will have more than one audience—the participants in the project might be one, the organisation involved or the funding body might be another. Each may be interested in different questions and open to different evidence. Part of what can help here is to:

1 Justify clearly and explicitly the method or methods you want to use. If you want to use an evaluation method that the funding body is not familiar with, for example, you need to be able to explain how and why this is a valid way to proceed. Using literature and other research particularly from reputable and respected researchers can help with this. Participatory and action research approaches, for example, have greater credibility now that they have been used broadly and by many established researchers.

2 Involve your audience/s in making the decisions about methods and how results will be produced. If your audiences are part of the process they are more likely to support and advocate for the way the research has been carried out and how it is written up.

3 Make some compromises. This might simply be about carrying out the research in a way that has multiple methods or, for example, has a combination of quantitative and qualitative data. Most research and evaluation has at least some data that is readily quantifiable, which often makes results more easily understandable. As well as providing descriptive information, summarise qualitative interviews to say, for example, 50 per cent of those interviewed felt the service needed to expand to include a wider geographic area. Such a finding provides both quantitative and qualitative information. Be clear about what you are prepared to compromise and what you are not and why.

4 Articulate the value and limits of particular methods. To convince your audience of the value of your approach you may need to be quite explicit about its advantages and disadvantages. For example, will statistical data showing improvement in mental health through involvement in a group process give enough information about what was significant in the process? Will data showing there has been an increase in child protection notifications show that a community program has not been successful or that it has successfully generated attitudes of shared community responsibility leading to increased notifications? Both these examples suggest the need for a combination of qualitative and quantitative data—a more postmodern or integrated both/and rather than an either/or approach. As well as articulating these it can also help to use questions so that the audience grapples with these too, asking them what a particular approach will demonstrate and what its limits will be.

5 Present the results in ways that are illuminating. In spite of the managerialist preference for specific outcomes, the audience—including

funders—are likely to be impressed by stories that illuminate the findings. Finding a particularly focused and representative story that makes a lasting impact can be as influential as statistical data. Combining relevant data with pertinent stories can be very effective and remembered by all of the audience.

How workers can move to seeing research and evaluation as a way of furthering their work

The next section briefly outlines some of the approaches to research and evaluation and gives examples of how these might be incorporated into practice.

Action research

Essentially, action research is a cyclical process (Wadsworth 1997), which begins with the researcher and those interested meeting to agree on what they want to explore or what they want to develop and how they will do it. This usually includes participants or users of a service as well as other people or their representatives likely to be affected in an organisation or community. Generally, those involved form an ongoing reference or advisory group. Once agreement is reached, the research begins, and the reference group continues to meet and discuss ongoing issues and processes. When the research is completed, the group discusses the results and makes suggestions about a next stage or future projects. Ideally the action research cycle then continues with the identifying of new questions or new aspects of implementation.

Carr and Kemmis (1983) stress the connection between involving people and seeing improvement in practice. Improvement includes greater understanding of practice and the situation in which the practice takes place as well as in the practice itself. Cherry (1999:xiv) identifies three strands:

- an action strand which is about making change, making useful and noticeable differences to the world outside of oneself...(the 'outer journey')
- a knowledge strand which is about enriching our collective wisdom about how and why things and people work
- a learning strand which is about developing individual and collective practice, enhancing our capability to do the same or different— possibly harder—things in the future. The learning strand offers the

possibility of an inner journey, one which involves the unconscious acquisition of skills and the acquisition of highly self-conscious and self-reflective processes for gaining wisdom about self.

Cherry's view is that all three of these must be present, though often one will be emphasised, and this is reflected in the varied approaches to action research (Reason and Bradbury 2001).

Case scenarios

Cheryl worked at a community health agency. Various clients across the region had expressed concern about their experience of giving birth. She called together a reference group made up of two midwives, three consumers of birthing services, two local general practitioners, and an obstetrician. The group decided to develop a survey and send it out to local hospitals and maternal and child health and community health centres inviting people to respond. Nearly 200 responses were received and the group met to look at the data and develop a plan of action. The group continued to meet to implement and review the plan.

Binnie and Titchen (1999) used action research in a hospital ward to implement patient-centred nursing—that is, a style of practice where the focus is respect for the patient as a person and the 'acknowledgement and valuing of each patient's own way of perceiving and experiencing what is happening'. One acted as the 'outside' researcher, the other as the 'inside' researcher/colleague. They involved the nurses on the ward and senior management in planning and implementing the change in a series of 'action spirals'—cycles of implementing, seeking feedback, examining data, and further implementing. They found that action research (Binnie and Titchen 1999:231–2) 'provided a discipline which made us more thoughtful, sensitive and rigorous than we might otherwise have been....The practice of regularly and systematically reviewing progress in relation to each of the action spirals committed us to seeking feedback on every aspect of the development work'. They identify challenges of the process—the amount of data collected that needed to be considered, the tension between the democratic group process and keeping up the momentum, and living with the unpredictable nature of action research. However, they conclude that 'involvement in the action research process enhanced the professional development of participants, including ourselves....sharing project data with staff was a valuable way of stimulating reflection and creative thinking. In the action planning that followed, we were able to involve nurses in negotiation and decision making. The skills that nurses acquired through this process were readily transferable to their increasingly independent practice' (Binnie and Titchen 1999:232).

Identifying program logic

This is a form of evaluation, again with various names. It is often called program or formative or design evaluation, and in Owen and Rogers's categories, clarificative evaluation. Remember this is what they call 'Clarifying the internal structure and functioning of a program or policy' (Owen and Rogers 1999:42–3). The aim is for the evaluator and interested staff and/or clients to meet to identify the key typical processes and stages of delivering a program or service. This is particularly useful when a program is being developed or when an organisation wants to reflect on a program that has evolved to articulate how it operates. The group also links principles and hoped-for outcomes to each stage. This approach affirms the value of involving staff and clients in articulating the program's processes. The results are often written up in a diagram so that it is easy to see how the process works.

For example, St Luke's (see Chapter 7) developed a model of integrated practice for working with families using a solution-focused, competency-based approach that had developed organically over several years. The agency wanted to articulate the model more clearly and John Owen and I were asked to help work on this. In order to unearth the logic of the program—that is, the sense staff had about how it worked—I met with staff over several weeks. At the first meeting, we talked about what a typical progression of work with clients might look like, while acknowledging that this would not always happen, and what assumptions would be linked to each step. After the meeting, I wrote up what I thought people had said, then at the next meeting they refined this further. This continued in cycles until we had a clear picture of the steps taken and the assumptions or principles for each step. For example, early in the process, workers had identified a principle they named as 'clients make all the decisions for themselves', but as they discussed this further, it was clear that this could not always be the case. Some clients had been referred as part of a court process and so their decision-making was limited from that perspective; others wanted resources that St Luke's either did not have or did not feel able to offer to the client or at this point given the needs of other families. The principle then became 'clients will make decisions for themselves as much as possible'.

Cooperative inquiry

Cooperative inquiry can seem very similar to action research, in that it too is a participatory approach that works in cycles. What is distinctive about this, particularly in its most 'pure' form, is the emphasis on equal involvement as co-researchers of what might otherwise be called the researcher and participants or those being researched. Heron stresses that this form of research is '*with* people not *on* them or *about* them....In its most complete form, the inquirers engage fully in both roles, moving in cyclic fashion between phases of reflection as co-researchers and of action as co-subjects. In this way they use reflection and action to refine and deepen each other' (Heron 1996:19). This means that the researcher must be interested in the issue in a way that means they can participate directly, rather than guiding the process for other people. However, while Heron's preference is that researchers are fully involved in the experience, he acknowledges that at times researchers may be fully involved in sharing decision-making about the research questions, but not as much in the experience of the research.

Cooperative inquiry does have stages, put simply as:

- the first reflection or inquiry phase where people meet to work out exactly what the dimensions of the inquiry will be
- the action phases where people meet to carry out the tasks or actions that have been agreed to—this may be in two stages with greater depth in the second stage

Case scenario

Mandy worked in a hospital outpatients department as an occupational therapist. She had experienced chronic pain for many years and was interested in researching how other people dealt with it. She invited past participants of chronic pain management courses to a meeting and explained that she was interested in meeting for seven sessions over three months to carry out a cooperative enquiry into what helped people deal with chronic pain. Eight people agreed to participate. In the two meetings (the enquiry stage), people shared how they perceived chronic pain, strategies they had used, and what they would like to happen in the enquiry process. In stage two (the action phase), each person who wanted to tried out new ideas they had gained from the group and reported back. At the end of each meeting, the group reflected on what had happened and where they wanted to go in the next week. In the third reflective stage (week seven), they talked about the value of the process. Several people had tried a new strategy and found it helpful, and all said they had found belonging to the group positive and something they looked forward to. They decided to write up the results and agreed to meet in a month to think about other activities they might be interested in.

- the second reflection phase where the group looks back over the process and decides to review or modify the topic or chooses to explore the same aspect further or move on to a new aspect of the issue
- these action and reflection phases continue to cycle until the final reflection phase, which clarifies outcomes and explores what should happen next, including whether to write a report, cooperatively.

Strategies for integrated practice

This section briefly identifies some potential strategies for integrated practice.

Reinforcing goals and linking them to practice

In education, Schon explored the idea of espoused theory and theory in action. What he meant by this was that we frequently identify our ideal way of working or how we believe we should work, but what we do in practice is different (Schon 1983). Similarly in organisations, we may identify clear overall goals for the organisation, which are often broad and may express some of the values of the organisation. These can seem very distant to workers on the ground, who operate according to program aims. Revisiting the agency's fundamental goals can lead to a change in what is seen as valid work.

For example, take a social worker or psychologist working in a school in what has been defined as a casework or counselling role. The overall goals for the school might be to provide a harmonious environment in which students can learn and develop. Part of this might be a goal around enabling students to learn to work cooperatively together. In practice, the worker is seeing a lot of children who are being bullied and, as a result, are reluctant to come to school. Rather than continuing to work with what is becoming an overwhelming number of children individually, the worker could encourage the School Council to reflect on its goals and what that means in terms of bullying, in narrative terms creating alternative stories so that the school community might work on celebrating difference. This might lead to class and whole school activities on valuing diversity, communicating constructively about difference through peer mediation, or harmony days celebrating diversity.

Arguing effectiveness

Essentially this means being able to convince decision-makers that using different strategies can meet the same goals at least as effectively or preferably with greater success. For example, an agency may offer several different kinds of counselling programs, such as a combination of generalist counselling, gambling counselling, and mediation, each funded separately. A staff member interested in working across these areas could point out what they have in common, and the advantages of staff being able to work across programs in terms of mutual support, such as covering when staff are on leave, building a broader skill base etc. For managers using a systems perspective, there would be some clear advantages: if one staff member leaves, others will still be able to cover some of the work, and there could be greater flexibility in providing services as needed so that outcomes are maintained. This linking can create its own momentum over time, generating shifts in perception about how work can be managed.

Actively making links

Staff and managers in agencies are often so busy with existing work tasks that they find it hard to stop and think about what they are doing and why. Funding often separates programs and activities rather than connecting them. This tends to create an environment in which people do not see links between actual or potential programs or activities. Pointing out those links can enable the agency to perceive programs and work practices in a different way.

A community health worker in a relatively isolated community began by seeing whoever wanted generalist counselling as well as people referred by the local hospital and other health workers. Gradually, she also visited people who seemed to be interested in talking about the community and how it operated. Initially, she felt overwhelmed by the range of issues that seemed to emerge from what had seemed like a placid, easy-going community with few problems. She invited a group of people to meet and talk together about their impressions of the community and gradually they started to look at how they might work on common issues.

Alternatively, you may realise that you are seeing a number of people with children—often adults who have a mental illness. Many of them want emotional support and you begin to wonder whether that would come better from each other rather than from you. You invite them all to afternoon tea to meet each other and also advertise the afternoon tea in the agency newsletter. Ten people come and there are many lively conversations. You ask how people would feel about meeting as a group for mutual support and seeing you only as needed. There is general agreement that people have much to offer each other and a date is set for another meeting.

Using and creating opportunities

Occasionally, an opportunity of some kind will arise in the workplace. Reasons may be internal to the agency or external. An unexpected funding round, for example, can present an opportunity to do something quite different, that complements and builds on existing practice. Keeping possible developments in mind and having active networks that can be used as needed can help you use new chances well. A change of management or new workers can be an opportunity too to suggest trying something new.

Imagine, for example, that you are a counsellor in community health in a rural community. After a prolonged drought, the number of women from farms you are seeing has increased significantly. A major issue for many of them is their husband's depression and reluctance to seek help. You have extensive networks with key players in the local community and begin meeting with them. Soon the local churches are involved. A funding round becomes available for community activities in drought-affected areas. A series of barbecues is funded to provide places for people to meet and talk informally. Feedback suggests that the people in the community, including the men, are feeling less isolated and are starting to talk about what can be done.

Pushing the boundaries

Not all workers have narrow job descriptions that make it hard to manage integrated practice. Some positions have broad descriptions that at least in theory allow diverse practices. The issue is more about assumptions about how things should and perhaps have been done in the past. The challenge then is to push your own and the agency's boundaries about what can be done and how. Rural agencies, for example, may be broader in their expectations because of the lack of other workers in a community, but there are also urban agencies that tend to have wider expectations, such as community health services.

I worked once with a foster care worker. She had enormous energy and commitment to improving foster care services. As she worked with children and families, she realised that the foster parents shared that commitment and energy and that some of them particularly wanted to work with her. A foster care association was formed, people supported each other with children in their care, and together she and the foster parents lobbied for more and better services.

A program development worker began a project by meeting with all of the people identified as key informants in terms of their power and influence in the regional community. It soon became clear that she was missing important perspectives in relation to the program area: potential clients and carers were rarely seen as influential. She decided she needed to start meeting individuals and families who understood the issues from their own experience. This meant the timelines for the project had to be extended, but after seeing the results of her initial interviews, the managers involved agreed that this would be necessary for the project to be effective.

Summary

This chapter aimed to ground ideas about how to work in human service organisations, particularly in thinking about an integrated approach. Three approaches with specific tools were suggested:

- Using critical reflection to reflect on and change practice. Critical reflective enables organisations and workers to think critically about their practice, identifying underlying assumptions in a way that leads to change. Particular tools for critical reflection illustrated here were:
  - critical incident analysis—using a specific experience to explore practice using a framework of questions that help deconstruct the experience, then reconstruct with an expectation of change
  - reflective writing—using writing or journals to explore practice experiences, either using the actual experience or writing in a more fictional way. Again this can then be used to articulate assumptions and values and lead to changed practice
  - using a set of questions that enables workers to critically reflect on integrated practice in particular.

- Networking in the sense of finding ways to engage in mutually supportive and challenging relationships with other people wanting to develop integrated practice. This might be through existing teams or work groups in an organisation; other workers might need to initiate their own networks inside and/or outside the organisation. Such groups could be opportunities for critical reflection as illustrated above or could be used for other forms of mutual support and exploration of practice issues.

- Research and evaluation creating opportunities for working collaboratively and reflectively in developing and maintaining an integrated approach to practice. Creating such opportunities provides another way for workers and organisations to explore practice. This would also mean that research and evaluation become part of practice rather than an optional extra. Collaborative research and evaluation involving clients can have many benefits for workers, clients, and their organisations in terms of shared knowledge and learning as well as developing more effective practice.
- Specific strategies to consider for extending roles in the direction of integrated practice. The chapter ends with some specific strategies encouraging workers to be active in seeking integrated practice. These include: reinforcing the organisation's broad goals and linking these to practice, arguing that other ways of operating can be at least as effective, actively making links across work domains and demonstrating these to the organisation or community, using and creating opportunities for change, and pushing the boundaries so that different perspectives can be seen as possible.

Reflective practice

Thinking about your own work situation, what tools could you use to further integrated practice for yourself? How did you react to the tools suggested here, that is:

- critical reflection?
- ideas about networking?
- using research and evaluation?
  How might you be able to use each of these—in supervision, team meetings, on your own, meeting with a peer, as part of a specific group?

- What is likely to work within your organisation? From outside your organisation?
- Are some approaches more likely to be seen sympathetically?
- How will different people react?
- What beginning steps could you take?

10

Conclusion: Moving Towards Integrated Practice

Practitioners themselves have an important role as catalysts in education and stimulating all levels of their own organisation. While it is important to have senior management behind any initiative—as all textbooks on organisational change stress—it is not a precondition for gearing up your agency to combat exclusion. Within their organisations practitioners should not wait for a message from the top; worry less about where the message comes from and more about getting it across. A negative consequence of the big silo culture is that issues and social problems are largely seen as 'out there' and 'not down to us' or to do with 'economics—which we have no control over' or 'community development which is not our role'.

This is your business and that or your organisation. If not yours, whose? If not now, when? (Pierson 2002:214)

The dynamic relationship between an organisation and its workers is a central theme in organisational life. Working in human service organisations is an integral part of working in the human service field. For the vast majority of workers, managing to interact constructively with their employing organisation is a key focus in their working lives. Workers also have to engage with a range of other organisations, often on behalf of their organisation or for their clients. To be effective, I have suggested here that workers need to have a sense of agency or capacity to engage actively with the organisation and its processes. Such agency implies 'more than simply movement, but impulsion towards some intention based on our values and ideologies' (Adams 2002:10).

This desire for change based on values generates tensions for workers in human service organisations, discussed in the first chapter of this book. Such workers generally have established values about their role, reflecting professional training as well as their own experience and beliefs. They are seeking empowerment for clients, have expectations of fair and just practice, and a desire to create a better world. These aims often seem to be in conflict not with the organisation's explicit aims, but with its more implicit aims of efficiency, maintaining funding, and simply avoiding conflict and risk. This is particularly so in the current managerialist climate with its emphasis on a business-oriented approach: funding according to narrowly defined categories, pressure to work to established procedures, focus on outcomes, and fear of risk.

However, this awareness of limitations and tensions needs to be balanced with a sense of possible change, also explored in Chapter 1: a growing recognition of the importance of community context, interest in critical reflection and reflective practice, and a return to working in partnerships. This chapter also explores two areas that generate a sense of tension and possibility for workers: what it means to be a professional and new perspectives on research and evaluation, including evidence-based practice.

In this concluding chapter, I will explore two main questions. First, given these tensions, how can workers can become active agents in their organisations? This section effectively summarises the discussion in the book. The second question focuses on what using an integrated approach might mean for human service organisations and their managers. This connects back to some of the current tensions in organisations and suggests some ways forward, including the need for training and support and ongoing research.

How can workers deal with these tensions and maintain a positive sense of how their own values as workers can be expressed; how can they be 'active agents' either generating change in their organisation or advocating for maintaining a valued perspective or activity?

Reframing tensions as allowing possibilities for change

Part of the answer here lies in recognising current tensions so that it becomes possible to work with them. A common theme for human service workers is the demanding nature of their direct service work—whether this is with clients as individuals and families and/or communities, or in policy or program development. The focus of their activity is rightly on their work with clients, but this can mean that not enough attention is paid to the organisational context that impacts on their work. Being able to name these tensions and to see tensions of some kind as to some extent inevitable, can mean that workers feel more able to engage with them. A narrative approach talks about 'externalising the problem': naming the issues as distinct from the person involved, which reduces the power of the issue. Most of us are used to living with, juggling, and maneouvering tensions—the work/family or leisure tension is a frequently named one in our current culture. Naming these tensions can begin the process of making change seem possible.

As active agents, it is important to recognise possible prospects for change as well as tensions, partly because this gives a more realistic picture of what is happening. It can also give a sense of hope—if change is happening in some areas, it is possible for it to happen in others. It reminds workers to see the organisation's situation as dynamic and fluid, even when it seems fixed and rigid. A systems approach helps here to see how all of the parts of the organisation are connected and in turn affected by the external environment. The two issues that can be seen as both positive prospects for change and potential tensions are current views about professionals and changes in research and evaluation.

Using a variety of perspectives to see the organisation as a client

Workers have a considerable capacity to use their professional knowledge, experience, and intuition in assessing and engaging in client work. Generally, workers are fluent in the language of a variety of frameworks and approaches that enable them to practice well. Sometimes this capacity appears to be lost when workers are considering their organisation. Instead of feeling they can critically assess and engage with the organisation, workers feel overwhelmed and powerless. As we explored in the first half of the book, workers need to bring their knowledge of approaches and frameworks to help them stand back from the organisation and explore what is happening, to see the organisation from different perspectives. This helps create a distance between the worker and the organisation: the worker becomes less entangled and can see the organisation as a complex entity. The worker can then, as they would with clients, use their awareness of their own and other people's emotions to work effectively.

I have suggested here that this can partly come from developing an understanding of human service organisations and how they operate on a number of levels:

- the complexities of their purpose, auspice, and technology, and the opportunities and limitations created by particular structures (Chapter 2)
- the culture of the organisation; how culture is developed and maintained; the value of a learning culture that can respond quickly to change, culture, and supervision; the influence of personality; and recognising and working with a culture of fear and risk (Chapter 4)
- processes of change and the influence of power and authority, what these might mean in terms of being an active agent for change or maintaining the expression of important values (Chapter 5).

Using relevant theoretical perspectives—both broad theory and practice theories—can also help by providing a variety of lenses through which to see the organisation and the relationships and dynamics within it. Chapter 3 considers two broad theories first:

- Postmodernism suggests the need for a flexible and open approach, understanding multiple perspectives rather than seeking 'one truth'. For workers seeking to be active agents, this reinforces that the predominant view is not the only possible one. Using deconstruction can enable workers to see how their and the organisation's assumptions can be articulated in a way that leads to constructive change.
- Critical social theory explores the impact of dominant social structures in terms of power and cultural expectations for individuals and organisations, including how these become internalised by individuals. A feminist critical theory, for example, would focus on how expectations about gender are perpetuated in social structures and how these are 'taken on board' by individuals, often limiting what they see as options. Active workers can use this theory to see how the organisation and general social structure maintain particular power relationships and expectations, and so challenge these.

I have also explored how three practice theories could be used by workers to understand and work more effectively with human service organisations (Chapter 3). These are:

- A psychoanalytic approach reminds us of the place of emotion and the influence of history as well as providing tools for exploring and using these dynamically for change. To be an active agent, workers need to recognise how history is part of what influences the present and to be able to name and engage with feelings that impact on work in general and on the process of change. This might mean, for example, recognising that even desired change can bring feelings of loss and that encouraging discussion of these feelings will enable people to move to the new system.

- A narrative approach emphasises working on the whole person, including awareness of relevant history and context, separating the 'person from the problem', acknowledging what works as well as what does not. For an active worker this might mean, for example, identifying what happens when the organisation works well and building on this to generate change.
- A systems approach encourages thinking about how workers, the organisation, and the environment are interconnected. Because all the parts of the system are connected, change in one area will affect others. However, the organisation as a system tends to move towards equilibrium, so workers seeking change need to be conscious of, for example, the value of working on several areas at once depending on the area for change.

Affirming the centrality of values

Values are fundamental to working in human service organisations, but are sometimes lost in the pressure to achieve work goals and follow routines and procedures. Organisations will often make their underlying values explicit in their mission statements, but implicit values and expectations may contradict these. Workers need to remember for themselves and remind their organisation about the place of values. In Chapter 6, values as principles for integrated practice that can be used as the basis for approaching change in organisations were identified. These include:

- maintaining a breadth of vision, seeing the whole context for the organisation, its workers and clients
- seeking a fair and just society
- working across domains—seeing connections between types of work in order to respond in the most fitting way to each situation
- working towards wholeness
- being aware of context—seeing work in the context of broader social and cultural issues as well as the organisation's community context

- actively articulating the importance of values
- valuing reciprocity and shared knowledge
- celebrating difference
- valuing connecting skills and knowledge
- acknowledging the place of specialist skills and knowledge.

Wrestling with questions constructively—using knowledge, skills, and tools

Organisational efforts often focus on how to deliver services in ways that are most efficient for the organisation and acceptable to funding bodies. Active workers need to remind organisations that there are also other questions to wrestle with—for example, a more important question might be how do clients experience this organisation? Would clients agree that the organisation's aims and vision are being reached? What suggestions would clients have about how services or programs can be accessed and how they are delivered? The history of human service organisations shows that there are no easy answers to questions of management and changes do happen sometimes without clear rationale (Liddell 2003). However, it is important to keep asking questions and debating the issues, so that change is oriented towards client-centred practice.

Using knowledge and skills effectively is important here. Often knowledge and skills are learnt in discrete boxes in training courses or staff development workshops. Chapter 8 aims to identify common skills and knowledge so that workers can see that skills and knowledge from one area can be applied in another. This can widen the scope of what workers feel able to do, what they can suggest, initiate, or develop within or outside their organisations. Tools to further practice in this way are explored in Chapter 9:

- the capacity to use tools for critical reflection, including reflection on integrated practice
- the facility to build and use networks for support and change
- the ability to use research and evaluation to validate and improve organisational practices.

Using a model of integrated practice

This book also suggests that working towards integrating practice is a way for workers to be active agents in their organisations (see Chapter

8). Integrating practice can be thought about on a number of levels. For some people integration has negative connotations of assimilation or amalgamation—bringing separate entities together with the danger of having them all become the same. What I mean by integrating practice here is about seeing the whole rather than the parts, making connections so that work is more effective. What this means in practice would depend on the particular situation. The aim is not to have a definitive and prescriptive model, but to think about such practice as dynamic and responsive to change. In integrating practice, it is useful to think about what practice looks like from a client perspective, whether the client is an individual, family, or community. Practice is likely to be seen as better when:

- people or communities are seen as whole and complex, with strengths and resources as well as issues and needs
- the context is taken into account and is part of the work
- connections are made across issues rather than issues being dealt with separately
- it is flexible, creative, and open, and encourages working in a variety of ways
- recognises the importance of working from values that are enabling, and celebrate diversity and fairness.

How such practice operates will depend on the nature of the work and the organisational and community context. In Chapter 8, three dimensions of integrated practice are identified:

- Community dimension—all organisations will relate to a geographic and/or a community of interest. Clearly some may relate to both —for example, a focus on working with older people in a particular town.
- Practice dimension—this includes fields of practice: the types or categories of clients such as families seeking counselling, or young people seeking support and housing as well as practice domains—the kinds of work done that might vary from work with individuals or groups, to community work or policy development.
- Agency dimension—integrated practice might happen through individuals or teams, be initiated by individuals or the organisation, and be formal or informal.

Workers and their organisations then can think about integrating practice in terms of the community in which they operate, the agency's preferences for integration by individuals or teams, and the range of practice fields and domains that can be integrated. From a worker perspective, a worker might request to be able to work across two or three program areas that have obvious goals and work styles in common. Another might ask for a time allocation to make connections in a local community that might lead to community resources for clients.

One agency might start, for example, by thinking about the issues typically faced by their clients, then look at the skills and capacities of workers to decide what range of issues could be worked with by individual workers. Another might decide to start by allocating workers to focus client work in particular communities, allowing time for establishing wider community contact as well as client work.

What using an integrated practice model might mean for human service organisations and their managers

Funding and accountability

Funding sources and accountability are obvious issues for agencies in considering integrated practice. Currently, funding frequently comes in narrowly defined packages. Even within a field of work, such as working with families, funding can come from state or federal government, and from several different programs within each of these. Each area of funding is likely to have different criteria about such areas as how money is to be spent, who is eligible, criteria to be used, time to be allocated, etc. Because of this agencies often find it easier, at an operational level, to maintain these divisions, having separate workers to carry out each program. However, this does take extra time, and therefore money, at an administrative level as well as creating duplication for individuals and families (Martinez-Brawley 1992).

There are two main approaches for agencies to deal with this that can happen simultaneously. The first is to continue to raise, with government and other funding bodies, the advantages of integrating practice both at an administrative and service delivery level. It is easy for people more removed from services on the ground to lose sight of the disadvantages of segregated program funding. Governments have had times of consciousness in the past about the need for more integration across government departments and it seems that there may again be some awareness of this.

The second is to start integrated practice on the ground while still keeping records about separate program interventions. What this would mean in practice is that rather than having, for example, one worker for family counselling, one worker for mediation, and one worker for parent–adolescent work, all three workers would provide family counselling, which would include mediation and parent–adolescent work. Each worker would need to maintain statistics, as they most likely already do, documenting how many of each service type they have provided. Given that the agency would continue to advertise all three services, the supervising worker would simply continue to make sure that target figures are reached. To give what you would hope would be an absurd example, this means that rather than a family starting with a family counsellor, looking at relationship issues, moving on to the mediation worker to agree how to end the relationship, and finally going to the parent–adolescent worker because the adolescents in the family are reacting to the decisions, the family could simply work with one person. There are obvious benefits to this: for the client who only has to deal with one worker, rather than developing a relationship with three; for the workers in following through with families; and for agencies in saving time from duplicated work. The case scenario from St Luke's in chapter 7 is an example of this.

Structures to support integrating practice

Ideally, for integrated practice, agencies will create structures that ensure that workers are well supported, with realistic workloads. Depending on the agency's approach, workers will need time allocated for the variety of work roles they are expected to cover. From my own experience, there can be considerable tension for workers in dealing with what may feel like competing demands. One of the most positive dimensions of integrated work is the linking of casework and community work. Each can inform and extend the other. However, it is also potentially the most stressful. How do you justify having cups of tea and building community relationships when court reports need to be done? Workers need managers with an understanding of effective integration work and supervision structures that support both dimensions. Given this, integrated work can be effective and satisfying for staff. Hadley and Leidy (1996) report that using what they call a patch approach in an American county human services agency was felt to be predominantly positive by staff in relation to improved understanding of local communities and the development of more positive relationships with communities and families. They conclude that 'the beginnings of a more accessible and relevant service have been established and the first moves have been made to try to engage the wider community' (Hadley and Leidy 1996:833).

Political implications

Agencies also need to be realistic about what activities such a model might generate. A commitment to community work as part of integrated practice may be tested by the direction a community (and so workers) decide to engage in. Gulati and Guest (1990) write about the Local Community Service Centres in Quebec where workers are based in particular geographic areas. In the early years:

> community organisers mobilized citizen groups around such issues as unemployment...dilapidated housing...and used tactics that, over time, generated considerable hostility and opposition from established groups in the communities....the radicals...were silenced and in an effort to avoid controversy, social action as a major strategy was underplayed and replaced with what came to be called the community approach...(which) is based on the premise that natural helping networks are important and that efforts should be made to create and support them (Gulati and Guest 1990:64).

Agreeing to integrate practice can mean having less control over outcomes and this can make organisations nervous in relation to funding. While governments are becoming more interested in community or neighbourhood programs to foster community participation and capacity building, they are not always interested in open agendas following community interests. This is another potential tension for both workers and organisations. Again there are no easy answers to this; it can help to remind governments of their espoused values and goals that often articulate a desire for communities to make their own decisions and take action.

Training and ongoing support

Training and support are issues for workers individually as well as for organisations. Both can play a significant role in organisational life by ensuring that workers feel equipped for their work. Most training courses provide a solid foundation of general skills, but workers often need specific knowledge and skills for their workplace. The organisation needs to consider how this can best be provided given the agency's role and context. A large organisation may have its own staff development unit and large numbers of staff needing similar programs, so it makes sense to run some of its own programs. A small rural agency might only have one worker at a time needing training, so it is likely to make more sense for the person to go elsewhere. For organisations taking integrated practice seriously, attention needs to be paid both to the training staff already have and what they will need to be supported in integrated practice.

One of my own early experiences of introducing a patch system had mixed success. Each staff member was allocated a geographic area in which to carry out a broad range of casework, including general family counselling, work with families where children were at risk, probation and parole, substitute care, and family support. The amount of client work allocated was carefully assessed to make sure that staff really did have time to network, explore general issues, and develop partnerships within their patch, with one day a week being allocated for community work of some kind.

When we evaluated the results, what was clear was that working effectively in a patch generally requires a reasonable degree of confidence and training in how to work in an integrated way. Staff who did not have training that was broad enough found it difficult to develop a patch or integrated perspective. For some their training was primarily focused on working with individuals, particularly young people at risk, and it is important to recognise that they did work across a range of casework areas in an integrated way. However, the concept of broader networking with a community was new and somewhat unwelcome. Most staff felt they were being asked to carry out significantly different roles that they were not necessarily interested in and did not see as part of their job description. The two staff who did express satisfaction about this approach had both had broad social work training. They found it easier to grasp the basis concept and already had relevant training.

We concluded that for this approach to work, staff needed:

- training in the general concept of an integrated approach
- specific skills to carry out the work
- supervisors who were sufficiently skilled to be able to provide support and guidance about this approach
- agency structures that reflected an integrated approach.

Organisations that have decided to use integrated practice formally are more likely to build in support systems for staff in existing supervision or group meetings, for example. Some agencies will have people who have worked in an integrated way themselves and so are able to provide imaginative and creative supervision.

In other organisations, staff are likely to have to develop their own forms of support. The use of critical reflection is particularly helpful in thinking about integrated practice, offering both theory and tools or processes that enable workers to explore their practice in depth. Creating opportunities for mutual support through formal or informal supervision or meetings and/or using research or evaluation to reflect on and explore practice are other possibilities (for more detail see Chapters 6 and 9).

An integrated approach clearly has considerable implications for training, such as the need for workers to have skills and knowledge for working effectively across a range of domains, from work with individuals, families, and groups to community work and social policy. Some courses already encompass many of these, but this would vary considerably depending on the discipline and the institution.

Students do not necessarily find it easy to think in terms of integrated practice. My impression is that it is unusual to have lecturers, for example, who can teach across domains, and so encourage students to think about links in practice. Secker (in Payne 1997:44) found that students who had particular social skills were more fluent in integrating theory. These were students who listened well and 'could develop ideas, drawing on a range of different courses and seeing connections, rather than seeing pieces of knowledge as separate'. Payne suggests that 'It may be, then, that successful application requires social and interpersonal skills, and the self-confidence to discuss ideas actively as part of practice'. A healthy development in the course I used to teach in was a new final year subject called an 'Integrative Seminar', unfortunately also now a victim of funding and curriculum narrowing. The aim of this subject was to encourage students to look at a scenario and to consider how they might respond to it from the perspectives of individuals and/ or families involved, the community the family lives in, and the current social policy agendas. Student feedback suggests that this was often an 'aha' experience enabling students to see the links between domains that have previously felt quite separate. Student placements or field experience is an important vehicle for a student learning about working across domains. Integrative seminars where students come together and share experiences can be used to help students make such connections.

Ongoing research and evaluation

Some work has been done on the effectiveness of integrating practice. Martinez-Brawley's work at the Centre for Rural Pennsylvania (Martinez-Brawley 1992) demonstrates some of the costs of not integrating practice and the relative savings from integration at an administrative level. Pierson (2002:221) says early efforts at a patch system were not successful, partly because the 'notion of joining services together was not thought through...'. The management strategy for staff was not well developed, so that workers were not well supported and community involvement was thwarted by bureaucratic impediments that meant local people could not really participate. He suggests in England currently, 'with this experience to draw on, and with a greater understanding of how to empower multi-agency front-line teams, reconfiguring services around a neighbourhood agenda has become the decisive element in public service's strategy for tackling exclusion' (Pierson 2002:222). Such experiences need to be evaluated; positive results will encourage change and provide more specific ideas about what strategies are effective. More work clearly needs to be done in looking at what works in integrating practice, in documenting organisational systems that work.

Conclusion

Finally, we need to return to where we started this final chapter: how to have workers and organisations who work in dynamic relationships with each other. Organisations do have a life and vigour of their own, but ultimately they are composed of workers who bring their own sense of purpose and energy. Active workers have a powerful and enabling sense of their own knowledge, skills, and values. These can be used to make their voice heard in the organisation to generate change or consolidate important values. Organisations and their workers operate in a particular context that brings both tensions and opportunities for change. The hope is that organisations and workers can work within this context to fuel a mutual desire for creative and empowering change for clients and communities.

Bibliography

Adams, R. (2002). 'Developing Critical Practice in Social Work'. *Critical Practice in Social Work*. R. Adams, L. A. Dominelli, and M. Payne, Eds. Houndmills, Hampshire and New York, Palgrave.

Adams, R. (2003). *Social Work and Empowerment*. Houndmills, Basingstoke, Palgrave Macmillan.

Allan, J., B. Pease, and L. Briskman, Eds (2003). *Critical Social Work: An Introduction to Theories and Practices*, Crows Nest, Allen & Unwin.

Argyris, C. A. and D. A. Schon (1996). *Organisational Learning 11: Theory, Method and Practice*. Reading, Massachusetts, Addison-Wesley.

Bacchi, C. (1999). *Women, Policy and Politics: The Construction of Policy Problems*. London, Thousand Oaks, California, Sage.

Badwall, H., P. O'Connor, and Rossiter, A. (2004). 'Living out Histories and Identities in Organizations: A Case Study from Three Perspectives'. *The Learning Organization and Reflective Practice: The Emergence of a Concept*. N. A. Gould and M. Baldwin, Eds. Aldershot, Ashgate.

Baldwin, M. (2004). 'Critical Reflection: Opportunities and Threats to Professional Learning and Service Development in Social Work Organizations'. *Social Work, Critical Reflection and the Learning Organization*. N. A. Gould and M. Baldwin, Eds. Aldershot, Ashgate.

Banks, S. (2002). 'Professional Values and Accountabilities'. *Critical Practice in Social Work*. R. Adams, L. A. Dominelli, and M. Payne, Eds. Houndmills, Hampshire and New York, Palgrave.

Barclay, P. (1982). *Social Workers: Their Roles and Tasks: The Report of a Working Party Set Up in October 1980*. London, National Institute for Social Work, Bedford Square Press.

Barnett, R. (1999). 'Learning to Work and Working to Learn'. *Understanding Learning at Work*. D. Boud and J. Garrick. London, Routledge.

Beer, J. and E. Stief (1997). *The Mediator's Handbook*. Gabriola Island, British Columbia, New Society Publishers.

Berger, A. A. (2003). *The Portable Postmodernist*. Walnut Creek, Lanham, New York and Oxford, Altamira Press.

Berry Street (2004). Principles. Victoria, Australia, http://www.berrystreet.org/about_vision.htm.

Binnie, A. A. and A. Titchen (1999). *Freedom to Practise: The Development of Patient-centred Nursing*. Oxford, Butterworth Heinemann.

Bolman, L. G. and T. E. Deal (1997). *Reframing Organisations: Artistry, Choice and Leadership*. San Francisco, Jossey-Bass Publishers.

Bolton, G. (2001). *Reflective Practice: Writing and Professional Development*. London and Thousand Oaks, Paul Chapman Publishing Ltd, Sage.

Borden, W. (1992). 'Narrative Perspectives in Psycho-social Interventions Following Adverse Life-events'. *Social Work* 37(2):135–41.

Boud, D. and J. Garrick, Eds (1999). *Understanding Learning at Work*. London, Routledge.

Boud, D., R. Cohen, and J. Sampson (2001). *Peer Learning in Higher Education*. London, Kogan Page Limited.

Braye, S. (2000). Participation and Involvement in Social Care. *User Involvement and Participation in Social Care*. H. Kemshall and R. Littlechild, Eds. London, Jessica Kingsley.

Bridges, W. (1991). *Managing Transitions: Making the Most of Change*. Reading, Massachusetts, Addison-Wesley Publishing Company.

Briskman, L. and C. Noble (1999). 'Social Work Ethics: Embracing Diversity?'. *Transforming Social Work Practice*. B. Pease and J. Fook, Eds. St Leonards, NSW, Allen & Unwin.

Briskman, L., et al. (1999). *Challenging Rural Practice: Human Services in Australia*. Geelong, Victoria, Deakin University Press.

Brockley, B., M. Rogers, and R. Abson (2004). Bringing Art and Science Together in the Classroom: A Community Wide Learning Approach at Slaty Creek Presentation at Regional Research Forum, La Trobe University, Bendigo.

Brodsky, A. E., P. J. O'Campo, and R. Aronson, (1999). 'PSOC in Community Context: Multi-level Correlates of a Measure of Psychological Sense of Community in Low-Income, Urban Neighborhoods'. *Journal of Community Psychology* 27(6):659–79.

Brookfield, S. (1987). 'Significant Personal Learning'. *Appreciating Adults Learning: From the Learners' Perspective*. D. Boud & V. Griffin, Eds. London, Kogan Page.

Brookfield, S. D. (1995). *Becoming a Critically Reflective Teacher*. San Francisco, Jossey-Bass Publishers.

Brown, A. and I. Bourne (1995). *The Social Work Supervisor: Supervision in Community, Day Care and Residential Settings*. Buckingham, Open University Press.

Brown, T. and L. Jones (2001). *Action Research and Postmodernism Congruence and Critique*. Buckingham, Open University Press.

Canadian Nurses Association (2004). Code of Ethics, http://cna-aiic.ca/cna/documents/pdf/publications/CodeofEthics2

Carr, W. and S. Kemmis (1983). *Becoming Critical: Education, Knowledge and Action Research*. Geelong, Deakin University.

Cherry, N. (1999). *Action Research: A Pathway to Action, Knowledge and Learning*. Melbourne, RMIT Publishing.

Compton, B. and B. Galaway (1999). *Social Work Processes*. Pacific Grove, California, Brooks/Cole Publishing Co.

Cooper, A. (1996). 'Psychoanalysis and the Politics of Organisational Theory'. *Journal of Social Work Practice* 10(2):137–45.

Coughy, M. O. B., P. J. O'Campo, and A. Brodsky (1999). 'Neighborhoods, Families and Children: Implications for Policy and Practice'. *Journal of Community Psychology* 27(5):615–33.

Coulshed, V. and A. Mullender (2001). *Management in Social Work*. Houndmills, Palgrave.

Cousins, J. B. and L. M. Earl (1992). 'The Case for Participatory Evaluation'. *Educational Evaluation and Policy Analysis* 14(4):397–418.

Cowan, J. (1998). *On Becoming an Innovative University Teacher*. Buckingham, Society for Research into Higher Education & Open University Press.

Cowley, S. (1999). Nursing in a Managerial Age. *The Changing Nature of Nursing in a Managerial Age*. I. Norman and S. Cowley, Eds. Oxford, Blackwell Science.

Cox, E. (1995). *A Truly Civil Society*. Sydney, Australian Broadcasting Commission.

Darling, R. B. (2000). *The Partnership Model in Human Services Sociological Foundations and Practices*. New York, Boston, Dordrecht, London, Moscow, Kluwer Academic/Plenum Publishers.

Delgado, M. (2000). *Community Social Work Practice in an Urban Environment*. New York, Oxford, Oxford University Press.

de Shazer, S. (1991). *Putting Differences to Work*. New York, Norton.

Dominelli, L. (2002). 'Feminist Theory'. *The Blackwell Companion to Social Work*. M. Davies, Ed. Oxford, Blackwell Publishing.

Duke, S. and G. Copp (1994). The Personal Side of Reflection. *Reflective Practice in Nursing: The Growth of the Professional Practitioner*. A. Palmer, S. A. Burns, and C. Bulman, Eds. Oxford, Blackwell Scientific Publications.

Dwyer, M. (1988). *Wake up the Sun*. Thornbury, Victoria, Desbooks.

Elliott, B., L. Mulroney, and D. O'Neil (2000). *Promoting Family Change: The Optimism Factor*. St Leonards, NSW, Allen & Unwin.

Everitt, A. and P. Hardiker (1996). *Evaluating for Good Practice*. London, Macmillan.

Ewing, R. and D. Smith (2001). 'Doing, Knowing, Being and Becoming: the Nature of Professional Practice'. *Professional Practice in Health, Education and the Creative Arts*. J. Higgs and A. Titchen, Eds. Oxford, Blackwell Science.

Fagenson, E. A., Ed. (1993). *Women in Management: Trends, Issues, and Challenges in Managerial Diversity*. Women and Work: A Research and Policy Series. Newbury Park, London and New Delhi, Sage.

Family and Community Services Department, Commonwealth Government (2000). *Family and Community Networks Initiative: FaCS Evaluation Requirements*. Canberra, Commonwealth Government.

Family and Community Services Department, Commonwealth Government, Australia, (2004). Vision, Purpose and Outcomes, http://www.facs.gov.au.

Fetterman, D. M. (2000). *Foundations of Empowerment Evaluation*. Thousand Oaks, California, Sage.

FitzRoy, L. (1999). 'Offending mothers: Theorising in a Feminist Minefield'. *Transforming Social Work Practice*. B. Pease and J. Fook, Eds. St Leonards, Allen & Unwin.

Fook, J. (1993). *Radical Casework: A Theory of Practice*. St Leonards, NSW, Allen & Unwin.

Fook, J. (2002). *Social Work Critical Theory and Practice*. London, Thousand Oaks, New Delhi, Sage.

Fook, J., M. A. Ryan, and L. Hawkins (2000). *Professional Expertise: Practice, Theory and Education for Working in Uncertainty*. London, Whitney and Brisk.

Frances, R. (1997). *Another Way of Knowing, Another Way of Living: Participatory Evaluation in a Community Setting, Melbourne*. Melbourne, Preston Creative Living Centre: 98.

Francis, D. (1997). 'Critical Incident Analysis: A Strategy for Developing Critical Practice'. *Teachers and Teaching: Theory and Practice* 3(2):169–88.

Francis, D. and P. Henderson (1992). *Working with Rural Communities*. Basingstoke, Macmillan.

Galbally, R. (2004). *Integration, Quick Smart: Disability and Community*. Sir John Quick Bendigo Lecture, Bendigo, Victoria.

Garbarino, J. and F. Barry (1997). 'The Meaning of Maltreatment'. *Understanding Abusive Families: An Ecological Approach to Theory and Practice*. J. E. Garbarino and J. Eckenrode, Eds. San Francisco, Jossey-Bass Publishers.

Garbarino, J. and J. Eckenrode, Eds (1997). *Understanding Abusive Families: An Ecological Approach to Theory and Practice*. San Francisco, Jossey-Bass Publishers.

Gardner, F. (2003). 'User Friendly Evaluation in Community-Based Projects'. *The Canadian Journal of Program Evaluation* 18(2):71–89.

Gardner, F. and J. Lehmann (2002). '"But wait! There's still more!" Some Unaccounted for Aspects of Qualitative Evaluation and Research'. *Australian Qualitative Research* 2(2):16–27.

Geertz, C. (1973). *The Interpretation of Cultures*. Hutchinson of London, The Anchor Press.

Germain C. B. and A. Gitterman (1980). *The Life Model of Social Work Practice*. New York, Columbia University Press.

Gilley, T. (1990). *Empowering Poor People*. Melbourne, Brotherhood of St Laurence.

Gould, N. (2000). 'Becoming a Learning Organisation: A Social Work Example'. *Social Work Education* 19(6):585–96.

Gould, N. (2004). The Learning Organization and Reflective Practice: The Emergence of a Concept. *Social Work, Critical Reflection and the Learning Organization*. N. A. Gould and M. Baldwin, Eds. Aldershot, Ashgate.

Gulati, P. and G. Guest (1990). 'The Community-Centered Model: A Garden-Variety Approach or a Radical Transformation of Community Practice'. *Social Work* 35(1):63–8.

Guransky, D., J. Harvey, and R. Kennedy (2003). *Case Management Policy, Practice and Professional Business*. Crows Nest, NSW, Allen & Unwin.

Gurman, A. and D. Kniskern (1981–91). *Handbook of Family Therapy*. New York, Brunner/Mazel.

Hadley, R. and B. Leidy (1996). 'Community Social Work in a Market Environment: A British-American Exchange of Technologies and Experience'. *British Journal of Social Work* 26:823–42.

Hampden-Turner, C. and F. Trompenaars (1993). *The Seven Cultures of Capitalism*. New York, Doubleday.

Harvey, L. (1990). *Critical Social Research*. London, Unwin Hyman Ltd.

Hasenfeld, Y. (1992). *Human Services as Complex Organisations*. Newbury Park, California, Sage.

Hawken, D. and J. W. Worrall (2002). 'Reciprocal Mentoring Supervision. Partners in Learning: A Personal Perspective'. *Supervision in the Helping Professions*. M. McMahon and P. Patton, Eds. French's Forest, NSW, Prentice Hall, Pearson Education. pp. 43–53.

Hawkins, P. and R. Shohet (1989). *Supervision in the Helping Professions*. New York, Open University Press.

Healy, K. (2000). *Social Work Practices Contemporary Perspectives on Change*. London, Sage.

Healy, K. and A. Hampshire (2002). 'Social Capital: A Useful Concept for Social Work?'. *Australian Social Work* 55(3):227–38.

Herda, E. A. (1999). *Research Conversations and Narrative: a Critical Hermeneutic Orientation in Participatory Inquiry*. Westport, Praeger.

Heron, J. (1996). *Co-operative Inquiry Research into the Human Condition*. London, Sage.

Higgs, J. and A. Titchen, Eds (2001). *Professional Practice in Health, Education and the Creative Arts*. Oxford, Blackwell Science.

Hilmer, G. (1993). *National Competition Policy Report by the Independent Committee of Inquiry*. Canberra, Australian Government Publishing Service.

Hollister, R. G. and J. Hill (1995). Problems in the Evaluation of Community Wide Initiatives. *Roundtable on Community Change: New Approaches to Evaluating Community Initiatives: Vol 1: Concepts, Methods and Contexts*. J. P. Connell, A. C. Kubisch, L. B. Schorr, and C. H. Weiss, Eds. USA, The Aspen Institute, Aspen, Colorado.

Holman, R. (1988). *Putting Families First: Prevention and Child Care: A study of Prevention by Statutory and Voluntary Agencies*. Basingstoke, Macmillan.

Ife, J. (1997). *Rethinking Social Work*. South Melbourne, Longman.

Ife, J. (1999). 'Postmodernism, Critical Theory and Social Work'. *Transforming Social Work Practice*. B. Pease and J. Fook, Eds. St Leonards, NSW, Allen & Unwin.

Ife, J. (2002). *Community Development*. French's Forest, NSW, Longman.

Illich, I. (1972). *Disabling Professions*. London, Salem, Boyars.

Ivey, A. E. and M. B. Ivey (1999). *Intentional Interviewing, Counseling: Facilitating Client Development in a Multi Cultural Setting*. Pacific Grove, California, Brooks/Cole Publishing Company.

Jackson, A. C. and F. Donovan (1991). *Managing Human Service Organisations*. St Leonards, NSW, Prentice Hall.

Jarvis, P., J. Holdford, and C. Griffin (2003). *The Theory and Practice of Learning*. London and Sterling, Virginia, Kogan Page.

Johns, C. and D. Freshwater, Eds (1998). *Transforming Nursing Through Reflective Practice*. Oxford, Malden, Blackwell Science.

Johnson, R. (1986). *Inner Work*. San Francisco, Harper and Row.

Johnson, R. (1993). *Owning Your Own Shadow*. San Francisco, Harper.

Johnson, Y. M. (1999). 'Indirect Work: Social Work's Uncelebrated Strength'. *Social Work* 44(4):323–34.

Jones, A. and J. May (1992). *Working in Human Service Organisations: A Critical Introduction*. South Melbourne, Longman.

Jones, C. (2001). 'Voices From the Front Line: State Social Workers and New Labour'. *British Journal of Social Work* 31:547–62.

Jung, C. G. (1964). *Man and His Symbols*. London, Aldus Books Ltd.

Kadushin, A. (1985). *Supervision in Social Work*. New York, Columbia University Press.

Kaye, M. (1996). *Myth Makers and Story Tellers*, Sydney, Ligare Pty Ltd.

Kenny, S. (1994). *Developing Communities for the Future*, Melbourne, Nelson.

Kleiner, A. (1996). *The Age of Heretics*, New York, Doubleday.

Kondrat, M. E. (1999). 'Who is the "Self" in Self-Aware: Professional Self-Awareness from a Critical Theory Perspective'. *Social Service Review* 3:451–77.

Lancaster, R. (1997). 'The Meaning of Spirituality and the Nurse's Role in Providing Spiritual Care to the Dying Patient'. *Spirituality: The Heart of Nursing*. S. Ronaldson, Ed. Ascot Vale, Victoria, Ausmed Publications.

Lawrence, G. (1993). *People Types and Tiger Stripes*. Gainseville, Florida, Centre of Applications of Psychological Type.

LeCroy, C. W. (1999). *Case Studies in Social Work Practice*, 2nd edn, Pacific Grove, California, Brooks/Cole ITp.

Liddell, M. (2003). *Developing Human Service Organisations*. French's Forest NSW, Pearson SprintPrint.

Lipsky, M. (1980). *Street-Level Bureaucracy: Dilemmas of the Individual in Public Services*. New York, Russell Sage Foundation.

Markiewicz, A. (1996). 'Panacea or Scapegoat: The Social Work Profession and its History and Background in Relation to the State Welfare Department in Victoria.' *Australian Social Work* 49(3):25–32.

Martinez-Brawley, E. E. (1992). *Program Integration: An Alternative for Improving County Rural Human Services Delivery*. Centre for Rural Pennsylvania.

Martinez-Brawley, E. E. (2000). *Close to Home: Human Services and the Small Community*. Washington, DC, National Association of Social Workers, Harrisburg, PA.

Matheson, C. (1996). 'Organisational Structures in the Australian Public Service'. *Australian Journal of Public Administration* 55(2):36–46.

Matheson, C. (1998). 'Is the Higher Public Service a Profession?'. *Australian Journal of Public Administration* 57(3):15–27.

McDonald, J. (2002). 'Contestability and Social Justice: The Limits of Competitive Tendering of Welfare Services'. *Australian Social Work* 55(2):99–108.

McDrury, J. and M. Alterio (2002). *Learning Through Storytelling*. Palmerston North, New Zealand, Dunmore Press.

McKnight, J. L. (1997). 'A 21st Century Map for Healthy Communities and Families'. *Families in Society* 2: 117–27.

McMahon, L. and A. Ward, Eds (2001). *Helping Families in Family Centres Working at Therapeutic Practice*. London and Philadelphia, Jessica Kingsley Publishers.

McMillan, D. W. and D. M. Chavis (1986). Sense of Community: A definition and theory. *Journal of Community Psychology* 14:6–23.

McSherry, W. (2000). *Making Sense of Spirituality in Nursing Practice: An Interactive Approach*. London, Churchill Livingstone.

Mellors, J. (1996). 'Managing and Leading in the Next Century'. *Australian Journal of Public Administration* 55(3):83–9.

Mezirow, J. (1991). *Transformative Dimensions of Adult Learning*. San Francisco, Jossey-Bass Publishers.

Mintzberg, H. (1989). *Mintzberg on Management: Inside Our Strange World of Organizations*. New York, The Free Press.

Mitchell, J. (2000). *Psychoanalysis and Feminism*. London, Penguin.

Mullaly, R. (1997). *Structural Social Work: Ideology, Theory and Practice*. Toronto, New York, Oxford University Press.

Murphy, K. and S. Atkins (1994). 'Reflection with a Practice-led Curriculum'. *Reflective Practice in Nursing: The Growth of the Professional Practitioner*. A. Palmer, S. Burns, and C. Bulman, Eds. Oxford, Blackwell Scientific Publications.

Nathan, J. (2002). 'Psychoanalytic Theory'. *The Blackwell Companion to Social Work*. M. Davies, Ed. Oxford, Blackwell Publishing.

New Fulford Family Centre (2002). *Annual Report*. Bristol, Barnardo's.

Norman, I. and S. Cowley, Eds (1999). *The Changing Nature of Nursing in a Managerial Age*. Oxford, Blackwell Science.

O'Looney, J. (1998). 'Mapping Communities: Place-based Stories and Participatory Planning'. *Journal of the Community Development Society* 29(2):201–36.

Ooijen, E. (2000). *Clinical Supervision: A Practical Approach*. Edinburgh, London, Sydney, Churchill Livingstone.

Orme, J. (2002). 'Managing the Workload'. *Critical Practice in Social Work*. R. Adams, L. Dominelli, and M. Payne, Eds. Houndmills, Hampshire and New York, Palgrave.

Owen, J. M. and P. J. Rogers (1999). *Program Evaluation Forms and Approaches*. St Leonards, NSW, Allen & Unwin.

Page, S. and V. Wosket (2001). *Supervising the Counsellor*. East Sussex, Brunner Routledge, Taylor & Francis.

Palmer, A., S. Burns, and C. Bulman (1994). *Reflective Practice in Nursing: The Growth of the Professional Practitioner*. Oxford, Blackwell Scientific Publications.

Parton, N. and P. O'Byrne (2000). *Constructive Social Work*. London, Macmillan Press.

Patton, M. Q. (1997). *Utilization-focused Evaluation*. Thousand Oaks, California, Sage.

Payne, M. (1997). *Modern Social Work Theory*. Houndmills, Basingstoke and London, Macmillan.

Payne, M. (2000). *Narrative Therapy: An Introduction for Counsellors*. London, Sage.

Payne, M., R. Adams, and L. Dominelli (2002). 'On Being Critical in Social Work'. *Critical Practice in Social Work*. R. Adams, L. A. Dominelli, and M. Payne, Eds. Palgrave, Houndmills, Hampshire and New York.

Pease, B. and J. Fook, Eds (1999). *Transforming Social Work Practice*. St Leonards, NSW, Allen & Unwin.

Peck, M. S. (1987). *The Different Drum: Community Making and Peace*. London, Arrow.

Pierson, J. (2002). *Tackling Social Exclusion*. London and New York, Routledge.

Popple, K. (1995). *Analysing Community Work: Its Theory and Practice*. Buckingham, Open University Press.

Pusey, M. (1991). *Economic Rationalism in Canberra: A Nation Building State Changes Its Mind*. Cambridge, Cambridge University Press.

Putnam, R. D. (2000). *Bowling Alone*. New York, Simon & Schuster.

Reason, P. and H. Bradbury (2001). *Handbook of Action Research: Participative Inquiry and Practice*. London, Thousand Oaks, New Delhi, Sage.

Renzetti, C. M. and R. M. Lee, Eds (1993). *Researching Sensitive Topics*. Sage Focus Edition. Newbury Park, California, Sage.

Rolfe, G. (2000). *Research, Truth and Authority: Postmodern Perspectives on Nursing*. Houndmills, Basingstoke, Hampshire, Macmillan.

Rolfe, G., D. Freshwater, and M. Jasper (2001). *Critical Reflection for Nursing and the Helping Professions: A User's Guide*. Basingstoke, Palgrave.

Ronaldson, S., Ed. (1997). *Spirituality: The Heart of Nursing*. Ascot Vale, Victoria, Ausmed Publications.

Ronen, T. (2002). 'Cognitive Behavioural Therapy'. *The Blackwell Companion to Social Work*. M. Davies. Oxford, Blackwell Publishing.

Rosenau, P. M. (1992). *Post-modernism and the Social Sciences: Insights, Inroads and Intrusions*. Princeton, New Jersey, Princeton University Press.

Saleeby, D., Ed. (1997). *The Strengths Perspective in Social Work Practice*. New York, Longman.

Schein, E. H. (1992). *Organizational Culture and Leadership*. San Francisco, Jossey-Bass Publishers.

Schon, D. A. (1983). *The Reflective Practitioner: How Professionals Think in Action*. New York, Basic Books, Perseus Books Group.

Scott, D. (1995). 'Child Protection: Paradoxes of Publicity, Policy and Practice'. *Australian Journal of Social Issues* 30(1):71–94.

Scott, D. and D. O'Neil (1996). *Beyond Child Rescue*. St Leonard's, NSW, Allen & Unwin.

Scott Peck, M. (1987). *The Different Drum: Community-making and Peace*. London, Melbourne, Rider.

Senge, P. M. (1990). *The Fifth Discipline: The Art and Practice of the Learning Organization*. New York, Doubleday Currency.

Shields, K. (1991). *In the Tiger's Mouth: An Empowerment Guide for Social Action*. Newtown, NSW, Millennium Books.

Sinclair, A. A. and V. Wilson (2002). *New Faces of Leadership*. Carlton South, Melbourne University Press.

Smale, G., G. Tuson, and D. Statham (2000). *Social Work and Social Problems: Working Towards Social Inclusion and Social Change*. Houndmills, Hampshire, UK, Palgrave.

Smith, S. (2002). 'What Works for Whom: The Link Between Process and Outcome in Effectiveness Research'. *Australian Social Work* Vol. 55(2):147–55.

Stace, D. and D. Dunphy (1992). *Transitions, Turnarounds and Transformations: Alternate Paths in Strategic Change*. Sydney, Centre for Corporate Change, Australian Graduate School of Management.

Stanley, J. and C. Goddard (2002). *In the Firing Line: Violence and Power in Child Protection Work*. Chichester, John Wiley & Sons, Ltd.

Stones, C. (1994). *Focus on Families: Family Centres in Action*. Houndmills, Macmillan and British Association of Social Workers.

Stones, C. (2001). The Family Centre and the Consolidation of Integrated Practice. *Family Centres and their International Role in Social Action*. C. Warren-Adamson, Ed. Aldershot, UK, Ashgate.

Street, A. (1990). *Nursing Practice: High, Hard Ground, Messy Swamps and the Pathways in Between*. Geelong, Deakin University Press.

St Vincent's Health (2004). *Mission and Values*. Melbourne, http://www.svhm.org.au/infoabout/svh/missionvalues.htm.

Swenson, C. (1998). 'Clinical Social Work's Contribution to a Social Justice Perspective'. *Social Work* 43(6):527–37.

Talbot, A. (1990). 'The Importance of Parallel Process in De-briefing Crisis Counselors'. *Journal of Traumatic Stress* 3(2):265–77.

Taylor, B. J. (2000). *Reflective Practice: A Guide for Nurses and Midwives*. Allen & Unwin.

Taylor, C. and S. White (2000). *Practising Reflexivity in Health and Welfare: Making Knowledge*. Buckingham Philadelphia, Open University Press.

Taylor, I. (2004). Multi-professional Teams and the Learning Organisation. *Social Work, Critical Reflection and the Learning Organization*. N. Gould and M. Baldwin, Eds. Aldershot, Ashgate.

Thompson, N. (2001). *Anti-discriminatory Practice*. Basingstoke, Palgrave.

Thompson, N. et al. (1996). 'Stress and Organizational Culture'. *British Journal of Social Work* 26:647–65.

Thomson, L. (1998). *Personality Type: An Owner's Manual*. Boston & London, Shambhala.

Trompenaars, F. and C. Hampden-Turner (1998). *Riding the Waves of Culture: Understanding Cultural Diversity in Global Business*. New York, McGraw Hill.

Twelvetrees, A. (1991). *Community Work*. Basingstoke, Macmillan.

Vaill, P. B. (1996). *Learning as a Way of Being: Strategies for Survival in a World of Permanent White Water*. San Francisco, Jossey-Bass Publishers.

Vince, R. (2001). 'Power and Emotion in Organizational Learning'. *Human Relations* 54(10):1325–51.

Vince, R. (2002). 'The Politics of Imagined Stability: A Psychodynamic Understanding of Change at Hyder plc'. *Human Relations* 55(10):1189–1208.

Vinson, T. (2004). *Community Adversity and Resilience: The Distribution of Social Disadvantage in Victoria and New South Wales and the Mediating Role of Social Cohesion*. Richmond, Victoria, Jesuit Social Services.

Von Franz, M. L. (1993). *Psychotherapy*. Massachusetts, Shambhala Publications.

Wadsworth, Y. (1997). *Do It Yourself Social Research*. Collingwood, Victoria, Victorian Council of Social Services.

Wadsworth, Y. (1998). '"Coming to the table": Some Conditions for Achieving Consumer-focused Evaluation of Human Services by Service Providers and Service Users'. *Evaluation Journal of Australasia* 10(1 & 2):11–29.

Weber, M. (1964). *The Theory of Social and Economic Organization*. New York, The Free Press, Paperback Edition.

Webster, J. and S. Osborne (2005). Using the right type of evidence to answer clinical questions. *Evidence for Nursing Practice*. M. Courtney, Ed. Marrickville, NSW, Churchill Livingstone.

Weeks, G. and S. Treat, Eds (1992). *Couples in Treatment: Techniques and Approaches for Effective Practice*. New York, Bruner-Mazel.

Weeks, W. in Collaboration with Women in Women's Services (1994). *Women Working Together: Lessons from Feminist Women's Services*. Melbourne, Longman Cheshire.

Weinbach, R. W. (1990). *The Social Worker as Manager: Theory and Practice*. New York, Longman.

Weiner, M. E. (1990). *Human Service Management: Analysis and Applications.* Belmont, California, Wadsworth.

White, C. and D. Denborough (1998). *Introducing Narrative Therapy.* Adelaide, Dulwich Centre Publications.

Whitely, A. (1995). *Managing Change: A Core Values Approach.* South Melbourne, Macmillan Education.

Winter, R. and C. Munn-Giddings (2001). *A Handbook for Action Research in Health and Social Care.* London and New York, Routledge.

Wood, A. (2001). 'The Origins of Family Systems Work: Social Workers' Contributions to the Development of Family Theory and Practice'. *Australian Social Work* 54(3):15–29.

Yalom, I. D. (2000). *Momma and the Meaning of Life: Tales of Psychotherapy.* London, Judy Platnus Publishers Limited.

Zohar, D. A. and I. Marshall (2004). *Spiritual Capital: Wealth We Can Live By.* London, Bloomsbury.

Index